The Churches of Medieval Exeter

The Churches of Medieval Exeter

Nicholas Orme

For John Allan

First published 2014
by Impress Books Ltd
Innovation Centre, Rennes Drive,
University of Exeter Campus, Exeter EX4 4RN

© Nicholas Orme 2014

The right of the author to be identified as the originator of this work has been asserted in accordance with the Copyright, Designs and Patents Act 1988.

Typeset in 10/13.5 Palatino by Swales and Willis Ltd, Exeter, Devon

Printed and bound by Short Run Press, Exeter, Devon

All Rights Reserved. No part of this book may be reprinted or reproduced or utilised in any form or by any electronic, mechanical, or other means, now known or hereafter invented, including photocopying and recording, or in any information storage or retrieval system, without permission in writing from the publishers.

British Library Cataloguing in Publication Data
A catalogue record for this book is available from the British Library

ISBN: 978-1-907605-51-2 (pbk)
ISBN: 978-1-907605-52-9 (ebk)

Contents

List of Illustrations and Maps	vii
List of Abbreviations	xi
Preface	xiii

Introduction   1

Exeter and Its Medieval Churches	1
Church and Chapel Foundations before 1100	7
Church and Chapel Foundations of the Twelfth Century	16
The Early Church and Chapel Foundations: an Analysis	19
The Creation of Parish Churches	28
The Religious Houses	34
Chapel Foundations after 1222	40
The Parish Churches and the Clergy, 1300–1530	47
The Parish Churches and the Laity, 1300–1530	57
The Reformation	63

Gazetteer of Religious Houses, Churches, and Chapels in Exeter, 400–1550   67

Bibliography	191
Index	203

List of Illustrations and Maps

The author and publishers are grateful for permission from those listed below to reproduce cartography and illustrations from works in their copyright or possession.

Religious sites in the city of Exeter before 1222 (Based on material in *Historical Atlas of South-West England*, ed. R. J. P. Kain and W. L. D. Ravenhill, published by University of Exeter Press, 1999)	4
Religious sites in the city of Exeter, 1222–1548 (Based as above)	8
Religious sites in Heavitree parish (Based on Nicholas Orme, 'The Medieval Chapels of Heavitree Parish', *Devon Archaeological Society Transactions*, 49 (1991, publ. 1993), 121–9)	15
Religious sites in Cowick (St Thomas) parish	20
View of Exeter city, 1587 (John Hooker, *Isca Damnoniorum* ([London?], 1587))	27
St Sidwell's Fee, late sixteenth century (The dean and chapter of Exeter Cathedral, Cathedral Archives, D&C 3530 ff. 37–8)	179
Seals of Exeter religious houses (George Oliver, *Monasticon*, plates 1–3)	32
All Hallows Goldsmith Street, interior, 1906 (Beatrix F. Cresswell, *Exeter Churches*, opp. p. 7)	37
St Anne, 2014 (Photograph: Caroline Watson)	180
Castle Chapel, before 1792 (Drawing by R. B. Vidal reproduced in C. J. G. Sprake, *Gates and Other Antiquities of the City of Exeter*)	41
Cowick and St James Priories, agreement of 1208–9 (The provost and fellows of King's College Cambridge, College Archives, SJP/53)	46
St David, 1756×60 (Devon Heritage Centre, Exeter City Archives, Books 58/2. Photograph: Gary Young)	180

Dominican Friary, plan (Exeter Archaeology)	51
Dominican Friary, head of an effigy of a knight (Now in the Royal Albert Memorial Museum, Exeter)	181
St Edmund, before 1833 (E. I. C., 'Church of St Edmund', *The Gentleman's Magazine* (February, 1835), pp. 148–50)	62
St George, 1843 (Drawing by George Townsend, *Sketches of Bygone Exeter*, p. 1)	71
Grendon's Almshouse, before 1879 (J. Crocker, *Sketches of Old Exeter*, plate 18)	78
Heavitree church, 1840 (Devon Heritage Centre, West Country Studies Library M SC1147, engraving by Augustus de Niceville)	85
Hospital of St John, 1756×60 (Devon Heritage Centre, Exeter City Archives, Book 58/13. Photograph: Gary Young)	181
Church of St John Bow, 1864 (Devon Heritage Centre, West Country Studies Library OD, drawing by Edward Ashworth)	92
St Katherine's Almshouse, 2014 (Photograph: Caroline Watson)	182
St Kerrian, 1756×60 (Devon Heritage Centre, Exeter City Archives, Book 58/12, 14. Photograph: Gary Young)	182
St Laurence, 1906 (Beatrix F. Cresswell, *Exeter Churches*, opp. p. 75)	97
St Leonard, *c*.1830 (Devon Heritage Centre, West Country Studies Library MPh: EPR S0680)	103
St Loye, 1839 (George Oliver, *Ecclesiastical Antiquities*, i, 44–5)	110
St Martin, 2014 (Photograph: Caroline Watson)	183
St Mary Arches, 1908–16 (John Stabb, *Old Devon Churches*, ii, plate 78)	117
St Mary Major, before 1865 (Painting by Edward Ashworth, The Royal Albert Memorial Museum, Exeter)	184
St Mary Steps (Photograph: Exeter City Council)	185
St Mary Magdalene, before 1851 (The Devon and Exeter Institution, Diocesan Society Scrapbook, i, plate 19)	124
St Nicholas Priory (Exeter Archaeology, reconstruction by Richard Parker)	131
St Olave, 2014 (Photograph: Caroline Watson)	186

St Pancras, 2014 (Photograph: Caroline Watson)	186
St Petroc, 2014 (Photograph: Caroline Watson)	187
St Petroc, plan 1882 (Robert Dymond, 'The History of the Parish of St. Petrock, Exeter', *Devonshire Association Transactions*, 14 (1882), opposite p. 402)	138
Polsloe Priory (Exeter Archaeology, reconstruction of the west range by Stuart Blaylock)	146
St Roche, confraternity letter, *c.*1510 (*Short Title Catalogue of Books Printed in England 1475–1640*, 14077c)	154
St Sidwell, 1756×60 (Devon Heritage Centre, Exeter City Archives, Book 58/7. Photograph: Gary Young)	162
St Stephen, 2014 (Photograph: Caroline Watson)	187
St Thomas, 2014 (Photograph: Caroline Watson)	188
Topsham, 2014 (Photograph: Caroline Watson)	189
Holy Trinity, *c.*1820 (Devon Heritage Centre, West Country Studies Library LD, painting)	190
Wynard's Almshouse, seventeenth-century plan (The Devon and Exeter Institution, D17)	170

List of Abbreviations

×	An unknown date between two known dates
BL	British Library
Bodleian	Oxford, Bodleian Library
Cresswell	Beatrix F. Cresswell, *Exeter Churches* (Exeter, 1908)
D&C	Exeter Cathedral Archives, Dean and Chapter documents
DCRS	Devon and Cornwall Record Society
DHC	Devon Heritage Centre (formerly Record Office), Sowton, Exeter
ECA	Devon Heritage Centre, Exeter City Archives
ECC	Exeter City Council (Heritage Environment Record references)
Hedgeland	Caleb Hedgeland, model of Exeter, 1824 (Exeter, Royal Albert Memorial Museum)
HER	Heritage Environment Record
MCR	Mayor's Court Rolls
MDV	Devon County Council (Heritage Environment Record references)
Sherwood	Robert Sherwood, Map of Exeter, 1630s (ECA, L618)
Stabb	John Stabb, *Some Old Devon Churches*, 3 vols (London, 1908–16)
TNA	The National Archives, Kew
VCH	*Victoria County History*

Preface

This work, like my previous publications on Devon, could have not been achieved without the kindness and assistance of the staff of the Bodleian Library, the British Library, the Devon Heritage Centre, the Devon and Exeter Institution, Exeter Cathedral Archives and Library, Exeter University Library, the National Archives, and the West Country Studies Library. Marrina Neophytou of Devon County Council and Andrew Pye of Exeter City Council most generously provided me with the relevant entries from the Heritage Environment Record. I am glad to acknowledge how much the Exeter city entries owe to the work of Stuart Blaylock, John Allan, and others. Stuart Blaylock and Tony Collings have also kindly supplied me with advice from their own researches, and Charlotte Coles of Devon County Council with images. My colleagues Julia Crick and Robert Higham have given me much wise advice and saved me from numerous errors, while my excellent publishers, Impress Books, have offered unfailing support especially in the procurement of maps and illustrations. Finally I am grateful for the friendship, guidance, and generous help over many years of John Allan to whom this book is dedicated.

Nicholas Orme
Oxford
2014

Introduction

Exeter and Its Medieval Churches

Exeter has its origins in a Roman city that served as the administrative centre of the South-West of England. The city was elaborately walled in the third century but virtually deserted by the early fifth, after which it underwent a slow revival. A Christian minster was founded in about 670, the defences were improved or restored from the late 800s, and a functioning urban community existed by the tenth century.[1] From the latter date the city was the administrative capital of the county of Devon, and in 1050 it became the bishop's seat and diocesan centre of the diocese of Exeter, covering Devon and Cornwall. Exeter owes its importance to its defensible site on a hill above the lowest crossing point of the Exe, the principal river of Devon. The crossing was originally made by a ford but this was supplemented with a bridge by the twelfth century. The city's location is close to the sea, from which vessels unloaded and loaded at Topsham during the Middle Ages, three and a half miles away. It also lies at the meeting point of major roads from London and Bristol that lead onwards to Plymouth, north Devon, and Cornwall. In 1068 the city was strong enough to negotiate a surrender to William the Conqueror, after which a royal castle was built that became the headquarters of the crown in Devon and the seat of its principal officer, the sheriff.

The walled city covered an area of only 92 acres (37 hectares), but there were suburbs beyond all four sides of the walls by the twelfth century, and these seem to have grown in size and prosperity during the later Middle Ages. In the period mainly covered by this book, from about 1000 to about 1550, the city and suburbs housed

---

[1] For a summary of the city's medieval history see C. Henderson, 'The City of Exeter from A.D. 50 to the Early Nineteenth Century', in *Historical Atlas of South-West England*, ed. R. J. P. Kain and W. L. D. Ravenhill (Exeter, 1999), 482–98, with bibliography on p. 498. W. G. Hoskins, *Two Thousand Years in Exeter* (Exeter, 1960), is still useful.

a varied community of merchants, tradesmen, artisans, and labourers engaged in a wide range of trades, manufactures, services, and agriculture. By the fifteenth and sixteenth centuries the trade in wool and the manufacture of cloth were important activities. Self-government was achieved by the twelfth century, with a principal officer, called the mayor by 1205, assisted by a 'chamber' or council, the records of whose weekly court survive from 1263. The size of the population is difficult to estimate but may have reached 2,000 by the Norman Conquest, and the city's infrastructure of defences, streets, suburbs, and churches suggests that there were 5,000–6,000 inhabitants from the thirteenth to the fifteenth centuries. Lower estimates based on the poll-tax returns of 1377–81 are undoubtedly distorted downwards by large numbers of people omitted from the returns. By 1525 the total may have reached 8,000, making Exeter the fifth or sixth largest of the English provincial cities. The resident population was further increased by those who came from the South-West or further afield to trade, shop, or do business with the authorities and courts of the county town and diocesan centre.

Apart from being the seat of a bishop and his administration, Exeter was not of national importance in religious terms because it occupied a peripheral location in the kingdom and had no shrine or relics to attract pilgrims from outside its region. Nevertheless it resembled the other chief cities of England in possessing a large number of religious buildings in the Middle Ages: a cathedral, monasteries, hospitals, parish churches, chapels, and almshouses, many of which originated in about the eleventh and twelfth centuries.[2] There were some forty-three religious houses, churches, and chapels in and around Exeter by about 1220, and another fourteen appeared during the next three hundred years as well as private oratories and almshouses without chapels. Some of these institutions began to disappear as early as the thirteenth century, and the religious houses and most of the chapels followed them at the Reformation. Other religious buildings were removed during the development of the city in modern times, so that the twenty ancient parish churches that existed in 1800 are now reduced to ten, and not all of these are in use, but together with the cathedral and two medieval chapels they still form a prominent part of the townscape as one walks around the centre of the city.

---

[2] Relevant work on other major towns includes *Historic Towns* (also *Atlas of Historic Towns*), ed. Mary D. Lobel, 3 vols (London and Oxford, 1969–89); William Urry, *Canterbury under the Angevin Kings* (London, 1967), 207–13; Francis Hill, *Medieval Lincoln* (Cambridge, 1948, repr. Stamford, 1990); Norman P. Tanner, *The Church in Late Medieval Norwich 1370–1532* (Toronto, 1984); H. E. Salter, *Medieval Oxford*, Oxford Historical Society, 100 (1936), 113–31; *Winchester in the Early Middle Ages*, ed. Martin Biddle (Oxford, 1976), 329–35; Derek Keene, *Survey of Medieval Winchester*, part i (Oxford, 1987), 106–36; and *VCH Yorkshire: City of York*, ed. P. M. Tillott (London, 1961), 337–57 (minster), 357–65 (religious houses), 365–404 (parish churches).

This array of religious foundations has not escaped the attention of historians. Apart from individual studies and incidental references in works of wider compass, one might mention Beatrix Cresswell's *Exeter Churches* (1908), Frances Rose-Troup's *Lost Chapels of Exeter* (1923), the present author's account of 'The Medieval Chapels of Heavitree Parish' (1993), and *Lost Churches* by David Francis (1995).[3] The subject is a wide one, supported by enough evidence from surviving buildings, written records, maps, illustrations, and archaeological research to occupy scholars for years and to generate more than one substantial volume. This present study is necessarily more limited in scope, and historical rather than archaeological. It aims to provide a general inventory and description of the religious houses, churches, chapels, hospitals, and almshouses of Exeter up to the Reformation in about 1550, with dates of first record and a selection of relevant information, chiefly from documentary sources. The object is to enable the foundations to be easily identified with regard to their locations and nature, to clear up some of the confusions that have arisen in writings about them, and to explain their nature and activities in broad terms. An attempt has been made to indicate the main locational and spatial characteristics of the buildings, but lack of time and technology has regrettably made it impossible to research and produce the measured and dated plans that are ideally required for each one. In addition, since this is a study of the churches up to the Reformation, it includes only brief accounts of their later history.

The geographical area of the study consists of the historic walled city of Exeter and certain districts around and outside it. The principal church of the city, the minster that became the cathedral in 1050, seems once to have had a large parish that extended well beyond the city walls to the north, east, and south. In about 1200 this parish was considered to embrace what later became the separate parishes of Heavitree and Topsham, and they are therefore included in this account.[4] The western suburb of St Thomas across the River Exe constituted a different parish, that of Cowick which lay under the control of Cowick Priory from the mid twelfth century. However this area was united with the city of Exeter in 1900, and as it is now an integral part, its churches and chapels are also listed and referred to in the following pages. In 1966 the city's boundaries were further extended to take in the formerly rural parish of Alphington. That parish has not been included except for

---

[3] Beatrix F. Cresswell, *Exeter Churches* (Exeter, 1908); Frances Rose-Troup, *Lost Chapels of Exeter*, History of Exeter Research Group, 1 (Exeter, 1923); Nicholas Orme, 'The Medieval Chapels of Heavitree Parish', *Devon Archaeological Society Proceedings*, 49 (1991, publ. 1993), 121–9; David Francis, *Lost Churches*, Discovering Exeter, 7 (Exeter, Civic Society, 1995).

[4] *English Episcopal Acta*, vol. XII: *Exeter 1186–1257*, ed. Frank Barlow (London and Oxford, 1996), 172–4.

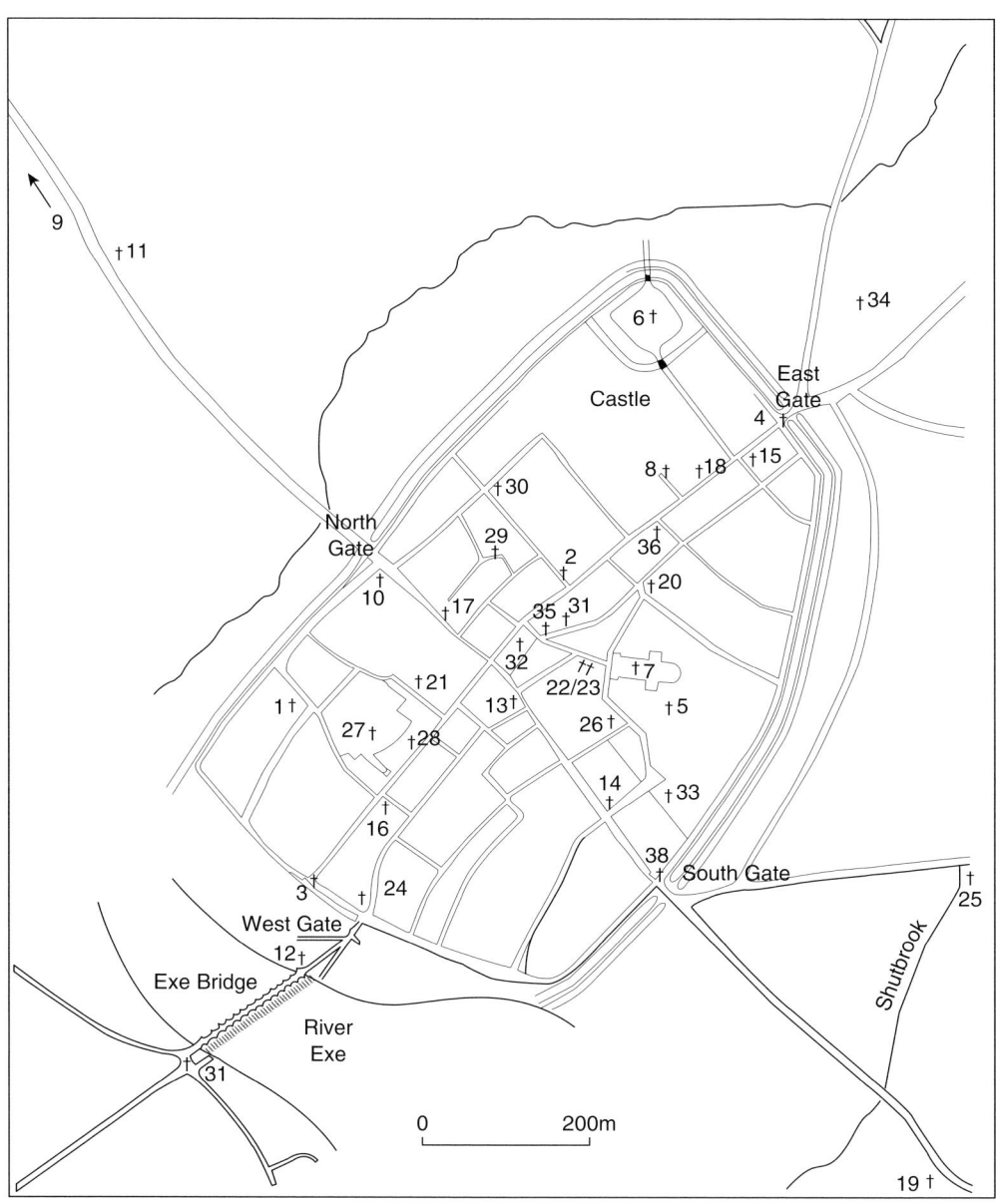

Religious sites in the city of Exeter before 1222.

MAP IDENTIFICATIONS

1 St Alexius Hospital	20 St Martin
2 All Hallows (Goldsmith Street)	21 St Mary Arches
3 All Hallows-on-the-Wall	22 St Mary Major
4 St Bartholomew	23 St Mary Minor
5 Bishop's Chapel (St Faith)	24 St Mary Steps
6 Castle Chapel (St Mary)	25 St Mary Magdalene Hospital
7 Cathedral (SS Mary and Peter)	26 St Michael
8 Christchurch	27 St Nicholas Priory
9 St Clement	28 St Olave
10 St Cuthbert	29 St Pancras
11 St David	30 St Paul
12 St Edmund	31 St Peter Minor
13 St George	32 St Petroc
14 St James	33 St Radegund
15 St John Hospital	34 St Sidwell
16 St John Bow	35 SS Simon and Jude
17 St Kerrian	36 St Stephen
18 St Laurence	37 St Thomas
19 St Leonard	38 Holy Trinity

the priory of St Mary Marsh at Marsh Barton which lay within it, on the grounds that the priory had a close connection with the church of St John Bow and other urban property in Exeter.

Before addressing the subject, it is necessary to say something about the names that will be used for the various foundations. The commonest word for a religious building or organisation in the Middle Ages was 'church' (Latin *ecclesia*), which was used for a wide range of foundations. It could be applied to cathedrals, abbeys, priories, friaries, or hospitals, both to the buildings used for worship and to the institutions as a whole: 'the church of St Nicholas' as an alternative to 'St Nicholas Priory'. Parish churches were also known as 'churches' by the tenth and eleventh centuries, and so were religious buildings of lower status which did not possess parishes or were more private in nature. In Domesday Book, for example, two such buildings in and near Exeter – St James and probably St Stephen – are referred to as churches, and St John Bow is similarly named as late as the 1160s.[5] During the early twelfth century, however, the words 'chapel' and 'oratory' came into use to describe lesser places of worship that were not parish churches. 'Oratory' tended

---

[5] *Domesday Book: Devon*, ed. Caroline and Frank Thorn, 2 vols (Chichester, 1985), 15/1, 52/50; below, p. 117.

to be applied to rooms set aside for prayer in private houses and 'chapel' to purpose-built places of worship, either inside churches or as free-standing buildings, but 'chapel' is also found being used for private rooms which on other occasions might be described as 'oratories'.[6]

The word 'chapel' has a distinctive history at Exeter because the cathedral was considered to be the parish church of the walled city up to the early thirteenth century, as well as of the districts outside the walls that became the parishes of Heavitree, St Leonard, and Topsham. Other lesser churches existed within this area and functioned like parish churches in most respects, but they did not possess parishes. As the usage of the word 'chapel' increased during the middle of the twelfth century, they came to be called by that word rather than 'church' and it was the normal term for them by the 1190s. Then in 1222 many of these lesser churches inside and outside the city walls were given the status of parish churches and provided with territories. This made them technically churches again, although they continued to be regarded as chapels in some respects until at least the early sixteenth century, chiefly because they had no rights of funeral or burial. The change of 1222, however, brought about a clearer distinction between churches and chapels in Exeter. Churches had parishes, acquired parish organisations, and formed part of the public structure of the Church. Chapels were essentially private buildings with restricted rights and activities, and they were subject to the authority of the parish church and clergyman in whose parish they lay.

The terminology of the present volume largely follows the historical sources, while trying to make the nature of each institution clear to the reader. Religious houses are usually referred to by the words used for them at the time: cathedral, friary, hospital, minster, monastery, nunnery, or priory. The lesser churches in and around Exeter are generally called chapels before the introduction of parishes in 1222, and churches thereafter if they were given parishes but chapels if they were not. The word 'chapel' is also applied to sections of religious buildings that contained altars, and to private places of worship in houses rather than calling them oratories.

---

[6] E.g. A visitation of canons' houses in 1301 refers to their 'chapels', whereas Bishop Stapledon's register (1307–26) prefers the word 'oratory' for similar places, but sometimes talks of 'chapels or oratories' (*The Register of Walter de Stapeldon, Bishop of Exeter*, ed. F. C. Hingeston-Randolph (London and Exeter, 1892), 153–4, 298–302). On the Latin words *capella* and *oratorium*, see *Dictionary of Medieval Latin from British Sources*, ed. D. R. Howlett and others (London, 1975–2013).

Church and Chapel Foundations before 1100

The dates at which the Exeter churches and chapels originated are usually hard to identify. Up to about 1200 we possess only scattered evidence about their existence from documents, small survivals of masonry, and burials. The earliest signs of a church are the burials found in the south-west corner of the Cathedral Close which date from the fifth century and point to a building for Christian worship in the area of the Roman forum.[7] These are followed chronologically by a reference of the eighth century to a monastery where the young St Boniface is said to have been based in about the 680s, a monastery that may have been founded by a king of the West Saxons in 670. By the time that the church is next mentioned in about the 890s, the monastery is likely to have evolved into a minster of clerks or canons who lived a more worldly life than monks in separate houses, often with wives and families. The minster of the 890s was under royal patronage. It was reorganised and perhaps re-endowed by King Æthelstan, probably in the year 932 and still as a community of clerks, but in 968 King Edgar appointed an abbot 'to rule the monks gathered at Exeter'. This signified an intention to turn the church back to a monastery, but the monastic community did not last and by the early eleventh century it had given way once more to a body of clerks or canons. In 1050 the king gave the minster to the bishop of Crediton, who moved his seat there so that it became the cathedral of Devon and Cornwall. From this time onwards it was staffed by a group of canons.[8]

Today the words 'minster' and 'cathedral' evoke the thought of a single great building. When the site of the church of St Mary Major was excavated in the 1970s, west of the cathedral, it revealed the foundations of a late Anglo-Saxon church which was identified as *the* minster church that became the cathedral in 1050.[9] The building was indeed of some size,[10] but major religious sites of that era often had more than one church, and although no second church has yet been discovered, there are signs that it might have existed, perhaps further east on the site of the present cathedral. One such sign is the dedication of the minster jointly to Mary and Peter, since some other major churches with two patron saints had a building for each of them.[11] Another is the likelihood that the minster required two buildings in order

---

[7] P. T. Bidwell, *The Legionary Bath-House and Basilica and Forum at Exeter* (Exeter, 1979), 2, 111–13.

[8] On the early history of the minster, see Nicholas Orme, *Exeter Cathedral: the first thousand years, 400–1550* (Exeter, 2009), 1–17.

[9] C. Henderson and P. T. Bidwell, 'The Saxon Minster at Exeter', in *The Early Church in Western Britain and Ireland*, ed. Susan M. Pearce (Oxford, 1982), 145–76.

[10] Estimated at 32.4 metres in length externally (ibid., 162).

[11] John Blair and Nicholas Orme, 'The Anglo-Saxon Minster and Cathedral at Exeter: twin churches?', *Friends of Exeter Cathedral 65th Annual Report* (1995), 24–6.

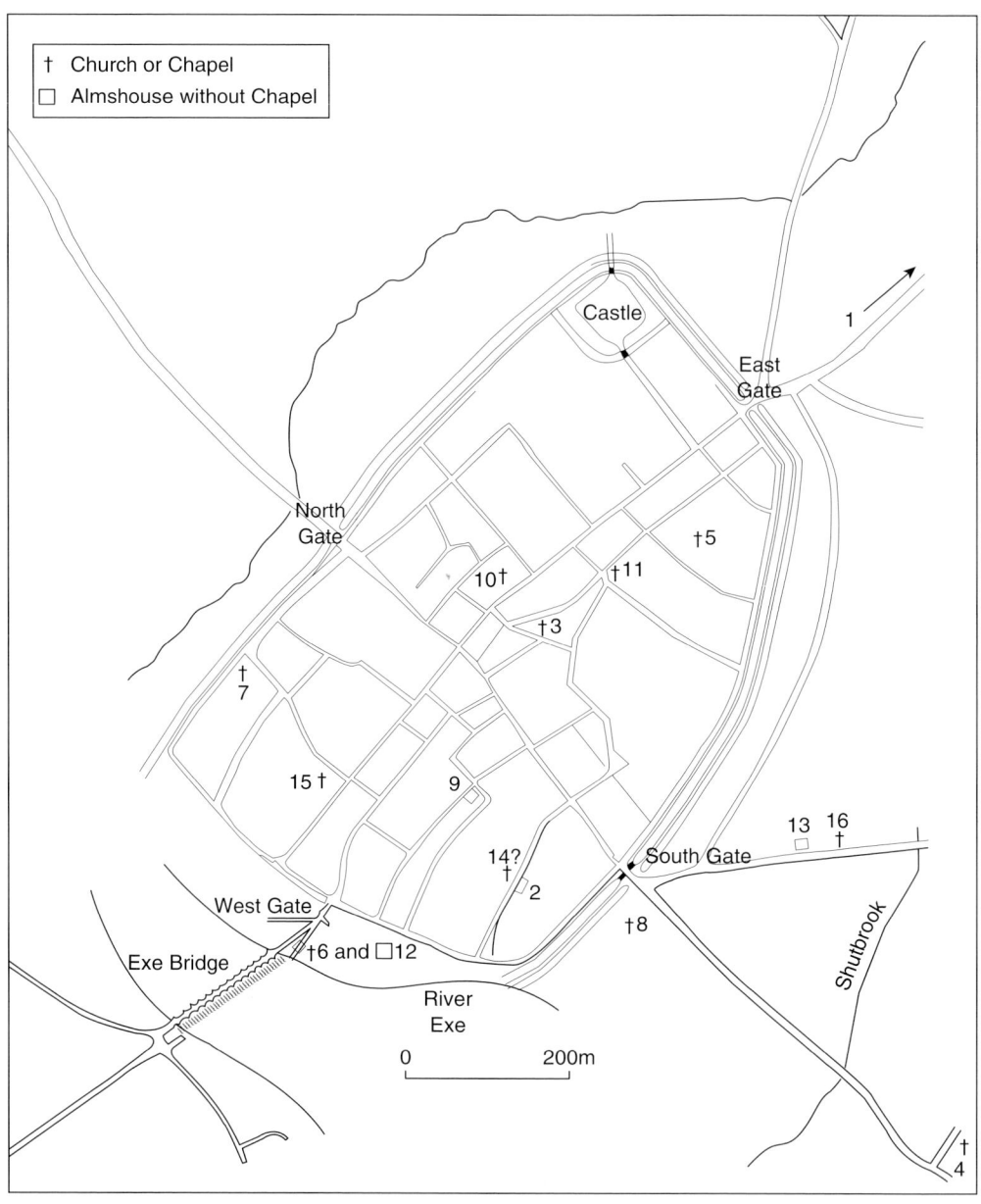

Religious sites in the city of Exeter, 1222–1548.

MAP IDENTIFICATIONS

1 St Anne
2 Bonville's Almshouse
3 Charnel Chapel
4 St Clair
5 Dominican Friary
6 Exe Bridge Chapel
7 Franciscan Friary (I)
8 Franciscan Friary (II)
9 Grendon's Almshouse
10 Guildhall Chapel
11 St Katherine's Almshouse
12 More's and Fortescue's Almshouse
13 Palmer's Almshouse
14 St Roche Hospital
15 Tuckers Hall
16 Wynard's Almshouse

---

to function. When the monks were introduced in 968, it is unlikely that the resident clerks or canons were immediately removed. They remained until they should die out or be bought out, but since monks and clerks performed their services in different ways, the two groups would have had to do so separately. Worcester, with a similar situation, had two churches for the purpose.[12]

A second church would have been helpful to cater for lay people too, because monks lived in relative seclusion and their services were elaborate ones. The minster and its successor the cathedral were the parish church of the city and its eastern hinterland until the early thirteenth century. It is probable that most funerals took place at the minster, followed by burials in its churchyard, as they certainly did later on at the cathedral.[13] In addition the minster, as we shall see, would have had houses and tenants in the city, and it was usual to require tenants to attend their landlord's church. It is conceivable therefore that the building on the site of St Mary Major was this more public church, called St Mary, and that a more private church for clergy, named St Peter, lay further east of it. Even after a new cathedral was built on the eastern site, beginning in 1114, a second church was still required to the west of it, since St Mary (later St Mary Major) was retained and partly rebuilt during the twelfth century. This must have been to fulfil some general role with respect to the cathedral or the city, since it did not become a parish church until 1222.

No other religious site in Exeter is recorded in documents until the eleventh century. However there are indications that other churches may have existed before that date. The strongest is the discovery of graves attributable to the late Anglo-Saxon

---

[12] John Blair, *The Church in Anglo-Saxon Society* (Oxford, 2005), 351–2, which argues that it was unusual for clerks to be expelled in favour of monks.
[13] David Lepine and Nicholas Orme, *Death and Memory in Medieval Exeter*, DCRS, new series 46 (2003), 6–8.

period (ninth to eleventh centuries) on the site of Exeter Castle.[14] Graves imply a church standing in much the same area as the later Castle Chapel, and Dr Robert Higham has made cogent suggestions about the context for such a church and graves.[15] Since the churchyard of the minster was probably the normal place of burial in Exeter because the other city churches did not have burial grounds, the church on the castle site must have had an unusual privilege in this respect. Dr Higham observes that the castle area may have been chosen for fortification by William the Conqueror in 1068 because it was already a royal residence or headquarters. This would fit with the presence of a church having burial rights, since these would have been easier to acquire at a site belonging to the king, especially as the minster itself was a royal possession.

Three other pieces of evidence are less tangible. The Life of St Paul Aurelian, the patron saint of St Pol-de-Léon in Brittany, which was written in that province in 884, claims that the saint had a virgin sister named Sitofolla who lived near the English Channel.[16] Sitofolla may be a variant form of *Sativola*, the Latin version of Sidwell who is recorded as a saint in Exeter in later times. Paul's life dates were not known to the author of his Life and are not known today, so the most that can be gathered from this source is that the Breton author may have been aware of a cult of Sidwell in Exeter in the late 800s, presumably with some kind of cult centre: chapel or holy well. The second is a document of the first half of the tenth century which contains a set of rules for a guild of wealthy men. The guild held meetings in the city three times a year, including the celebration of mass by a priest, but the rules do not specify where the masses should take place. They could have been said at the minster or at some other church.[17] The third is the shaft of a tenth- or eleventh-century Saxon cross found in the ruins of Exe Bridge and now in the Royal Albert Memorial Museum, Exeter. This is certainly a piece of Christian art and probably once stood in the city, but its original site and purpose are unknown.[18]

---

[14] *Exeter Castle: history, fabric analysis and excavation*, ed. Stuart R. Blaylock (forthcoming).
[15] R. A. Higham, *Making Anglo-Saxon Devon* (Exeter, 2008), 188; idem, 'William the Conqueror's Siege of Exeter in 1068', *Devonshire Association Transactions*, 145 (2013), 67–106; idem, 'The Origins and Context of Exeter Castle', in *Exeter Castle*, ed. Blaylock (forthcoming).
[16] Nicholas Orme, *The Saints of Cornwall* (Oxford, 2000), 212, 234.
[17] P. W. Conner, *Anglo-Saxon Exeter: a tenth-century cultural history* (Woodbridge, 1993), 168–9; *English Historical Documents c.500–1042*, ed. Dorothy Whitelock, 2nd ed. (London and New York, 1979), 605.
[18] Rosemary Cramp, *Corpus of Anglo-Saxon Stone Sculpture*, vol. VII: *South West England* (London, 2006), 86–7.

The shortage of records before about 1000 needs to be emphasised because in 1873 a romantic writer named Thomas Kerslake proposed a theory that many of the Exeter churches existed as early as Æthelstan's reign.[19] His starting point was a statement by the historian William of Malmesbury, who visited Exeter in the 1120s, that Æthelstan evicted the Cornish from Exeter 'where they had lived until then on an equal footing with the English'.[20] Supposing the city to have been divided into distinct areas inhabited by 'Celts' and Saxons, Kerslake assigned some of the Exeter churches recorded in the twelfth and thirteenth centuries to an imagined 'Celtic' area on the basis of their dedications (notably David, Kerrian, and Petroc) and others to a 'Saxon' area (including George, Laurence, Martin, and Stephen). The theory convinced some local historians but it does not bear examination.[21] William tells us that he heard stories about Æthelstan from local people, and the division of the city was evidently one of these stories and as such a piece of folklore. It is not compatible with the rest of our knowledge about the history of Exeter, and the city could not have had a large community of Cornish people in Æthelstan's reign. The only indubitable 'Celtic' church dedications in Exeter are the three mentioned above, and it will be argued in due course that they are just as likely to have arisen between the tenth and twelfth centuries. There may indeed have been more churches in Exeter than the minster by Æthelstan's reign, and these churches may have included some of those recorded later on. But no later church has yet been attested so early, either in writings or material remains.

Historians must work from evidence, and we reach safe ground in this respect only after about 1000 when places of worship other than the minster come into view in documentary records or material remains. Between then and the Norman Conquest in 1066, there is evidence for six and possibly seven churches in Exeter besides the cathedral. The first is the postulated church at the Castle and the second St Sidwell, whose saint appears more clearly than before with references to her in relic lists and in an inventory of English shrines from about the early part of the century. These imply the existence of a church containing her tomb by that date. St Olave was probably endowed by 1063, St Martin was dedicated in 1065, and both these churches include some Anglo-Saxon masonry as did St Stephen and the now-vanished St George. An unnamed church, which we shall suggest was St Stephen,

---

[19] T. Kerslake, 'The Celt and the Teuton in Exeter', *Archaeological Journal*, 30 (1873), 211–25, reprinted in *Saint Richard the King of Englishmen and his Territory A.D. 700–720* (Clevedon, 1890), 75–96.

[20] William of Malmesbury, *Gesta Regum Anglorum*, ed. R. A. B. Mynors, R. M. Thomson, and M. Winterbottom, 2 vols (Oxford, 1998–9), i, 216–17.

[21] E.g. Cresswell, *Exeter Churches*, 1–2.

appears in Domesday Book as having belonged to King Edward the Confessor in 1066,[22] and a further candidate is St Mary Steps. This church possessed the alternative name of St Edward who can only have been King Edward the Martyr (died 978). His cult spread widely during the next hundred years or so, and is likely to have been most popular at Exeter in the eleventh century.[23]

The next resource for the history of Exeter's churches is Domesday Book of 1086. Its compilers were not concerned with churches unless they possessed landed property subject to tax. Five achieved mention in Exeter, a number that is roughly comparable with the evidence from other major cities. Two of these were included because they were associated with urban property or landed estates: St Olave and the Castle Chapel, to be described in a following paragraph.[24] A third is revealed by an estate called *Jacobescherche*, named from a small private church that later became the priory church of St James and lay outside the city to the south-west.[25] Finally two churches were mentioned but not identified. One was owned by the bishop and located 'in Exeter' according to the local or 'Exon' version of Domesday, and 'in the city' as stated by the national or 'Exchequer' text of the Book. It was linked with forty-seven houses in the city that also belonged to the bishop.[26] The other church was 'in Exeter' in both texts of Domesday, and in the ownership of Robert count of Mortain.[27] Until the early twentieth century the bishop's church was believed to be St Stephen, because in later times it was his church and was connected with the houses he owned, while the count's was conjectured as St Laurence.[28] In fact there are grounds for rejecting both of these attributions. St Laurence appears to have belonged to the Pomeroy family, while the most reliable evidence about St Stephen states that it was given to Bishop William Warelwast by King Henry I. This gift took place between 1107, when William became bishop, and 1123, when the king confirmed the grant.[29] Henry is most likely to have acquired the church from William count of Mortain, Robert's son, whose property he confiscated in 1106, which suggests that St Stephen was the count's church in 1086. In any event it could not have been that of the bishop.

---

[22] *Domesday Book*, ed. Thorn, 15/1.
[23] D&C 2513; below, p. 18.
[24] *Domesday Book*, ed. Thorn, 9/2, 16/89–92.
[25] Ibid., 52/50.
[26] *Domesday Book: Additamenta*, ed. H. Ellis (London, Record Commission, 1816), p. 111 (f. 120v); *Domesday Book*, ed. Thorn, 2/1.
[27] *Domesday Book*, ed. Thorn, 15/1.
[28] For discussion of what follows, see below, pp. 123, 166–7.
[29] *Regesta Regum Anglo-Normannorum*, ed. H. W. C. Davis et al., 4 vols (Oxford, 1913–59), ii, 185.

The search for the bishop's church must therefore be extended to the other three churches with which he was linked in medieval Exeter: St Mary Arches, St Sidwell, and the cathedral. St Mary Arches is not recorded as belonging to the bishop until 1334, but its elaborate architecture suggests that his ownership can be traced back to at least 1200. However its poor documentary profile provides no basis for establishing its existence in 1086 and casts doubt on its role at that date as an important church associated with the bishop's houses in Exeter. The historian W. G. Hoskins proposed that St Sidwell was the church in question, on the grounds that it lay in property given by the bishop to the cathedral, to which one might add that Domesday Book would have attributed it to the bishop because the Book does not accredit the cathedral with any property of its own.[30] Nevertheless there are two reasons against accepting St Sidwell as the unnamed church. One is that most of the bishop's houses in Exeter, with which the church is linked, appear in later records as scattered within the city walls or outside them on the north and south sides.[31] It is hard to believe that he expected his tenants to relate to and attend a church as far away as St Sidwell beyond the East Gate. The other reason is the probable origin of the bishop's houses which, we shall now argue, are likely to have once belonged to the minster.

That leaves the cathedral (the former minster) as a candidate to be the bishop's church. It may seem strange that Domesday Book should refer to the cathedral as an unnamed church belonging to the bishop rather than a religious house in its own right. But the Book ignores the cathedral almost completely. The Exon Domesday contains a heading 'Lands of the Church of St Peter of Exeter' (the patron saint of the cathedral), but thereafter it only states that 'the bishop holds' each of the properties concerned. The Exchequer text does not even include this heading, but assigns all the cathedral's traditional lands to the bishop and makes a single allusion to the cathedral canons as having a share in their income.[32] The houses ascribed to the bishop in 1086 must surely have been ones that belonged to the minster before it became the bishop's church in 1050, for they are unlikely to have come into his hands by any other route. Their inhabitants would have been expected to relate to the minster, the church of their landlord, and they were probably still in habit the minster's tenants in 1086, although assigned to the bishop at that time and subsequently under his full control.

---

[30] W. G. Hoskins, 'Early Churches in Exeter', *Friends of Exeter Cathedral 29th Annual Report* (1959), 21.
[31] Muriel Curtis, *Some Disputes between the City and the Cathedral Authorities of Exeter* (Manchester, 1932), 88–91 and passim.
[32] *Domesday Book*, ed. Thorn, 2/8.

The unnamed bishop's church is therefore best identified as the church on the St Mary Major site. This would be equally so if it was the only cathedral church or the outer, western half of a pair of churches: the one that specialised in ministering to lay people. However St Mary, as we may call it, did not remain the church of the bishop's tenants in later years. By the early thirteenth century the bishop's houses and their tenants had become associated with the church of St Stephen which belonged to him in the city, and they now constituted 'St Stephen's Fee' over which the bishop claimed special rights against the powers of the city authorities. It is not clear when this change of church took place: it may have been between 1114 and 1133 at the time that the new Norman cathedral was being built east of St Mary, or at some time later in the twelfth century. The change was evidently remembered in the city, however, where the bishop's claim over St Stephen's Fee was obnoxious to the city authorities, and they seem to have considered that the change undermined or invalidated his claim. This would explain the fabrication of two charters at some point during the twelfth or thirteenth centuries, evidently on the part of the bishop or his officers, which attempted to backdate his ownership of St Stephen to the reign of William the Conqueror. The charters then allowed him to assert that the linkage of the church, the houses, and the rights claimed over them was both ancient and identical with the records of Domesday Book.[33]

Apart from the minster-cathedral, the majority of the churches in these early records were probably small institutions in terms of buildings, staffing, and endowments. Most had a single priest to hold regular or occasional services in return for payment by a landowner or from the donations of worshippers. Two of the churches, however, were more ambitious foundations. St Olave was endowed by one of the greatest women in England: Gytha, the Danish wife of Earl Godwin of Wessex and mother of Earl Harold (King Harold II). She gave it a hide of land at Sherford in the South Hams, which was valued at £3 per annum in Domesday Book, to which Edward the Confessor added a smaller property.[34] She must have meant her gift to support a well-paid priest or a small body of clergy to pray for and publicise the earls of Wessex, although this plan came to nothing after the Norman Conquest. The Castle Chapel was evidently erected and endowed by Baldwin fitz Gilbert (died 1090). He was a Norman invader: lord of Okehampton, sheriff of Devon, and as such the castellan of the new Exeter Castle built by William the Conqueror in or after 1068. The chapel was a new building in the approximate vicinity of the postulated Anglo-Saxon church, and was manned in 1086 by a group of 'canons' in 1086, a canon being a term of status which was also applied to the cathedral clergy. Baldwin too

---

[33] Below, p. 167.
[34] *Domesday Book*, ed. Thorn, 1/34; below, pp. 150–1.

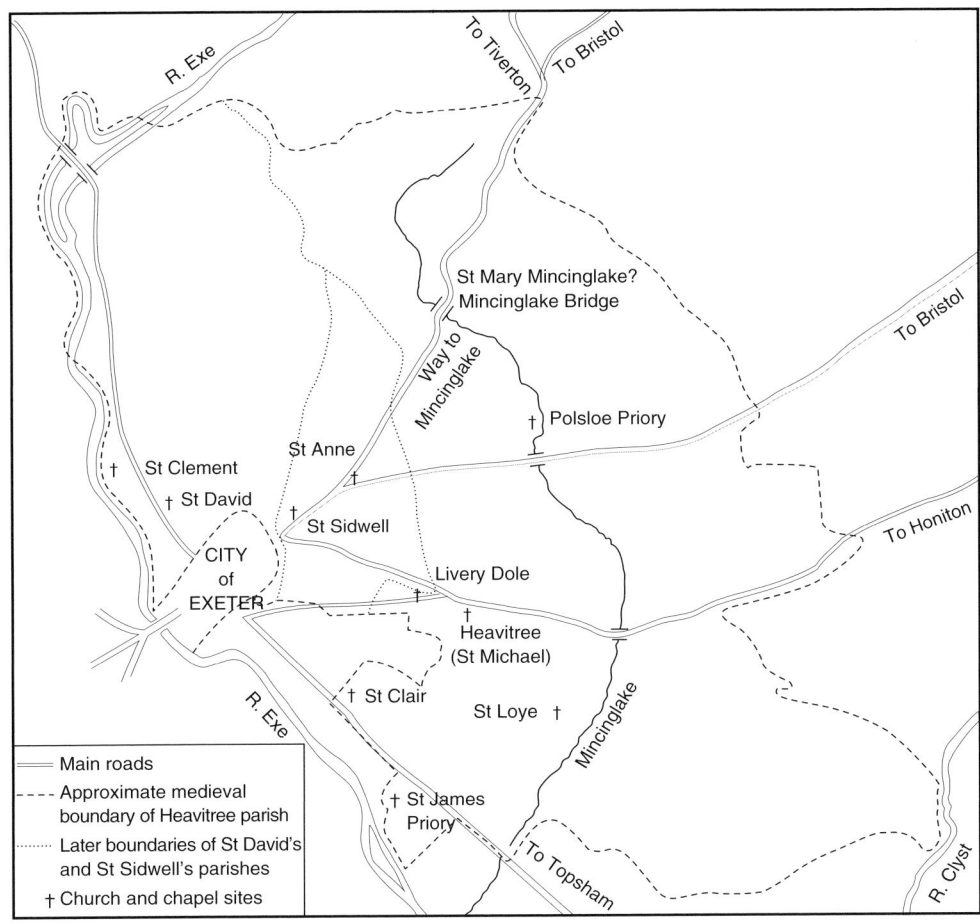

Religious sites in Heavitree parish.

endowed his clergy well with four estates in the Broadclyst area worth £3 15s. per annum according to Domesday Book.[35]

Norman lords valued monasteries more than their English counterparts had recently done, but Baldwin was probably deterred from founding one at the castle because the monastic life would not have fitted with the busy activities of the garrison. Instead the first Exeter monastery of the Norman period was founded in 1087, a

---

[35] *Domesday Book*, ed. Thorn, 16/89–92.

year after the compilation of Domesday Book, by William the Conqueror's abbey of Battle in Sussex. William granted property in Devon to Battle, including Gytha's church of St Olave and its two estates, and these were used to endow a daughter house in Exeter: the priory of St Nicholas, situated a little way below St Olave off Fore Street.[36] This was the first monastery to appear in the city since the days, a century previously, when there had briefly been monks in the minster. Its appearance was not welcome to the bishop of Exeter, Osbern, and the cathedral clergy, who evidently viewed it as a church over which they would have little control, unlike the small parochial chapels in the city. They obstructed St Nicholas from acquiring a burial ground or ringing bells in public, and the monks were obliged to appeal to the pope for support. Only after two popes had intervened did the archbishop of Canterbury, St Anselm, order the bishop and the cathedral to withdraw their opposition, and the monks acquired burial and ringing rights in 1100–2.[37]

Church and Chapel Foundations of the Twelfth Century

After Domesday Book there is a dearth of information about the Exeter churches that lasts until about the middle third of the twelfth century. Royal and episcopal documents rarely mention them, and private deeds have not begun to survive. It is only in 1123 that a reliable reference exists to St Stephen, after which the sources improve to reveal the Bishop's Chapel of St Faith (recorded by 1142); St Leonard (by about 1149); the leper hospital of St Mary Magdalene (by about 1150); St Pancras (by the 1160s); the hospital of St Alexius (founded c.1170); St Kerrian and one of the two chapels of All Hallows (by 1184); the hospital of St John (by 1185); St John Bow (by 1187, but probably earlier); and St Laurence (undatable, but likely to go back to the 1120s). Their appearance is accompanied by records of the foundation of four monasteries, the origins of which are easier to determine. The priory of St Andrew (Cowick) was established by 1137 as a daughter house of the Benedictine abbey of Bec-Hellouin, and that of St James in about 1141 as a dependency of the Cluniac priory of St Martin-des-Champs, both in France. St James occupied what was now called the 'chapel' of St James off Topsham Road but was evidently the same as the 'church' alluded to in Domesday Book.[38] The priory of St Mary Marsh at Marsh Barton in Alphington parish was created as a branch of Plympton Priory in 1142, and the priory of Polsloe, which came into existence in about 1160, was an independent house of Benedictine nuns.

---

[36] Below, p. 145.
[37] *English Episcopal Acta*, vol. XI: *Exeter 1046–1184*, ed. Frank Barlow (London and Oxford, 1996), 6–7.
[38] D&C 2074.

By about 1200 information increases much further through the survival of two lists of religious buildings in and around the city. Not only do the lists enumerate many or most of the extant churches and chapels (omitting the monasteries), but they follow a topographical order that sheds light on the locations involved. The first list, undated but datable between 1194 and 1204, relates to an adjudication by the bishop of Exeter, Henry Marshal, of a dispute between the cathedral chapter of Exeter and the archdeacon of Exeter.[39] The bishop decided that the cathedral chapter was to have jurisdiction over those chapels in and around the city whose clergy it appointed or from which it received revenues. There were seventeen such chapels. The list begins at Holy Trinity by the South Gate, proceeds along South Street to St James, and turns via Palace Gate into the Cathedral Close where it names St Michael, St Mary Major and St Mary Minor, St Petroc, SS Simon and Jude, and St Martin. Next it goes up the High Street to Christchurch near the castle, back to St Kerrian and St Cuthbert in North Street, and thence down Fore Street to All Hallows-on-the-Wall. Finally it leaves the city and travels clockwise round the outskirts to include St Clement, St David, St Sidwell, St Michael at Heavitree, and St Margaret at Topsham.

The second list occurs in a grant of about 1214 by an Exeter citizen, Peter de Palerna, of one penny a year to each of twenty-eight 'chapels' in Exeter in return for prayers to be said in each one on the anniversary of his death.[40] This list commences at St Sidwell outside the East Gate and proceeds through the gate to St Bartholomew which stood just inside it, down the south side of High Street (St Stephen) and into the Cathedral Close (St Martin, St Peter the Great (i.e. the cathedral), St Mary the Great (Major), St Mary the Little (Minor), St Peter the Little, and St Petroc). It then turns into South Street where it includes St James and Holy Trinity on the east side, and passes through the South Gate to St Mary Magdalene (the leper hospital), adding St Leonard whose parish later came up to this point. After this it returns to the west side of South Street (St George), continues down the south side of Fore Street (St John Bow and St Edward), and crosses Exe Bridge from St Edmund at the east end to the original church of St Thomas at the west end. From the bridge it travels back up the north side of Fore Street (All Hallows-on-the-Wall, St Olave, and St Mary Arches), down North Street (St Kerrian and St Cuthbert), and along lanes to St Pancras and St Paul. The final three chapels are Holy Trinity, St Laurence, and All Hallows (Goldsmith Street). These are out of sequence if the compiler was planning to go up the north side of High Street, but he may have been mentally

---

[39] *English Episcopal Acta,* vol. XII, ed. Barlow, 172–4.
[40] D&C 2513, printed in *The Registers of Walter Bronescombe ... and Peter Quivil*, ed. F. C. Hingeston-Randolph (London and Exeter, 1889), 451–2.

completing a circle or aiming to end at the city Guildhall in which case they are in the correct order.

Two churches in Palerna's list are not immediately recognisable. When Mrs Rose-Troup discussed the list in 1923, she argued that St Edward was the Charnel Chapel in the Cathedral Close and that the list-maker had forgotten to put it in its rightful place.[41] The Charnel Chapel was indeed dedicated to Edward, but it was not founded until 1286. St Edward appears where one expects to find St Mary Steps, but that name is absent from the list which indicates that Edward was an earlier name of the same church. Holy Trinity in (or rather off) the High Street is identical with Christchurch in Bishop Marshal's list. Churches dedicated to the Trinity were commonly known by both names and both were used for this chapel, so there is no need to postulate two foundations close together as was done by Rose-Troup and the late C. G. Henderson.[42] Palerna omitted the chapels of the hospitals of St Alexius and St John, those of St Michael and SS Simon and Jude within the Cathedral Close, and those of St Clement, St David, Heavitree, and Topsham outside the city walls, although all were in existence by that date. The latter two were perhaps not then regarded as relating to Exeter, but there is no obvious geographical reason for the exclusion of the others because Palerna included three extramural chapels. One or two of the omitted ones may have lacked a permanent priest, but this was not the case at the hospital of St John, apparently not at SS Simon and Jude, and unlikely at St David which later became a substantial chapel-of-ease. In short, Palerna's list is selective: it cannot be relied on as a complete account of the churches and chapels in and around the city.

Peter de Palerna was not the only person to arrange for sums of one penny to be given to a large number of chaplains in Exeter. The medieval cartulary of the hospital of St John contains some transcripts from 'an old missal' of the parish church of St Martin. These list twelve separate endowments (including Peter's) by which one penny was paid to a prescribed number of chaplains in the city on a particular day of the year. The names of their churches are not recorded. In all but one case the day was probably that of the anniversary of a person's death and the payment (like Peter's) was made in expectation of prayers for the donor's soul. The numbers of chaplains vary: twenty-four in one endowment, twenty-eight in two, twenty-nine in one, and thirty-two in eight. A thirteenth endowment does not mention prayers for the dead, although such prayers may have been involved, and was a payment

---

[41] Rose-Troup, *Lost Chapels*, 19–20, 34–7.
[42] *Historical Atlas of South-West England*, ed. Kain and Ravenhill, 487.

of 29*d*. by the provost of Exeter to twenty-nine chaplains: a sum alleged to have been given by 'King William from the collection of the stepgable (*stepgabuli*)', meaning the market dues.[43] If we could be sure that this payment was given by the Conqueror or by his successor William Rufus, we could conjecture most of the thirteenth-century churches and chapels back to at least the year 1100. However, the temptation should be resisted. The royal attribution may be only a conjecture or, if true, may have been an order to pay 1*d*. 'to each chaplain', which meant twenty-nine by the date of the missal entry, perhaps in the thirteenth century. Nor need the discrepancies between the other numbers represent stages in the numerical growth of religious foundations. As we have seen, Palerna's grant excluded several extant chapels, and others may have limited themselves in similar ways. Even thirty-two was not the largest potential total.

The significance of these payments is that they demonstrate their donors' awareness of the city and its clergy as a single entity. Legally this was the case, for, as we shall see, there were no parish churches in Exeter save for the cathedral until 1222. After parishes were established, people's horizons tended to narrow, and donors of charity in the later Middle Ages demonstrated more interest in their parish church or favourite religious house, and less in the city as a whole than their predecessors had done.

The Early Church and Chapel Foundations: an Analysis

By about 1214 there were some thirty-four public churches and chapels in and around Exeter as well as private chapels and nine religious houses which will be treated in later sections. Owing to the fragmentary evidence, it is not possible to say when most of them were founded. As we have seen, about ten were probably extant by 1100: the cathedral (perhaps with two buildings), the church at the castle, and those dedicated to St Edward alias St Mary Steps, St George, St James (the later priory), St Martin, St Nicholas (the priory), St Olave, St Sidwell, and St Stephen. Of these only the cathedral-minster and St Sidwell show signs of existence before 1000, while St Edward, St Martin, and St Olave look likely to be later than that date along with St Nicholas. Eleven or twelve foundations were made during the twelfth century: four of the monasteries, the three hospitals, and the non-monastic chapels of Christchurch, St Edmund, St Mary Major, St Thomas, and perhaps SS Simon and

---

[43] ECA, Book 53A f. 36r. Similar grants include 48*d*. to the parish chaplains of Exeter in 1293 (ECA, ED/M/170); 28*d*. to the rectors and vicars of the city in 1298 (ECA, 51/1/1/6); and 16*d*. to the parish chaplains of Exeter in 1314 (ECA, ED/M/223).

20 The Early Church and Chapel Foundations: an Analysis

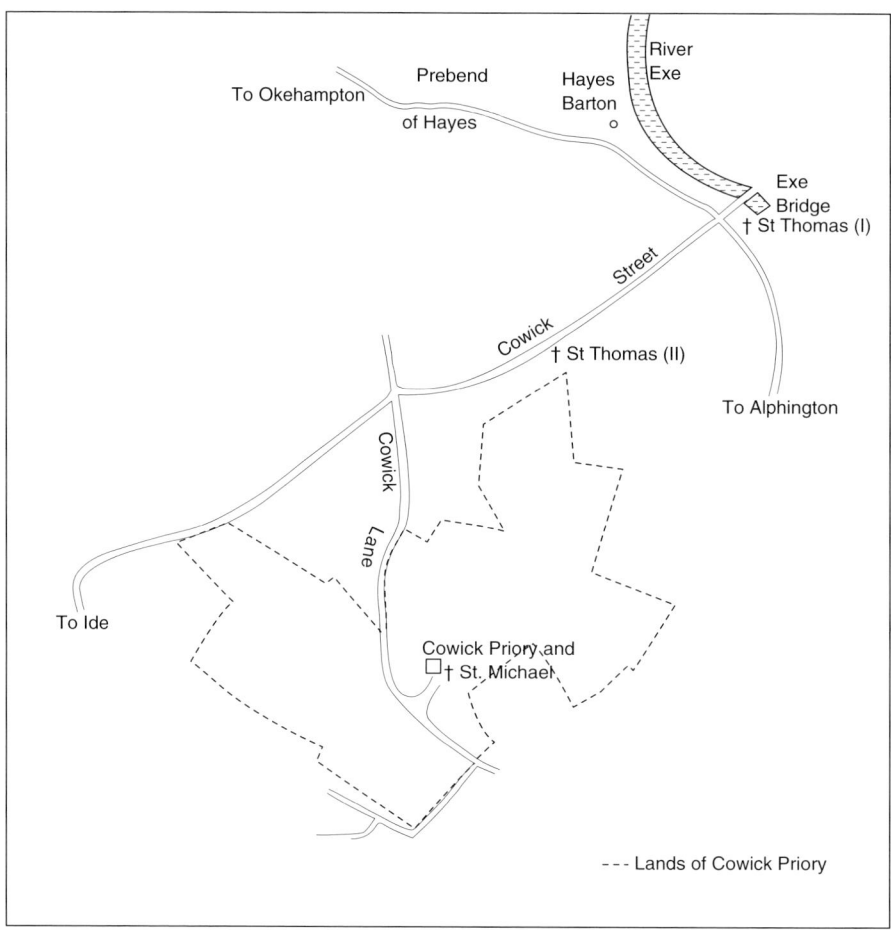

Religious sites in Cowick (St Thomas) parish.

Jude. The last to appear were probably St Edmund and St Thomas towards the end of the century. The origins of the rest cannot be traced, and their dedications offer no help in this respect because they are common ones that might have been given in either late Anglo-Saxon or Norman times. It is therefore impossible to gauge the rate of church foundations across the eleventh and twelfth centuries or to relate this to the growth of the city and its suburbs, except to observe that the monasteries and hospitals were all founded between about the 1080s and 1180s.

Officially the cathedral remained the only parish church of Exeter and its surroundings east of the River Exe until 1222 when, as we shall see, these areas were divided into parishes. In this respect it resembled the minsters and cathedrals of some other ancient cities, such as Winchester and Worcester, although Exeter was unusual in the length of time that the cathedral held on to its parochial monopoly.[44] As late as the early thirteenth century, Pope Innocent III (1198–1216) granted the cathedral canons the privilege that no-one might erect a mother church within their parish.[45] Even after 1222 everyone within the city walls of Exeter was obliged to be taken after death for a funeral in the cathedral, and all had to be buried in the cathedral cemetery (the green area within the Cathedral Close) unless they gained permission otherwise. This rule was not relaxed until 1637.[46] Only the Castle Chapel (in a privileged area of the city), the monasteries, the leper hospital of St Mary Magdalene (probably), and the extramural churches and chapels of Cowick, St David, Heavitree, St Leonard, St Sidwell, and Topsham acquired their own churchyards. The question therefore arises: if the clergy of the cathedral were so fiercely defensive of their funeral and burial rights, why did they tolerate the proliferation of so many other places of worship within the parochial area that they controlled?

They were not always tolerant. They resisted the foundation of St Nicholas Priory, prevented the hospital of St John from having a graveyard until the mid fourteenth century, and had sometimes strained relationships with the Exeter friaries. They were less concerned about the lesser churches in Exeter, on the other hand, since the cathedral remained officially the mother church of the city and the others as its subordinate chapels. Moreover a majority of these chapels ended up in the cathedral's ownership, having (one presumes) been given to it by the founders. The chapel functions too – daily prayers, masses, and probably pastoral services like baptism – were evidently not regarded as threatening the cathedral's status but rather as relieving it of responsibilities. Then there was the fact that some of the chapels were founded or owned by people of importance whose goodwill mattered and who could not be obstructed. The pre-Norman church on the castle site, as we have seen, is likely to have had a royal origin, and Edward the Confessor owned at least one other church which we have proposed as St Stephen.[47] St Olave, endowed or re-endowed by Countess Gytha, appears to have related to a nearby area known in the twelfth century as *Irlesbery*, 'the earl's enclosure', which belonged to her husband Earl Godwin of Wessex and their son Earl Harold, later King Harold II. Her foundation probably provided a place of worship for this area and any tenants

---

[44] Keene, *Medieval Winchester*, 107; *English Episcopal Acta*, vol. xxxiii: *Worcester: 1062–1185*, ed. Mary Cheney et al. (London and Oxford, 2007), 10–12.
[45] *Reg. Bronescombe*, ed. Hingeston-Randolph, 240.
[46] Lepine and Orme, *Death and Memory*, 3–24.
[47] *Domesday Book*, ed. Thorn, 15/1.

of the earls in the city.⁴⁸ Mention has been made of the count of Mortain's church, the probability of a church belonging to the Pomeroy family, and the Castle Chapel built by Baldwin fitz Gilbert. If the conjecture is right that St John Bow was once in the hands of Baldwin's granddaughter, it would have been another foundation or possession of his family.⁴⁹ Two other Domesday landlords, Geoffrey (bishop of Coutances) and Walter of Douai, held significant urban properties in Exeter and may have founded or annexed chapels for themselves and their dependents.⁵⁰ Two rural estate owners certainly did so at St James (the later priory) and St Leonard.

Many of the Exeter chapels were therefore 'seigneurial' in origin and had an important role in proclaiming the presence and status of their lordly founders or appropriators in the religious and secular capital of the region. Some of these lords had a house in Exeter at the time of Domesday and may have worshipped in their chapels while they resided. Prayers would have been said therein for them and their families, and the chapels provided meeting and bonding places for their tenants and servants. We may also classify St John Bow, St Mary Arches, and St Stephen as belonging to lords, although in their case the lords were the bishop and the priory of Plympton. But not all the Exeter chapels need have been founded or acquired by kings, lords, or prelates. It was possible for a wealthy local man or woman to build one as an act of private devotion and to increase the veneration of Christ or a saint. The twelfth-century martyrology of Exeter Cathedral records on 26 February the name of Algar whom it described as 'our brother', meaning a member of the cathedral's confraternity of supporters, with the comment 'he built Christchurch'.⁵¹ This was probably the chapel near the High Street which was subsequently owned by the cathedral, presumably through Algar's donation. The three hospitals also look like foundations by well-to-do Exeter citizens, and the bridge chapel of St Edmund may have been a civic enterprise to encourage funds for the bridge. Yet other chapels may have originated with a group of neighbours who wished to provide a place of worship for their street, or with a guild that required a place in which to worship together.

Two chapels certainly had links with guilds. Shortly after 1200 the canons of the cathedral made an agreement with 'the twenty brethren of the city of Exeter and the Kalendar brethren', who appear to have constituted two separate guilds that

---

⁴⁸ Higham, *Making Anglo-Saxon Devon*, 187. Part of the same area, around St Nicholas Priory, was known as 'Harold's Fee' in the fifteenth century (*Letters and Papers of John Shillingford, Mayor of Exeter 1447–50*, ed. Stuart A. Moore, Camden Society, new series 2 (1871), 10).
⁴⁹ Below, p. 118.
⁵⁰ *Domesday Book*, ed. Thorn, 3/1, 23/27.
⁵¹ D&C 3518; Lepine and Orme, *Death and Memory*, 250–8 at 251.

were federated or united at this time.[52] By the agreement the brethren granted the canons their rights in the chapels of St Peter the Little and St Paul, and the canons allowed them to hold their 'kalendar masses' in the chapel of St Mary Major.[53] Similar 'Kalendar' brethren or guilds are recorded in Bristol and Winchester in the thirteenth century.[54] They included clergy, men, and women, usually of higher status, and were so called because they met for the celebration of mass on the 'kalends' or first day of the month, at which prayers were said for the brethren whose anniversaries of death lay in that month. It is known that the Exeter guild of Kalendars received rent from a piece of land by the chapel of St Paul in 1254, which makes it look as though that chapel was the original venue of that guild.[55] If so, perhaps St Peter the Little was that of the 'guild of twenty'. Admittedly in neither case can we be sure that the guilds had founded these places of worship. They may have chosen existing buildings as suitable places to meet.

The sites of the early churches and chapels, as has been seen, are approximately traceable from the two topographical lists and more certainly from the later survival of some of their buildings in a standing form or on maps. The locations may be divided into three categories. Within the Cathedral Close there were six significant buildings: St Martin, St Mary Major, St Mary Minor, St Michael, St Peter the Little, and SS Simon and Jude, as well as the private chapel of the bishop and eventually those of the cathedral canons. Here a wish to be near the cathedral and its cemetery was no doubt a motive for the siting. Outside the Close but within the city walls there were twenty-one chapels. Most of these were on or just off the four major streets. Of these streets, North Street had St Cuthbert and St Kerrian; South Street Holy Trinity, St George, and St James; High Street All Hallows (Goldsmith Street), St Bartholomew, St John (hospital), St Laurence, St Petroc, and St Stephen; and Fore Street All Hallows-on-the-Wall, St John Bow, St Mary Steps, and St Olave, with St Edmund beyond on Exe Bridge. Four buildings were also close to the city gates, a feature commonly found in other walled cities. St Cuthbert was by the North Gate, St Bartholomew by the East, Holy Trinity by the South, and St Mary Steps by the West. Only a few sites were in minor streets or alleys: Christchurch, St Alexius, St Paul, St Pancras, and the Castle Chapel. With these exceptions a wish to give prominence to places of worship is apparent, which may be a sign of fairly early

---

[52] Guilds containing twenty members are recorded elsewhere in Devon in about 1100 (Lepine and Orme, *Death and Memory*, 259–61).

[53] Nicholas Orme, 'The Kalendar Brethren of the City of Exeter', *Reports and Transactions of the Devonshire Association*, 109 (1977), 153–69; idem, 'The Guild of Kalendars, Bristol', *Bristol and Gloucestershire Archaeological Society Transactions*, 96 (1978), 33–52.

[54] D&C 2078; Orme, 'The Kalendar Brethren', 154–5.

[55] ECA, ED/M/80.

origins when premium situations within the walls were still available. Siting was further assisted by the cathedral's monopoly of burials, since no building inside the city walls needed to acquire space for a churchyard save for St Nicholas Priory which had one for its members.

The third kind of location was outside the walls, where there were eleven chapels. Eight of these lay within the cathedral's jurisdiction: St Clement, St David, St Edmund, St Leonard, St Margaret (Topsham), St Michael (Heavitree), St Sidwell, and the chapel of the leper hospital of St Mary Magdalene. The other three were beyond the river in Cowick: the joint monastery and parish church of St Andrew with the chapels of St Michael and St Thomas. Most of the extramural churches or chapels served the city suburbs or other outlying settlements, although the function of St Clement (near the present St David's Station) is not clear in that respect. Nevertheless it is worth noting that three were sited a little way off main roads rather than beside them. These were St Clement, Heavitree, and St Sidwell, to which we might add St James Priory, which had an earlier existence as a non-monastic chapel, and Cowick Priory, which may have had one. Seclusion from a road was natural for a religious house and was chosen by all four of the priories established outside Exeter in the twelfth century, but it is more difficult to explain in respect of the non-monastic chapels. There were also some peripheral areas within the city walls where chapels were not built, either through the poverty of these areas or their usage for other purposes. This was true of the southern part of the 'West Quarter' between South Street and Fore Street, the north-west of the city near Bartholomew Street, the grounds of the Bishop's Palace, the south-east of the city (where the Dominican Friary was eventually built), and the Castle precinct.

The dedications of the early churches and chapels also merit attention, despite the lack of a timeline in which most of them can be placed. We think of dedications as limited to a single name – Holy Trinity, Christchurch, or a saint – but some if not all consisted of three or four names, of which only one was commonly used. Examples of this, with the dates on which the names are first recorded, include:

  St George: God, St Mary, St George, and All Saints (*c*.1330)
  St John hospital: God, Mary, John the Baptist, and All Saints (1224–35)
  St Martin: Jesus Christ, Holy Cross, Mary, Martin, and All Saints (1065)
  St Olave: Mary, Thomas the Apostle, and Olave (1063)
  St Roche hospital: Mary, the Eleven Thousand Virgins, and Roche (1521)

The church dedications of the major English cities were usually those widely used in the Middle Ages. Exeter's list of Holy Trinity, All Hallows or Saints, Mary, George, James, John the Baptist, Martin, Michael, Peter, Paul, and Thomas Becket includes names commonly found in Canterbury, Lincoln, Norwich, Oxford, Winchester, and York. Another four of Exeter's saints were English or Scandinavian but also common elsewhere. Cuthbert was a northern figure in origin and Edmund an East Anglian one, who both gained churches in the south and west of England. Edward, who we have argued was the Martyr, spread widely across the former territories of Wessex, and Olave (Olaf), king of Norway (died 1030), is said to have had some forty churches named after him in Britain. These lay chiefly in the north and east of the island but included one place, Poughill, in Cornwall.

Cities often honoured a local or regional saint: Mildred in Canterbury, Botolph and Etheldreda in Norwich, and Swithun in Winchester. Exeter had four such dedications: its own saint Sidwell and three from the 'Celtic' world: David, Kerrian, and Petroc. A fifth may be discounted, because there is no merit in the conjecture that St Paul was dedicated to the Breton St Paul Aurelian, alias Paul de Léon, rather than to Paul the apostle. The Breton saint was hardly known in England, whereas dedications to the apostle are found in several other English towns.[56] Petroc, although his cult was Cornish in origin, was adopted by at least fifteen churches in Devon including his Exeter chapel. These adoptions did not originate before the Anglo-Saxon conquest of the South-West as was once thought, but in or after about the tenth century by which time his chief shrine at Bodmin had come under the control of the kings of England, allowing his reputation and relics to make their way eastwards. Kerrian, whose festival was celebrated in Exeter on 5 March, was ostensibly the Irish St Ciarán commemorated on that date, but may rather have been inspired by Piran, another Cornish saint, who was identified with Ciarán and shared his festival day. Piran's principal church in Cornwall, Perranzabuloe, belonged to the cathedral by the mid twelfth century and may partly account for the Exeter link. The presence of David is harder to explain. One church in Cornwall was dedicated to him (Davidstow) and a minor one (Dotton) in Devon. His cult in Exeter may also come from the eleventh or twelfth centuries and reflect a greater knowledge of the Welsh Church among Anglo-Saxons or Normans.[57]

Little can be said of the early buildings of these churches and chapels. They could be of stone by about the middle of the eleventh century, in view of the Anglo-Saxon masonry at St George, St Martin, St Olave, and St Stephen. Most were probably small structures to begin with, limited to a modest chancel and nave with a bell-turret rather than a tower, like the surviving building of St Pancras. Even the Norman Castle Chapel, although planned for a group of four clergy, was of a similar size down to its demolition in 1792. The locations of chapels alongside a pattern of streets that did not follow the four cardinal points of the compass meant that they were

---

[56] Below, p. 155.
[57] On these saints, see Nicholas Orme, *English Church Dedications, with a Survey of Cornwall and Devon* (Exeter, 1996), 237–42 and passim; and idem, *Saints of Cornwall*, 102–3, 160, 214–19, 220–3.

sometimes obliged to deviate from a true easterly orientation to a significant extent.[58] Awkwardness of the site is also attested at Holy Trinity by the South Gate. Here the building was on two floors until it was reconstructed in the fifteenth century, the upper floor serving the congregation while the lower contained three side altars.[59] Three chapels stood out from the rest by 1200, however, in terms of their buildings. St Mary Major acquired a substantial Norman tower and was sometimes known as 'St Mary of the Tower'. St Mary Arches was a spacious building with two Norman arcades leading to narrow nave aisles, while St Stephen had an Anglo-Saxon crypt, rebuilt in the twelfth century, and may have gained similar aisles in that or the following century. The extra features in these buildings were doubtless due to the bishop or the cathedral clergy, who probably had relationships with each of them.

Most if not all of the other city churches and chapels had similar patrons: the cathedral, a monastery, or a lay person. The patron had the right to choose the priest of the church or chapel, and in the case of ecclesiastical patrons to take a 'pension' or annual sum of money from its income. The bishop appointed to St Stephen, to St Mary Arches by 1344, and to his private chapel of St Faith. The cathedral canons, as we have seen, held similar powers over the seventeen chapels mentioned in Bishop Marshal's award, to which St Paul and St Peter the Little were added after the agreement with the two guilds. The monks of St Nicholas Priory were patrons of St Olave, the monks of Cowick of the church and chapels of their parish, the canons of Plympton Priory of St John Bow, and the monks of Ste-Marie-du-Val in Normandy of St Laurence until they gave it to Merton Priory (Surrey) in 1267. The chapels in lay patronage may have been numerous when they were founded, but they declined in number between 1066 and 1200 through the conveyance of Christchurch, St John Bow, St Laurence, St Olave, St Paul, and St Peter the Little to religious houses. This reflected a national process by which lay lords gave churches as endowments to such houses. Thereafter only a minority of the Exeter chapels remained in the hands of lay patrons.[60] They included All Hallows (Goldsmith Street), the Castle Chapel, St Edmund, St George (eventually in crown patronage), St Leonard, St Mary Steps, St Pancras, and probably St Alexius. Two of them, the Castle Chapel and St Leonard, came to belong to the Courtenay earls of Devon.[61]

---

[58] Ethel Lega-Weekes, *Some Studies in the Topography of the Cathedral Close* (Exeter, 1915), plate 4 opposite p. 18.

[59] *The Register of Edmund Lacy, Bishop of Exeter: Registrum Commune*, ed. G. R. Dunstan, 5 vols, DCRS, new series 7, 10, 13, 16, 18 (1963–72), ii, 259–63.

[60] The decline of lay patronage is paralleled in other cities, e.g. Winchester (Keene, *Medieval Winchester*, 111).

[61] *Reg. Bronescombe*, ed. Hingeston-Randolph, 140; *Reg. Stapeldon*, 215–16; *The Register of John de Grandisson, Bishop of Exeter*, ed. F. C. Hingeston-Randolph, 3 vols (London and Exeter, 1894–9), iii, 1267, 1276.

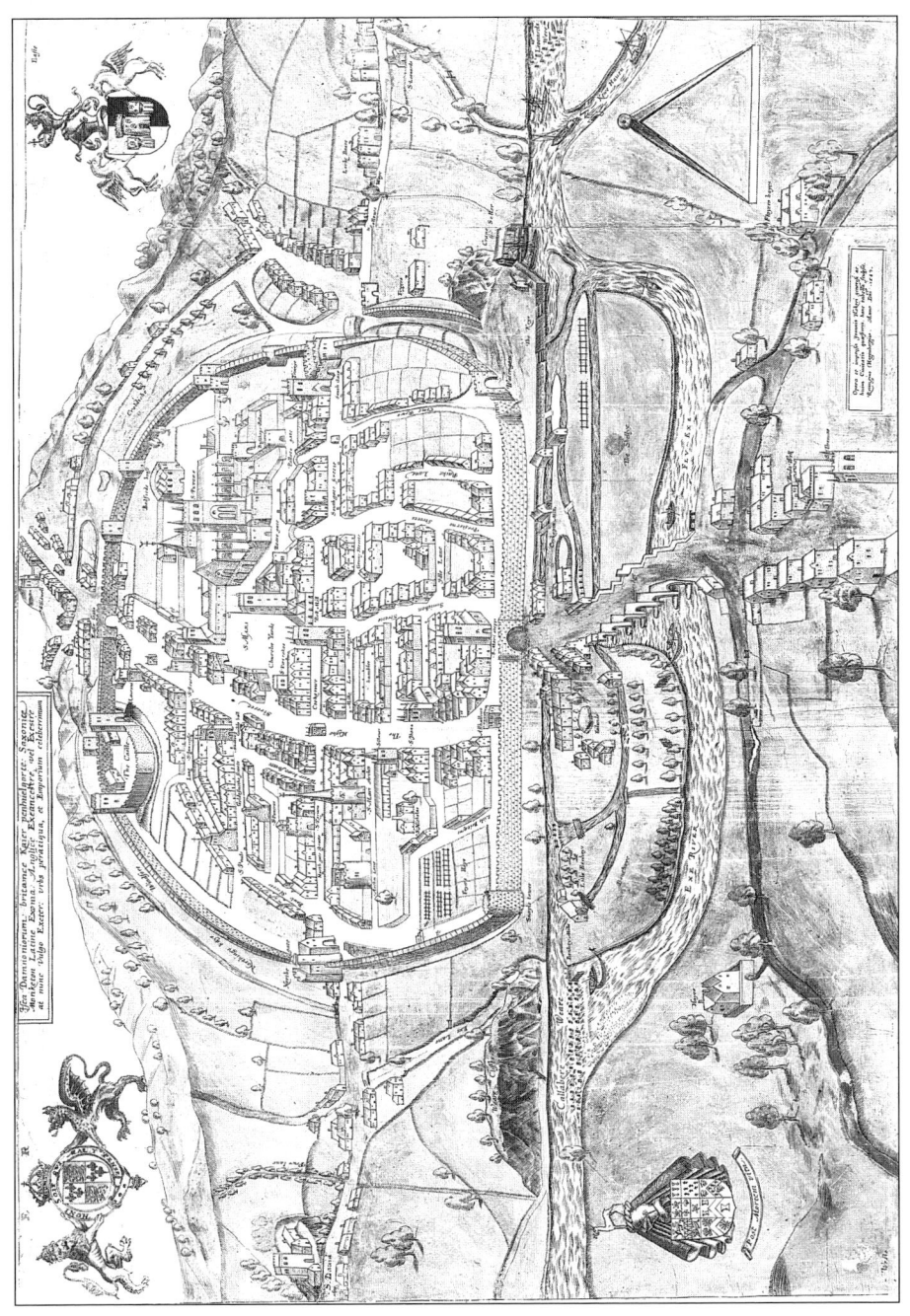

View of Exeter city by John Hooker and Franz Hogenberg, 1587. It depicts all the churches that were then in existence.

The activities of the chapels are obscure before the early thirteenth century. Clergy existed to serve them, known as 'chaplains' or 'priests'. Seven 'priests of the city' witnessed a deed in 1133.[62] The existence of Preston Street off South Street by the late twelfth century, a name that means 'the street of the priests', suggests that some of the clergy lived there and may have formed an informal community.[63] Some of the priests had enough status to become members of the Exeter guild of Kalendars, such as Thomas, chaplain of St Mary Major, and John, chaplain of St Paul.[64] By the thirteenth century the number of clergy receiving penny payments was close to that of the chapels on the city side of the River Exe, making it appear that most of the buildings had their own priest by this time. It is probably safe to assume that the clergy said daily prayers in their chapels and celebrated masses daily or every few days, but certainly on Sundays. Since the cathedral is not recorded as claiming a monopoly over baptisms, marriages, confessions, and the churching of women after childbirth, the clergy are likely to have performed these rites as well.

The Creation of Parish Churches

This first phase of Church history in Exeter came to an end in the early thirteenth century. According to a short Latin chronicle drawn up at Exeter Cathedral before 1308 and chiefly devoted to the bishops and the cathedral, 'In the year of the Lord 1222 the parishes of the city of Exeter were demarcated [*limitate*]'.[65] The bishop at the time was Simon de Apulia, and although no contemporary document survives to this effect, it is likely that he was responsible because nobody else could have carried out a measure that applied to so many foundations with different patrons. The chronicle makes the measure seem a simple one, but it must have been difficult and indeed controversial. Church ties in Exeter (apart from funerals and burials) were probably still largely voluntary or linked with land tenure. You worshipped at your neighbouring church, the church of your guild, or that of your landlord. Unpicking these relationships, establishing parishes that were economically viable, and deciding on their boundaries in a crowded city must have been an intricate operation and one that provoked opposition. We know nothing of the process or of the compromises that were needed to carry it out.

The bishop's motive was doubtless to bring the city into line with cities elsewhere and with the countryside of Devon, where people now all lived in territorial parishes. Most of the other large towns with a former single minster or cathedral parish were

---

[62] ECA, ED/88/2.
[63] J. E. B. Gover, A. Mawer, and F. M. Stenton, *The Place-Names of Devon*, 2 vols, English Place-Name Society, 8–9 (1931–2), i, 23.
[64] Orme, 'The Kalendar Brethren', 158.
[65] *Ordinale Exon*, ed. J. N. Dalton and G. H. Doble, 4 vols, Henry Bradshaw Society, 37–8, 63, 79 (1909–40), i, p. xxi.

probably subdivided by this time. Winchester had been so since at least 1143.[66] Exeter's nominal cathedral parish, overlapping with smaller voluntary churches, was an anomaly by the early thirteenth century when the Church required that everyone should be under religious discipline. Children should all receive baptism, adults should all attend worship and go to confession, and this could only be achieved by putting everyone into a designated area with its own church and clergyman. Clergy too would have been thought better supported by tithes and offerings from a predictable number of households than from voluntary payments as before. In the absence of a decree by the bishop, we have no direct knowledge of which chapels were made into parish churches and given a district to serve. However, subsequent references to churches in Exeter with parochial status suggest that about twenty-one chapels were given this privilege in the first instance, along with the hospital of St John, while two extramural chapels (St David and St Sidwell) gained partial parochial status.[67] The exceptions appear to have been the chapels of St Bartholomew, St Clement, St Michael, St Peter the Little, and SS Simon and Jude, those of the two other hospitals, private foundations such as the Castle Chapel and the Bishop's Chapel, and the chapels of Cowick to which the decision did not apply.

Most of the chapels that became parish churches were situated inside the city walls, and the parishes that they were given did not extend beyond the walls except for those of St Edmund and St Mary Steps, which included islands in the River Exe, and Holy Trinity, which reached some way southwards beyond Southernhay. St Leonard stood outside the walls on the south-east side of the city and acquired a small rural parish around itself. That left the large area north, east, and south of the city that had probably formed the outer part of the parish of the Anglo-Saxon minster. Most of this was made into a parish centred on the church of Heavitree, apart from a smaller piece at the southern end of it that became the parish of Topsham. Two of the chapels in this rural area, St David and St Sidwell, acquired an intermediate status between that of church and chapel. They were included in Heavitree parish, their revenues belonged to its church, and they were served by chaplains appointed by its vicar, but at some point they acquired their own recognised sub-parishes. They came to operate in a manner close to that of a parish church and were popularly regarded as such.[68]

The clergy of the new parish churches became technically 'rectors' rather than 'chaplains', but the new title took hold only gradually. At St Mary Major the priest

---

[66] Keene, *Medieval Winchester*, 116.
[67] In York the hospital church of St Nicholas was also given a parish (*VCH Yorkshire: City of York*, ed. Tillott, 397).
[68] E.g. the will of Roger Holand, 1506, refers to both as parish churches (TNA, PROB 11/15/2).

was still described as a chaplain in 1245 and as a 'vicar' in 1284, while his counterparts of St Pancras and St Paul were called chaplains as late as c.1250.[69] There remained a sense that their churches were not fully independent like parish churches elsewhere in Devon, but subordinate to the cathedral. In 1291 when the clergy of England were surveyed for taxation purposes in the process known as the 'Taxation of Pope Nicholas', the Exeter parish churches were still described as 'chapels'.[70] And as late as 1513 the bishop of Exeter referred to St Petroc as a 'parish church or chapel with cure [*capellam curatam*] . . . dependent upon the cathedral church of Exeter'.[71] The bishop's officers too seem to have been slow to regard them as on a par with other parishes. When Bishop Bronescombe's clerks began to keep a register of the institution of clergy to parish benefices in 1258, they recorded institutions to only six of the Exeter churches: the Castle Chapel, Cowick, St Edmund, Heavitree, St Mary Steps, and St Olave.[72] The register of the next bishop, Peter Quinil, which is incomplete, refers merely to two: Cowick and St Mary Major.[73] Since that of his successor, Thomas Bitton, has wholly disappeared, records of institutions to most of the city churches survive only after 1308 in the registers of Walter Stapledon and his successors.

The broad history of the churches and parishes of Exeter after 1222 resembles that of other cathedral cities and major towns. Most such places acquired many parish churches during the eleventh and twelfth centuries: London over a hundred, Norwich about sixty, Winchester over fifty, and Lincoln and York over forty.[74] Exeter fell short of these totals, but its original twenty-two (plus St David and St Sidwell) were comparable with the twenty-two of Canterbury and exceeded the seventeen of Bristol and Oxford, and the fourteen of Cambridge.[75] This profusion led to urban parishes being generally tiny everywhere, including Exeter. Its parish boundaries are not recorded until well after the end of the Middle Ages, but the later records probably represent the approximate extent and shape of the parishes in earlier times.[76] Most of Exeter's parish churches had a diminutive piece of territory around

---

[69] ECA, DD 67952; *Reg. Bronescombe*, ed. Hingeston-Randolph, 345; ECA, ED/M/38.
[70] *Reg. Bronescombe*, ed. Hingeston-Randolph, 451.
[71] DHC, Chanter XIII f. 177v. Churches in Winchester were also slow to gain full parochial status (Keene, *Medieval Winchester*, 107).
[72] *Reg. Bronescombe*, ed. Hingeston-Randolph, 127, 140, 143.
[73] Ibid., 345.
[74] *Historic Towns*, ed. Lobel, iii, 34–5 (on London); Tanner, *Church in Late Medieval Norwich*, 3; Keene, *Medieval Winchester*, 116; Hill, *Medieval Lincoln*, 147; *VCH Yorkshire: City of York*, ed. Tillott, 366.
[75] Urry, *Canterbury*, 207–13; *Historic Towns*, ed. Lobel, ii (Bristol, map 8; Cambridge, map 6); Salter, *Medieval Oxford*, 113.
[76] The map most easily consulted is in *Exeter in the Seventeenth Century: tax and rate assessments 1602–1699*, ed. W. G. Hoskins, DCRS, new series 2 (1957), reproduced in Wallace T. MacCaffrey, *Exeter, 1540–1640: the growth of the English country town* (Cambridge, Mass., 1958).

them and on the opposite side of the street, sometimes reaching out fingers to outlying properties that may have once belonged to owners who lived in the parish. St Martin, for example, contained the church, the block of housing that lay between Broadgate, High Street, St Martin's Lane, and the Cathedral Close, and a tenement on the opposite side of High Street. St George stretched raggedly down the south side of Smythen Street, while the territories of St Edmund, St Mary Steps, and Holy Trinity, as already stated, included lands outside the city walls. The oddest shape was that of St Mary Major. This comprised the church itself, a small area along Cook Row (the narrow north end of South Street), and a much larger area west of South Street, covering most of the southern part of the 'West Quarter' between that street and Fore Street.

The modest extents of most medieval urban parishes meant that the incomes for their clergy were correspondingly small.[77] This too was true of those in Exeter. The estimated incomes in the Taxation of 1291 throw some light on incomes, although its figures were greatly underestimated throughout England: very roughly at only half of what they should have been. The wealthiest benefice (or post for a clergyman) was reckoned to be that of St Mary Steps (£2 per annum), followed by St Mary Major (£1), St Kerrian and St Leonard (6s. 8d. each), and St George, St Paul, and St Stephen (2s. each). The other twelve city benefices listed in the Taxation were described as 'poor' or as 'scarcely sufficing to sustain one chaplain', and in the end the rector of St Mary Steps was the only cleric within the city who was required to pay any taxation at all, apart from the clergy of the cathedral, the monasteries, and the Castle Chapel.[78] In practice the incomes of the city rectors probably reached at least £2 or £3 per annum, but that was only equal to the wage of a hired chaplain of the day, the lowest sum on which one could survive. Their rise in status by becoming parish rectors was therefore not accompanied by gains of wealth.

The result of this poverty, not only of clergy stipends but of resources to maintain church buildings and activities, was the closure of churches and the amalgamation of parishes. This process took place in all the large cities, beginning as early as the twelfth century and continuing throughout the rest of the Middle Ages. Canterbury lost four churches, York five, Norwich six, and Winchester three by 1300 topped by an astonishing twenty-one in the fourteenth century.[79] The principal period of

---

[77] *Valor Ecclesiasticus tempore Henrici VIII auctoritate regia institutus,* ed. J. Caley, 6 vols (London, Record Commission, 1810–24), i, 27–8 (Canterbury); ii, 4–6 (Winchester); iii, 293–4 (Norwich); iv, 29 (Lincoln); v, 21–5 (York).

[78] *Reg. Bronescombe,* ed. Hingeston-Randolph, 451–2.

[79] Urry, *Canterbury,* 209–10; Tanner, *Church in Late Medieval Norwich,* 3–4; Keene, *Medieval Winchester,* 116–17; *VCH Yorkshire: City of York,* ed. Tillott, 365.

Seals of Exeter religious houses. From the top left, clockwise, the Franciscan Friary, St Alexius Hospital, St Mary Magdalene Hospital, St Nicholas Priory, St John the Baptist Hospital, and St James Priory.

reduction in Exeter was the 1280s and the chief initiator the bishop, Peter Quinil. In 1285 he united St Cuthbert to St Paul, and at about the same time he linked St Mary Minor to St Mary Major.[80] Two years later a third intervention joined the parish of the hospital church of St John to that of St Laurence.[81] One other church was closed before the Reformation: St James in South Street after the Black Death of 1349. As early as 1336 it was so poor that the bishop was obliged to give the benefice to a chantry priest of the cathedral to hold as an additional post.[82] By 1384 the church was vacant and although a visiting archbishop officiously appointed a rector, his initiative had only a brief effect and the benefice was subsequently united with that of Holy Trinity.[83] Three churches of the suppressed parishes – St Cuthbert, St James, and St Mary Minor – were eventually closed and their sites abandoned or developed for other purposes.

These disappearances, however, were not solely due to economic problems. A crucial reason was that the churches and parishes in question belonged to the cathedral. This allowed them to be united with other churches in its ownership, so that its loss of patronage was outweighed by gaining more viable benefices. In 1390 it considered even uniting the churches of St Martin, St Mary Major, and St Petroc although this idea came to nothing.[84] In the end these and the rest of the city churches survived, despite the poverty of many of them, until the Reformation and far beyond. Three factors saved them. One was the reluctance of the monastic and lay patrons of single churches to lose them, while a second was the growing prosperity of the city in the fourteenth, fifteenth, and sixteenth centuries. This produced more money for church offerings and tithes to support rectors, and for rebuilding and furnishing churches. A third factor was the availability of clergy to serve the city churches from the lower ranks of the cathedral clergy especially the vicars choral. At first the bishop and cathedral canons disapproved of the vicars acting as city rectors, but after the Black Death, when the number of clergy fell nationally, they became willing to allow the holding of a cathedral post along with a city church. Several of the city rectorships thereby became part-time posts, held by clergy who also had duties at the cathedral.[85]

---

[80] D&C 2111; *John Lydford's Book*, ed. Dorothy M. Owen, DCRS, new series 20 (1974), 105. The latter document, a later transcription, bears the date 1395, perhaps a mistake for 1285. However in 1284 the bishop had already instituted a vicar (*sic*) to St Mary Major with 'the chapels adjacent to it', perhaps including St Mary Minor, St Peter the Little, and SS Simon and Jude (*Reg. Bronescombe*, ed. Hingeston-Randolph, 345).
[81] ECA, Book 53A f. 8v.
[82] *Reg. Grandisson*, ii, 811.
[83] London, Lambeth Palace Library, Reg. William Courtenay f. 107r.
[84] D&C 3550 f. 63r–v.
[85] For details of these shared appointments, see Nicholas Orme, *The Minor Clergy of Exeter Cathedral: Biographies, 1250–1548*, DCRS, new series 54 (2013).

The legal status of the churches, chapels, and religious houses of Exeter remains to be considered. This is a complicated matter. We have seen that Bishop Marshal awarded jurisdiction to the cathedral chapter over the chapels to which it appointed clergy or from which it received payments of money, including Heavitree and Topsham. The archdeacon of Exeter had jurisdiction over the other chapels.[86] However by the late thirteenth century the cathedral's chapels (now parish churches) were not outside the normal diocesan structure in a separate 'peculiar jurisdiction' like its churches in the countryside of Devon. Instead all the churches within the city walls, together with St David, St Leonard, and St Sidwell outside, formed an ordinary rural deanery within the diocese, called the deanery of Exeter, supervised by a dean who was one of the city clergy holding the post for a year at a time in turn or by election.[87] In a variant of this, Heavitree (unlike its chapelries of St David and St Sidwell) and Topsham were not included in this deanery. They formed peculiar jurisdictions removed from the rural deanery and the archdeaconry, and were administered by the cathedral chapter. The bishops of Exeter had final overriding power over the churches of the rural deanery and most of the religious houses, including the Castle Chapel, Cowick, St James, St Mary Marsh, St Nicholas, and Polsloe. There were two exceptions to this in that both of the friaries founded in the thirteenth century possessed the privilege of exemption from the authority of the local bishop and his officers, although the cathedral chapter considered that this did not affect the cathedral's right to hold funerals of all save monks and friars who died in Exeter.[88] A third exception emerged in 1517 when the pope granted a similar privilege to Tavistock Abbey. It extended to Cowick Priory, by then its daughter house, and was in force until the Reformation.[89]

The Religious Houses

Towering above the parish churches in structure, wealth, and power stood the cathedral, its history too complex to be covered here and the subject of a separate study by this author.[90] Smaller but influential were eight more religious houses: the

---

[86] *English Episcopal Acta XII*, ed. Barlow, 172–3. The award was confirmed with slight alterations by two subsequent bishops (ibid., 228, 284–5).
[87] *Reg. Bronescombe*, ed. Hingeston-Randolph, 451; *Reg. Lacy*, ed. Dunstan, iii, 58. The modern title of the rural deanery, 'Christianity', is incorrect. All rural deaneries were known as 'deaneries of Christianity'; in Exeter, because there came to be a cathedral dean, it was often necessary to talk of 'the dean (or deanery) of Christianity of Exeter'.
[88] Below, p. 98.
[89] Below, pp. 91–2.
[90] Orme, *Exeter Cathedral: the first thousand years*.

monasteries of Cowick, St James, St Mary Marsh, and St Nicholas, the nunnery of Polsloe, and the hospitals of St Alexius, St John the Baptist, and St Mary Magdalene, of which St Alexius and St John were eventually united. In the mid thirteenth century these foundations were joined by Dominican and Franciscan friaries. Several of the major religious orders were represented: Benedictine monks and nuns (St Nicholas and Polsloe), Cluniacs (St James), Augustinian canons (St John and St Mary Marsh), and two of the orders of friars. The chief missing orders were the Cistercians, who usually avoided towns, and the Augustinian and Carmelite friars who were attracted to them. These two latter groups may have avoided Exeter through its relative remoteness but, with more likelihood, because its established religious houses, friaries, and parish churches left little room for the activities of any more clergy.

The four monasteries, as we have seen, were endowed by the Norman aristocracy. William the Conqueror gave the properties to Battle Abbey that allowed it to open St Nicholas, while William fitz Baldwin did likewise to the abbey of Bec-Hellouin, enabling the foundation of Cowick. St Mary Marsh emerged through grants of land to Plympton Priory by Baldwin's granddaughter Adeliz, and St James was the creation of Baldwin de Redvers, earl of Devon. All these houses were in place by the early 1140s. The next to appear, the priory of Polsloe for Benedictine nuns, in about 1160 was more of a collective enterprise. It was the first nunnery to be founded in the diocese of Exeter, and may have been the brainchild of the bishop, Robert of Chichester. Its endowments came from several hands, including those of the king, the bishop, and some men of knightly rank. The hospitals were created by people of lower status, chiefly clergy or citizens of Exeter, and their property centred on lands and tenements in and around the city. They also depended for part of their income on alms from members of the public. These characteristics were more pronounced in the case of the friaries. Their initial benefactors were wealthy local people who provided them with sites and no doubt helped with the costs of raising their buildings, but their ethos was to rely on voluntary donations not endowment income, and this shaped their life and work for the three centuries of their existence.

Of the monasteries only St Nicholas gained a site within the city walls and, as we have seen, its appearance there was not welcomed by the bishop or the cathedral. The Conqueror, who gave it the church of St Olave, is likely to have handed over all or part of the area of *Irlesbery* that appears to have belonged to the earls of Wessex, and St Nicholas was founded in or near this area. Cowick, St James, and St Mary Marsh were all situated outside the walls. St James took over an existing chapel and Cowick may have been built near an earlier parish church, but St Mary Marsh was on a virgin site. The detachment of the latter three houses meant that they had less contact with the people of the city, which was further reduced by the small size of St James and St Mary Marsh. Polsloe was also at a new location, probably chosen to be near the diocesan capital city but placed in a secluded spot about a mile away.

Two of the hospitals had peripheral sites: St Alexius, perhaps catering for the sick poor, in *Irlesbery*, and St Mary Magdalene for lepers well outside the city walls. Both, however, were still close enough to the city centre to benefit from almsgiving, and the third hospital, St John the Baptist, had a prominent site by the East Gate from which it too could profit in this way. The friars also sought to establish themselves inside the walls to be close to local people for pastoral work and fund raising. The Dominicans gained a good central site off the High Street, possibly with the help of the bishop, and the Franciscans went to *Irlesbery* where they appear to have replaced the hospital of St Alexius. This location proved to be unsuitable in the long term, and soon after 1300 the friars moved to a new one beyond the South Gate but still with ready access to the city.

None of the religious houses was truly independent. As we have seen, all save the friaries were within the diocese and under the bishop's authority. Polsloe was technically self-governing but recognised the bishop as its patron; he approved the election of prioresses and issued statutes for the nuns. St Nicholas, as a daughter house of Battle Abbey, received a prior and monks from that house but administered its own property. Cowick had a similar relationship with Bec-Hellouin until the mid fifteenth century when it became a mere cell or dependency of Tavistock Abbey and was wholly ruled from there. St James and St Mary Marsh were also fully dependent on their mother houses, St Martin-des-Champs and Plympton, although the distance between St James and St Martin meant that the former was largely left to its own devices. In the case of the hospitals, the status of St Alexius is obscure, but St Mary Magdalene fell under the bishop's supervision and St John under that of the city fathers until 1244. In that year the two authorities exchanged their patronage, perhaps because the bishop wished to control St John which had a staff of clergy. Each hospital thereafter had a supervisor representing the patron along with an internal head elected by the inmates. The friaries differed from all the other houses in belonging to international organisations. Whereas monks, nuns, and hospital clergy usually stayed in their houses for life, friars could be assigned to any place that their superiors wished. This meant that the friars in Exeter might have come from anywhere in England or even from the Continent, a feature paralleled at Cowick and St James whose monks were normally sent from France until at least the middle of the fourteenth century.

The Exeter houses were not very wealthy. In 1535, when the most accurate estimates of clerical incomes were made, Polsloe was valued at £164, St Nicholas £147, Cowick £124, St John £102, and St Mary Marsh £37. St James had disappeared in about 1429, but would hardly have been worth more than £30 or so, and there is no information about St Mary Magdalene or the friaries. These modest incomes meant that the staffing of the houses was correspondingly small. The friaries probably had the largest numbers of inmates, but there is no record of them until the

All Hallows Goldsmith Street. The church interior looking east, shortly before its demolition in 1906.

dissolution of the houses in 1538. At that time there were fifteen Dominicans and ten or eleven Franciscans, but the totals may have risen into the twenties or thirties in previous centuries. Polsloe had seventeen nuns before the Black Death, but the number fell thereafter; at the Reformation there were fourteen. St Nicholas usually had a prior and five monks, and Cowick the same up to the mid fourteenth century, after which it fell to three or four. St James had no more than two by that mid century, and St John, which may have started out with several brothers and sisters, evolved into a small religious house of a prior and two or three brothers. The inmates of St Mary Magdalene counted as brothers or sisters, but the only true cleric was a single chaplain.

The core activities of a religious house were the worship of God and the maintenance of the religious life. Unfortunately these have left little record so that we may only reconstruct them from what is known about England in general rather than Exeter in particular. Divine worship consisted of eight services said at intervals in the choir of the church from midnight until the late afternoon or evening. By about 1200 it is probable that mass was celebrated in the choir at least once every day in the middle of the morning. The nuns of Polsloe entered the priory as novices and were taught there to say the services. The friaries also took in young recruits and trained them, but because friaries operated within a wider organisation, the training might be done at other houses while their student friars might come to Exeter. The monasteries were too small to handle novices and largely depended on their monks being sent fully trained from their mother houses. The small Augustinian group at St John had links with a similar hospital at Bridgwater, and some training may have been done there. By the fourteenth century it was normal for monks and friars to be ordained as priests by the bishop, enabling them to celebrate mass and administer the sacraments. Nuns were not qualified to do that, and so Polsloe needed to employ a male chaplain for the purpose.

The religious life meant living as a community and sharing lodgings and meals under the disciplines of poverty (lack of personal possessions), chastity, and obedience. In fact poverty among monks was increasingly modified by allowances of money or personal possessions, and community life by the installation of private cubicles or chambers for sleeping and even eating. Study was encouraged, the pioneers in this respect being the friars who set up educational programmes from the thirteenth century. Monks followed in this path during the fourteenth, although it is not clear whether the Exeter houses went far in doing so. All the houses would have had books for study, the friars leading the field, but even St John is known to have owned several volumes. The friars also had close links with the universities. A few of their best students were sent to study there, and graduate scholars returned to act as lecturers at individual friaries. The Franciscan house at Exeter was designated a centre of study for friar students from the west of England in 1337. Priors and prioresses and their senior colleagues were also involved in administration. Inside and around the house servants had to be supervised in doing domestic or agricultural work. Hospitality would be offered to patrons and some travellers (the Courtenay earls of Devon had rooms at Cowick and the Dominican Friary) and charity was given to the poor. Externally property was managed, tenancies granted, and oversight given to the agents who collected rents. Houses kept records of their property and income, and cartularies or registers of evidence survive for St John, St Mary Magdalene, and St Nicholas.[91]

Most of the houses were involved pastorally with the world outside them. This was least so at St James, which was very poorly funded, and St Mary Marsh, which was chiefly an administrative centre. It was greatest among the friars whose vocation was to act as preachers and confessors to the laity and who needed to build personal

---

[91] G. R. C. Davis, *Medieval Cartularies of Great Britain* (London, 1958), 45.

relationships in order to elicit donations. Friars not only preached in their own churches but were invited to do so at the cathedral during Advent and Lent when sermons took place there. They could obtain bishops' licences to hear confessions throughout the diocese, and are recorded doing so at Polsloe and doubtless among many of the gentry of Devon and citizens of Exeter. Since friaries were free of the authority of the local bishop, some friars claimed the right to hold funerals in their churches and to bury people in their cemeteries who were not members of their houses. This was a challenge to the rights of the cathedral, and led to serious disputes between its canons and the Dominicans in 1281 and 1301. In the end there was a tacit agreement that funerals of others than friars must be held at the cathedral but that burials might take place at friaries with the permission of the cathedral canons. As a result a large number of wealthier citizens, men and women, arranged to have tombs in the friary churches. Excavation of part of the north nave aisle of the Dominican church has revealed a floor that was packed with burials.[92]

The monasteries were less involved with the general public, but by no means uninvolved. St Nicholas owned a surrounding area which was not part of any other parish, and when the churches of Exeter were valued for taxation purposes in 1291 it was listed both as a 'church' and as a priory, each with a separate income.[93] Some local people attended its priory church. We shall see that two of the city craft guilds envisaged holding services there, and when the priory was shut down in 1536 there was a famous episode in which women who had used the church for worship caused a riot at the demolition of the loft above the roodscreen.[94] Several of the gentry and citizens had tombs in the church and there are a few records of such people founding anniversary masses or 'obits' there to commemorate themselves. On the eve of the Reformation the monks dispensed food and drink to seven poor people each day, and gave the remains of their own dinner to others who were their tenants.[95]

The priory of St Andrew at Cowick had a strong parochial role. It was the sole parish church of that area until the late twelfth century when the church of St Thomas was built, and this at first was only a subordinate chapel. Until about 1300 Cowick church appears to have been shared by the monks in the choir and the parishioners in the nave, the latter perhaps with their own parish altar and chaplain.[96] Next to the priory stood the original parish burial ground of Cowick, and by 1278 there

---

[92] Lepine and Orme, *Death and Memory*, 12–13 and 44–119 passim.
[93] *Reg. Bronescombe*, ed. Hingeston-Randolph, 452, 475.
[94] ECA, Book 51 f. 343r.
[95] ECA, Chamber Act Book 4 f. 159v.
[96] Geoffrey Yeo, *The Monks of Cowick* (Exeter, 1987), 9, 11.

was a chapel of St Michael nearby, perhaps in order to serve the burial ground.[97] Gradually the parish services moved to St Thomas and, when that church was moved to a new site in Cowick Street in 1412, the new building took over most of the parish functions although the old cemetery remained in use for another three centuries. The hospital of St John, as we have seen, was made a parish church in 1222 and remained one until 1287. In that year its parish was united with that of St Laurence, but St John retained close links with the people of Exeter. It probably provided some hospitality and care of the sick, and eventually maintained a body of almsmen and poor scholars who attended the city High School. The church became a popular place of burial for richer citizens up to the Reformation, and a list survives that records the names of 146 of them.[98]

Chapel Foundations after 1222

The creation of a network of parish churches and parishes in and around the city of Exeter in 1222 made it difficult for anyone to establish any more churches with this status, and no new parish churches were created for several centuries. The same did not apply to chapels, provided that their founders, clergy, and users sought the permission and accepted the authority of the church of the parish in which they were situated. About thirteen new chapels (plus other more private oratories) came into existence in Exeter between the mid thirteenth and mid sixteenth centuries. The origins and purposes of these foundations are better recorded than those of their predecessors, and can be more easily fitted into the history of the Church. These new chapels also differed somewhat from those founded before 1222. Earlier chapels had competed only with the cathedral, which did not forbid their activities other than funerals and burials and allowed them to develop public worship and probably the administration of the sacraments. Once most of these chapels became parish churches, the other surviving chapels and those that were subsequently created had to find roles for themselves that did not threaten the churches. This meant that henceforth chapels developed specialities: serving individual institutions and social groups or promoting the veneration of particular saints.

Two new chapels were built in the city during the thirteenth century. One was erected by Walter Gervas, mayor of Exeter (died *c.*1258), at the western approach to the Exe Bridge which had been built or rebuilt towards the end of the twelfth century. The chapel was dedicated to the Virgin Mary, and Gervas gave an

---

[97] Ibid., 11; *The Register of Walter Bronescombe Bishop of Exeter 1258–1280*, ed. O. F. Robinson, 3 vols, Canterbury & York Society, 82, 87, 94 (1995–2003), ii, 116.
[98] ECA, Book 53A f. 8v; Lepine and Orme, *Death and Memory*, 39–43.

The Castle Chapel before its removal in 1792, from the north, showing chancel and nave (both with Norman features) and behind, trees in a probable cemetery.

endowment to the city to maintain a chaplain to celebrate mass there, appointed by the mayor of the city.[99] Chapels on or near bridges became popular in England from about 1200 onwards, and St Edmund originated in this way. There were other notable examples at London, York, and Bristol, and later at Bideford and Wadebridge in the South-West, where their proximity to passing traffic made it possible to solicit alms for their maintenance or that of the bridge itself. A second kind of chapel emerged at the same time in association with charnels. Larger populations in towns led to more burials in urban churchyards. The digging of frequent new graves often unearthed the bones from previous interments, which were then conserved in a charnel or storehouse to which a chapel was sometimes added as, for example, at Norwich, St Paul's (London), and Worcester. Exeter acquired its own Charnel Chapel in the Cathedral Close in 1286 at the expense of John of Exeter, alias Picot, a former dean of the cathedral. Picot was implicated in the murder of the cathedral precentor, Walter de Lechlade, in 1283: a notorious crime which brought Edward I to Exeter over Christmas in 1285–6 in order to supervise the trial of the alleged murderers. It appears that Picot's chapel was an act of penance and reparation on his part, the probability being strengthened by the dedication of the chapel to

[99] Lepine and Orme, *Death and Memory*, 140.

St Edward the Confessor, after whom King Edward was named.[100] It stood on the north side of St Mary Major church, opposite the west front of the cathedral, and survived until about 1550. Its usages included the celebration of mass, the meetings of a guild, the giving of theological lectures, and the preaching of open-air sermons from an exterior pulpit.[101]

Towards the end of the fourteenth century, a third class of chapels appeared in England in connection with almshouses. Almshouses differed from earlier hospitals like St John and St Mary Magdalene by addressing the needs of the infirm and elderly rather than the sick or lepers. They generally provided individual housing for such people, sometimes supplemented by meals or grants of money.[102] Exeter acquired seven or eight almshouses between about 1399 and 1520: Baker's, Bonville's, Grendon's, More's and Fortescue's, Palmer's, St Katherine, Wynard's, and possibly Obley's. Two of these included chapels while the remainder did not. The earlier was that of God's House or, as it is more often known, Wynard's Almshouse, founded in Magdalen Street by William Wynard in 1436. The chapel in his buildings is still extant and possessed an endowment for a chaplain.[103] The other chapel was in the almshouse of St Katherine in Catherine Street, a benefaction by John Stevens, canon of the cathedral, in about 1457. Its ruins remain on the site but there is no record of the employment of a full-time chaplain to serve it.[104] Finally there are several references between 1506 and 1521 to a hospital of St Roche, situated in Coombe Street off South Street. This appears to have been founded by a guild rather than a wealthy benefactor, and it evidently included a chapel dedicated to the Virgin Mary, the Eleven Thousand Virgins, and St Roche. The foundation may have been a hospital for the sick rather than an almshouse (St Roche was the patron of plague victims), but it and its chapel seem to have existed for only a short time.[105]

A fourth development of the later Middle Ages was a revival of guilds in Exeter. The old city guild of the Kalendars petered out in the fourteenth century, transferring its assets and the performance of its services to the vicars choral of the cathedral. After 1400 craft guilds were founded in Exeter as in other towns, chiefly to defend

---

[100] *John Lydford's Book*, ed. Owen, 106.
[101] Nicholas Orme, 'The Charnel Chapel of Exeter Cathedral', in *Medieval Art and Architecture at Exeter Cathedral*, ed. F. Kelly, The British Archaeological Association, Conference Transactions, 11 (1991), 162–71.
[102] Nicholas Orme and Margaret Webster, *The English Hospital 1070–1570* (New Haven and London, 1995), 138–9.
[103] Ibid., 242–4.
[104] Ibid., 244–6.
[105] Ibid., 247–8.

and regulate their members' work but with a religious dimension that involved meeting together for the celebration of mass at least once every year. Six of these guilds were formed in the fifteenth century, two of which used existing chapels for their masses while a third created a new chapel for the purpose. In about 1423 the guild of the shoemakers gained permission from the cathedral chapter to use the chapel of Christchurch and adopted the title of 'The Fraternity of the Trinity' from the name of the chapel.[106] They continued to worship there until the Reformation. The skinners are mentioned using the Charnel Chapel between 1426 and 1431, but seem to have gone elsewhere for their devotions thereafter.[107] The weavers, tuckers, and shearmen formed their guild in about 1471 as 'The Fraternity of the Assumption of the Blessed Virgin Mary', and acquired premises in Fore Street where Tuckers Hall now stands. These included a chapel which has become the hall of the guild, served by its own chaplain.[108] In about 1484–5 the governing body of the city, the chamber, rebuilt its Guildhall in High Street and added a chapel at the front of the upper storey: now the lord mayor's parlour.[109] The chapel was dedicated to St George, who became the national patron saint in the fifteenth century, and to St John the Baptist, perhaps because of the close relations between the citizens and the hospital of St John.[110] The chamber resembled a guild and by 1499 it had constituted itself as a formal fraternity or guild of St George comprising brothers and sisters (probably the twenty-four members of the chamber and their wives). In 1533 the chamber insisted that every member should belong to the guild.[111]

The remaining craft guilds arranged their religious activities in places other than chapels, as far as we know. The skinners may have transferred themselves from the Charnel Chapel to the church of St Martin. This is suggested by an undated fifteenth-century reference to a fraternity of Corpus Christi apparently in that church, a cult to which the skinners had a devotion.[112] The tailors formed their guild in 1466 in honour of St Mary, St John the Baptist, and All Saints.[113] They held their annual feast on the festival of St John the Baptist 'in harvest', i.e. 29 August, which implies that they did so in a church of the same saint: either the hospital of St John or the

---

[106] D&C 3550 f. 152r (or 133r). The document is another attestation of the fact that Christchurch and Trinity were interchangeable names.
[107] Orme, 'The Charnel Chapel of Exeter Cathedral', 166.
[108] Joyce Youings, *Tuckers Hall Exeter* (Exeter, 1968), 9–20.
[109] H. Lloyd Parry, *The History of the Exeter Guildhall and the Life Within* (Exeter, 1936), 21–9.
[110] Or because of the importance of the cloth trade in Exeter, the Baptist being associated with lambs.
[111] ECA, Chamber Act Book II f. 32v.
[112] D&C 2538/2.
[113] *Cal. Patent Rolls 1461–7*, 543.

church of St John Bow.[114] Their members also attended St Nicholas Priory on 26 January, but this was to observe the obit (anniversary mass) of one of their leaders, John Hamelyn, a former mayor of the city.[115] The bakers, who named themselves after St Mary and St Clement, arranged in 1483 to hold their festival at the Nativity of the Virgin (8 September), either at St Nicholas or at some 'other convenient church'.[116] The last of the craft guilds to be founded in the fifteenth century was that of the cappers or haberdashers, but the venue of its devotions has not yet been discovered.[117]

A fifth group of chapels to be considered is one of five that appeared outside the city walls in the parish of Heavitree. The earliest, St Loye, may have been founded in the thirteenth or early fourteenth century, to judge from its architectural features. It may have been a domestic chapel, since it is first mentioned in 1387 when the bishop of Exeter licensed Henry and Joan Tirelle to have services celebrated in the chapel which was described as lying within their house of Wonford.[118] Nonetheless it was not used solely for private purposes since it generated monetary offerings, implying that it was sometimes used by people from the neighbourhood or those with a devotion to St Loye, the patron saint of blacksmiths. Three other chapels were primarily cult chapels established to venerate a particular saint. St Anne's chapel in Old Tiverton Road was built in about 1418, largely through the efforts of John Wygwar, one of the chantry priests of the cathedral, with the support of the earl of Devon 'and other lords'.[119] Offerings in the chapel went to the cathedral canons as rectors of the parish, and from 1430 the account rolls that record these offerings mention others from a chapel of St Clair, described once as 'adjoining the church of St Leonard' and once as 'adjoining *Bokerell*'.[120] These references identify the chapel as having stood in Matford Lane by Parker's Well. Clair was a patron saint of eye disorders, and the well water was later believed to have healing powers in such cases. A 'new chapel of the Blessed Mary of Mincinglake' is first mentioned in 1465, and also produced offerings for the cathedral. It seems to have honoured the Assumption of the Virgin Mary, like that of the weavers and tuckers. The site is not recorded but the building may have stood near the bridge across the

---

[114] Toulmin Smith, *English Gilds*, Early English Text Society, original series 40 (1870), 313.
[115] Ibid., 325–7.
[116] Ibid., 335.
[117] John Hooker, *The Description of the Citie of Excester*, ed. W. J. Harte and others, 3 parts, DCRS (1919–47), iii, 824–7, 892.
[118] *The Register of Thomas de Brantyngham, Bishop of Exeter*, ed. F. C. Hingeston-Randolph, 2 vols (London and Exeter, 1901–6), ii, 636–7; Orme, 'Medieval Chapels of Heavitree', 124.
[119] Orme, 'Medieval Chapels of Heavitree', 124.
[120] Ibid., 125–6.

Mincinglake Stream that carried the road from Exeter to Tiverton and Bristol.[121] A fifth chapel appeared between 1428 and 1445 as a result of the closure of St James Priory. All or part of its church continued in use for worship until at least the end of the century, including the celebration of St James Day.[122] A sixth, that of Livery Dole, does not appear in records until the end of the sixteenth century, and seems likely to have been created in that period as an almshouse chapel.[123]

There were also chapels in private houses, or oratories as they were also called. They may have developed at an early date, since the Bishop's Chapel and Castle Chapel were in part private foundations of this kind. The archdeacon of Cornwall had a chapel of St Radegund in his house in about the 1220s, and by 1301 it was becoming common for the cathedral canons to follow suit in their dwellings. A survey of canons' houses in that year refers to five of them.[124] Later the bishops' registers contain licences for similar canons' oratories or references occur to them in wills, and the cathedral dean even annexed the older chapel of St Michael for his personal use by the early fifteenth century.[125] The house of the prebendary of Hayes in Okehampton Street was similarly provided with one.[126] We rarely hear if these chapels were dedicated to saints and many may not have been, but as well as those of St Michael and St Radegund there was a chapel of St Mary in the house of Canon William Fawell by 1539. He acted as a suffragan bishop and ordained clergy there.[127] Oratories in the houses of the gentry and leading merchants are also recorded but were less common. Within the city they were licensed for Roger atte Welle in 1376, Robert Wilford in 1392, Ricarda Grendon in 1414, and John Salter in 1433.[128] Outside the walls we hear of them in the houses of Nicholas Bowedon at Larkbeare and Richard Holand in Cowick Street, as well as at St Loye.[129]

Chapels do not exhaust the number of sacred sites in medieval Exeter. As in other towns and cities, holy wells and standing crosses were objects of religious veneration. The history of holy wells is a difficult subject, because most of the evidence comes from the nineteenth and twentieth centuries. At that time folklore and romantic

---

[121] Ibid., 122, 126.
[122] Below, p. 112.
[123] Orme, 'Medieval Chapels of Heavitree', 121, 127–8.
[124] *Reg. Stapeldon*, 153–4.
[125] D&C 3642.
[126] *Reg. Brantyngham*, ii, 680.
[127] DHC, Chanter XIV, ordination lists.
[128] *Reg. Brantyngham*, i, 366; E. Lega-Weekes, 'An Account of the Hospitium de le Egle, some Ancient Chapels in the Close, and some Persons Connected therewith', *Devonshire Association Transactions*, 44 (1912), 484; *The Register of Edmund Stafford*, ed. F. C. Hingeston-Randolph (London and Exeter, 1886), 275; *Reg. Lacy*, ed. Dunstan, i, 254.
[129] *Reg. Stafford*, 272; *Reg. Lacy*, ed. Dunstan, i, 220.

An indenture of 1208–9 between the priories of Cowick and St James, being the portion belonging to St James with the seal of Cowick.

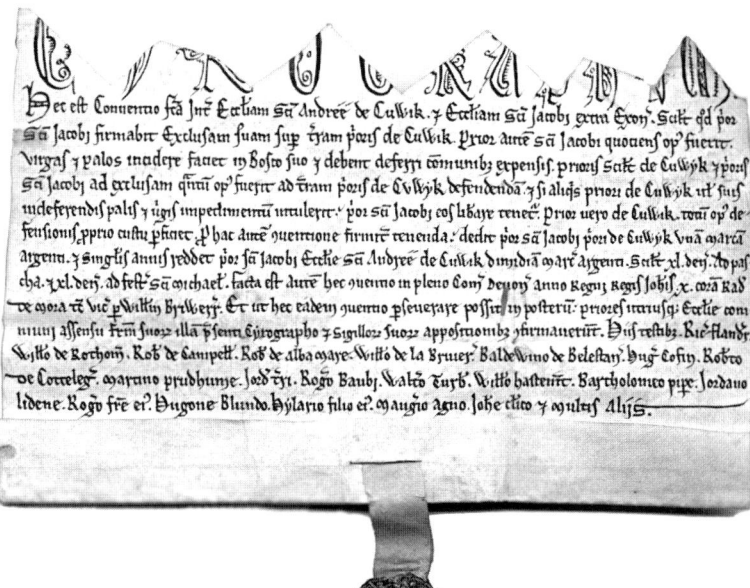

religion attributed holiness to wells that may not have such status in ancient times.[130] At least two wells in Exeter, however, were regarded as holy before the Reformation. St Sidwell's well in Well Street probably dated back to late Anglo-Saxon times, and land was donated for its upkeep in the thirteenth century. Its water was used for general purposes, but seems to have had some reputation for sanctity and the well eventually acquired a substantial well-house to protect it. Parker's Well in Matford Lane, as we have seen, was linked with the chapel of St Clair by the fifteenth century. A third well, at the junction of Paris Street and Heavitree Road, is described as that of St Catherine in 1806 when it was said to have once had an adjoining chapel, but the existence of the chapel and the antiquity of the well have yet to be established.

Crosses were more common than holy wells. Large crosses, elevated on a pyramid of steps, were often erected in town centres or market places. Small crosses were

[130] Nicholas Orme, 'Medieval Holy Wells in Devon', *Devonshire Association Transactions*, 145 (2013), 129–54 at 130.

placed along roads or on land where they acted as markers for travellers, indicators of boundaries, and resting places for bearers of coffins from outlying houses to the parish church. Churchyards normally contained a cross on a stepped base which was sometimes known as a 'palm cross' because it was decorated and visited during the ceremonies of Palm Sunday. The Franciscan Friary in Holloway Street had such a cross in its cemetery and this was probably the case at the cathedral, the other religious houses, and the extramural churches. The other kinds of crosses did not necessarily have a religious function, but it seems to have been common for people to say the Paternoster (Lord's Prayer) when passing them.[131] This association of crosses with Latin worship led to their disparagement after the Reformation. Many of the larger ones were removed, especially from churchyards, but at least three small medieval crosses survive in Exeter as well as the Anglo-Saxon shaft already mentioned, which is housed in the Royal Albert Memorial Museum. They include an example in Cowick Street, a cross formerly close to the chapel of St Loye, and Scarlett's Cross which once stood at the junction of Old Tiverton Road with Mount Pleasant Road and Rosebarn Lane.[132]

The Parish Churches and the Clergy, 1300–1530

More can be known about the Exeter parish churches in the fourteenth and fifteenth centuries, thanks to evidence from their buildings as well as from wills and records, especially churchwardens' accounts. This gives an impression of development in terms of their wealth and activities, which should be judged with caution because so little survives about them in earlier times. However most churches were at least partly rebuilt in the later Middle Ages and often enlarged to provide more room for towers, aisles, altars, images, processions, and congregational seating. A similar process is observable in all the larger English cities, by which churches shrank in number but expanded in size. St George, St John Bow, and Holy Trinity are all mentioned as acquiring extra land for this purpose, while St John Bow and St Stephen extended their chancels above an adjoining street. It is also worth pointing out that the size and status of a church building was not always limited to its religious activities. The manorial court of the bishop's properties, St Stephen's Fee, is likely to have met in St Stephen's church, and that of Plympton Priory's possessions may well have done so in St John Bow. The archdeacon of Exeter certainly held his court in St Mary Major during the fifteenth century.[133]

[131] Nicholas Orme, *The Church in Devon 400–1560* (Exeter, 2013), 125–7.
[132] HER refs. MDV17808 (SX 9098 9170), MDV17810 (SX 9461 9195), and MDV18262 (SX 9311 9388).
[133] Below, pp. 119, 136, 167.

At least fifteen churches appear to have gained aisles or chapels alongside their naves and chancels in or after the twelfth century. Eight had at least one (St David, St Edmund, St George, St John Bow, St Laurence, St Martin, St Mary Steps, and Holy Trinity), and seven at least two (Heavitree, St Mary Arches, St Olave, St Petroc, St Sidwell, St Stephen, and St Thomas). Sixteen churches are recorded or may be conjectured as possessing side altars in addition to their high altars. The locations of these are not always clear but they appear to have been usually placed at the east end of an aisle or chapel, or in one case (St Mary Major) under a west tower. The side altars numbered at least one at St David, St Edmund, St George, St James (parish church), St Martin, and St Mary Steps; at least two at Heavitree, St John Bow, St Mary Arches, St Mary Major, St Olave, St Sidwell, St Thomas, and perhaps St Kerrian; and at least three at St Petroc, Holy Trinity, and possibly St Stephen. Most churches gained towers in which to hang two or more bells, although St Kerrian, St Leonard, and St Pancras had only turrets for the purpose. Bells were privileges of parish churches that were sometimes denied to chapels, and most Exeter congregations seem to have regarded a tower as an essential mark of status by the fifteenth century. For reasons of space, however, several of the towers within the city walls were constructed within and above the nave rather than beyond its west end. Church towers were often described as 'steeples', but this word need not imply a structure with a cone-shaped spire. Hooker's and Hogenberg's map of Exeter, 1587, shows most of the city's towers with square castellated tops, although St Mary Arches and St Mary Major are credited with tall spires and St Olave and St Paul with lower ones.[134] Altogether the churches of Exeter were frequently renewed or added to. Each century saw changes and these continued after the Reformation, so that those that remained in the nineteenth century or exist today are not wholly accurate guides to the appearance of their medieval predecessors.

Each church in the city and suburbs with parochial status had a full-time clergyman, or should have done so. His usual title was 'rector', but St David, St John Bow, St Sidwell, and Topsham were served by chaplains who received small salaries rather than tithes and offerings like the rectors. A few churches contained an additional chaplain, deputising for an absent or busy rector, and some had the services of a chantry priest or two, usually for a limited period, but (as we shall see) there were not many such auxiliary clergy. In this respect Exeter resembled Winchester but differed from London, Norwich, and York with their large numbers of chantry and guild priests.[135] The staffing of the chapels is uncertain. Four had

---

[134] John Hooker, *Isca Damnoniorum* [map] ([London?], 1587). On Hooker's map of the Cathedral Close in DHC, ECA Book 53, St Stephen is shown with a small turret spire.
[135] Keene, *Medieval Winchester*, 122.

endowments to support permanent chaplains. These consisted of Exe Bridge Chapel and the Guildhall Chapel (although they came to share a single priest), Wynard's Almshouse, and (at least by the Reformation) Christchurch. The others are likely to have been served by clergy on an occasional basis, celebrating mass on one or more weekdays so as not to compete with the parish churches on Sundays.

The rectors of the city churches included men who were wholly occupied with their parish and those who were minor clergy of the cathedral: chiefly vicars choral but occasionally the chantry priests known at the cathedral as annuellars. In the case of the minor clergy, their parish work had to be done alongside their demanding duties in the cathedral choir which took place at intervals throughout the day. The cathedral may have granted them licences for absence, particularly on Sunday mornings to celebrate parish masses, but there is no surviving record of the fact. More rarely a cathedral canon held one of the city benefices in a similar way. The question of the rectors' accommodation has yet to be fully answered. As has been noted, the name of Preston Street suggests that some may have rented rooms or houses there up to 1222. Others may have done so elsewhere in later times. The rector of Holy Trinity, for example, leased a tenement in South Street in 1304, but the motive for such leases, whether for personal accommodation or profit, is usually unknown.[136] Nor is it clear whether or at what time most of the parish clergy acquired permanent designated houses. In the suburbs the bishop allotted a house to the vicar of Cowick in 1261, and another at Topsham is mentioned in 1281.[137] Within the city walls, on the other hand, no house was apparently assigned for the rector of St Kerrian until 1349–50 when he was allowed to build one next to the church on Trychay Street.[138] The rector of St Olave had none until 1408 which, it was said, prevented people from knowing where to find him, until in that year the parishioners allowed him to build a chamber at the west end of the church in which to live and sleep, and he seems to have taken his meals in St Nicholas Priory.[139]

In the early sixteenth century the stipends of the city rectors ranged from £4 13s. 4d. at St Pancras to £15 14s. 8d. at St Mary Major, most being between £8 and £10. A taxation record of 1522 also gives the personal wealth of some of them, based on the estimated value of their moveable goods. Thomas Banyster (St Olave) was reckoned to be worth £5, Thomas Acclom (St Petroc) £10, William Torre (St Martin)

[136] ECA, ED/M/200.
[137] D&C 3672A; *Reg. Bronescombe*, ed. Hingeston-Randolph, 127.
[138] ECA, ED/M/388.
[139] George Oliver, 'Extracts from Devon and Cornwall Deeds made by George Oliver in 1825 from a Manuscript in Powderham Castle', Devon Heritage Centre, unpublished volume, DD 23047.

£12, Thomas Benbow (St Kerrian and St Pancras) £20, John Tregethew (All Hallows Goldsmith Street) £20, John Bysshop (St Paul) £26 13s. 4d., Laurence Dobell (St Mary Major) £30, and Robert Fayreman (Holy Trinity) £40 6s. 8d.[140] Chaplains were less wealthy. The 1522 survey gives assessments for some of them, not always making it clear whether the amounts refer to stipends or goods. One unusually wealthy chaplain, William Redway, was rated at £40, presumably in goods and probably denoting private wealth. The rest were valued at £11 or below, and three at only £2. Below them John Gamonte was valued at only 10s., Thomas Fenton at 6s. 8d., and William Marys at nil. Clearly some of these chaplains were poorly paid and had little by way of savings. In 1362 the Church fixed the wages of parish chaplains (whom we would call curates) at £5 6s. 8d. per annum, and those of chantry priests at £4 13s. 4d.[141] The common rate for chantry priests in Exeter during the late fifteenth century was a little higher at £5 or 8 marks (£5 6s. 8d.), but such priests were often employed for only a limited period of time such as a year, under the provisions of a wealthy person's will.[142] When that period was over they had to find themselves another term of employment, and they were poorly equipped to face the problems of old age.

Each rector had a parish clerk to help him. The clerk rang the church bell, prepared the altar, read the epistle at mass, and said the responses in this and other services.[143] His original title was 'holy-water bearer' (*aquebaiulus*) because he carried and dispensed the holy water used in services such as baptisms, churchings of women after childbirth, and funerals. Until the end of the Middle Ages, clerks were usually adolescent youths aged between about fourteen and twenty-four. They were required to be unmarried and were often aspirants to become priests, their duties helping them to learn how to lead worship. In 1287 the bishop of Exeter ordered that the clerks of the cathedral city should be scholars, implying that the small income and fees attached to their office should support them while they studied at school.[144] This was still sometimes the case in the mid fifteenth century, when some Latin school exercises from Exeter mention a scholar who is responsible for censing the choir in church on a festival day, and a group of three students who complain that they have received only three halfpennies and a farthingsworth of thin ale for their

---

[140] *Tudor Exeter. Tax Assessments 1489–1595 Including the Military Survey 1522*, ed. Margery M. Rowe, DCRS, new series 32 (1977), 7–30.
[141] Orme, *Church in Devon*, 98.
[142] DHC, DD 22377; MCR 16–17 Edw IV mm. 9d, 32d; MCR 8–9 Hen VIII mm. 48–9.
[143] On parish clerks, see Nicholas Orme, *Medieval Children* (New Haven and London, 2001), 229–31, and idem, *Medieval Schools* (New Haven and London, 2006), 39–40, 205–7.
[144] *Councils & Synods A.D. 1205–1313*, ed. F. M. Powicke and C. R. Cheney, 2 vols (Oxford, 1964), ii, 1026–7.

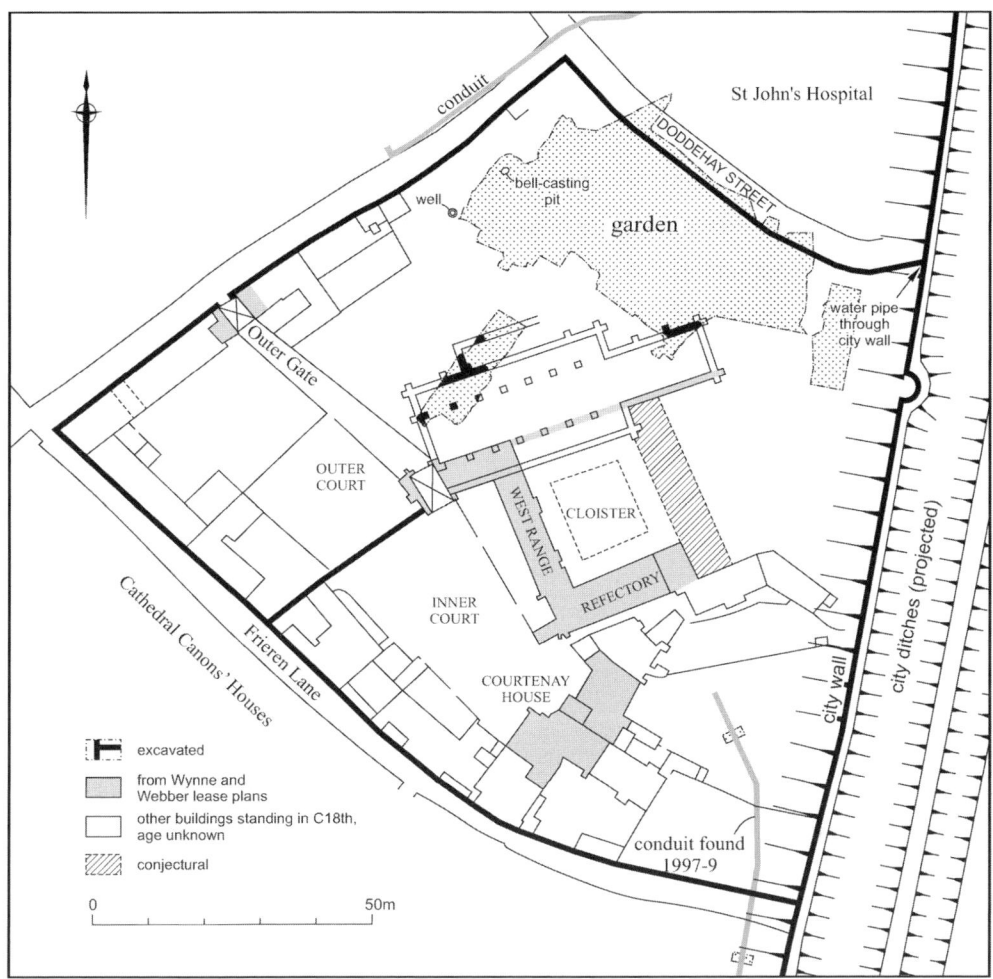

The Dominican Friary, showing the walled precinct with the church, cloister, grounds, and inner and outer gates.

work as clerks.[145] Two parish clerks are listed in the taxation of 1522: those of St John Bow and St Mary Arches. Not surprisingly, in view of the previous complaint, their goods or incomes were valued at nil.[146]

A little light is shed on some of the rectors of the fifteenth century by their wills. Roger Bernard of St Paul (died 1410–11) seems to have come from Davidstow

---

[145] Nicholas Orme, *English School Exercises 1420–1530* (Toronto, 2013), 117, 159.
[146] Rowe, *Tudor Exeter*, 21, 30.

(Cornwall). He was also a vicar choral and owned a tenement in Exeter, so that he was moderately prosperous. He had a wide acquaintance, giving bequests to a dozen friends who were mostly Exeter clergy and to the two Exeter friaries.[147] John Govys of Holy Trinity (died 1416) was another vicar choral. He too held a tenement, in his case by leasehold, and possessed two mazers (wooden drinking bowls) decorated with silver. He mentioned a dozen friends in his will, again chiefly clergy, and made donations not only to the friaries but the hospital of St John and the college of vicars choral. He asked for the residue of his estate to be given to poor priests and clerks.[148] Nicholas Collecote of St Laurence (died 1424) was a Devonian from Winkleigh. He requested burial in the hospital of St John and gave money to it and the friaries, but his horizons were wider since he left legacies not only to churches in Exeter but to the friars of Plymouth and the parish churches of Ashburton and Hatherleigh. He owned at least one musical service-book (an antiphonal), two ewers and basins, and a furred gown.[149] Finally Robert Lingham of St Mary Major (died 1428), was a former annuellar of the cathedral. He was the most prosperous of these clergy, owning several pieces of plate: a coconut cup mounted with silver, its cover topped with a griffin; a silver drinking bowl engraved with his initials; a silver cup bequeathed to him by a cathedral canon and inscribed 'In God is all my trust'; and other items. His bed was decorated with tapestry of fleurs-de-lys, and his possessions included a blue belt trimmed with silver and a baslard or dagger similarly decorated. His will mentions four of his books: a service-book for matins, a work of theology, one of canon law, and the *Pupilla Oculi* (a guide to the work of a parish priest), as well as referring to several city clergy.[150] All these wills give the impression of a modest but comfortable life-style, circles of friends (especially clergy), and a sense of a duty to give bequests to local churches and to the poor.

The religion of the parishes centred on Sunday services, when clergy were expected to say matins and celebrate mass in church during the morning, followed by evensong in the mid afternoon. They were also required to repeat all eight of the daily services each day, but it is not clear whether they did so in church or privately, and it is likely that they said the services in two or three blocks, morning and afternoon or evening, rather than at intervals like monks, so as to give time for other activities. Mass may have been celebrated daily as well, one stimulus to which was requests to do so (for a fee) by the relatives or executors of the dead. The religious houses and some of the parish churches acquired Lady chapels in

---

[147] *Reg. Stafford*, 396.
[148] Ibid., 415.
[149] *Reg. Lacy*, ed. Dunstan, iv, 1–3.
[150] Ibid., iv, 12–14.

which prayers were also said for the Virgin Mary.[151] During the fifteenth century, antiphons to be sung before her image were established at the cathedral, St Nicholas Priory, and St Petroc, while St Mary Arches had a mass in her honour by 1546. Another popular cult in that century and the next was the Name of Jesus. 'Jesus masses', usually held on a Friday, were established at St George and St Mary Arches by 1546, and the altars of Jesus in the hospital of St John and St Petroc probably figured in similar masses.

The regular round of services was varied in two ways. One was through music. Most of the daily services in religious houses and the Sunday ones in parish churches were sung to plainsong. During the fifteenth century, however, polyphony became popular, not so much in the regular services but for the masses and antiphons sung in honour of Jesus and the Virgin Mary. The cathedral led the way in this respect, appointing special 'clerks of the chapel' (meaning the Lady chapel) to compose and direct the polyphony, for which the cathedral had good vocal resources from its choristers, clerks, and adult clergy.[152] The other religious houses were poorly staffed, and would have had difficulties in performing polyphony except on an occasional basis. This was also true of most of the parish churches, but there are references to small organs at St Laurence, St Olave, St Paul, and Holy Trinity, and vestments for 'children' at St Mary Major: either altar boys or members of a small choir. More solid evidence survives from St Petroc. There the churchwardens' accounts record payments to a certain Master John Germyn for several years in the 1510s for playing the organs from time to time, and in 1526–7 John Glasyer was employed to write masses, antiphons, and sequences in five black books, suggesting the existence of a polyphonic choir at least on special occasions.

The second way that churches could diversify their worship was through religious cults. By installing images and sometimes altars beside them, the number of cults for veneration was greatly extended beyond the persons to whom the churches themselves were dedicated. At least fifty-six different cults of the Trinity, Christ, angels, and saints are recorded in medieval Exeter, not counting those of the cathedral (Table 1).[153] These were chiefly of such popular figures as Jesus, Mary, Michael, Christopher, James, John the Baptist, and Katherine. Christ, of course, was pictured on the crucifix above the roodscreen of every church, and the cult of the Name of Jesus was followed in some churches as we have seen, very likely in

---

[151] There were Lady chapels at the cathedral, St Mary Magdalene, St Petroc, and St Thomas, and possibly at St David, St Laurence, St Mary Arches, St Nicholas Priory, St Olave, St Sidwell, and other places.
[152] Orme, *Exeter Cathedral: the first thousand years*, 143–5.
[153] On the cults at the cathedral, see ibid., 171–87.

Table 1 Religious cults in medieval Exeter

This table omits the cathedral and its cults. Where a cult was named after more than one person, there is a separate entry for each excepting All Saints.

Cult name	Church/ religious house	Free-standing chapel	Altar and image	Image alone	Guild	Liturgical cult
Alexius	1					
All Saints	2					
Andrew	1		1			
Anne		1		1		
Anthony of Egypt				1		
Apollonia			1			
Bartholomew		1				
Christ/Trinity	1	2	2	1		
Christopher				4		
Clair		1				
Clement		1			1	
Corpus Christi					1	
Cuthbert	1					
David	1					
Dominic	1					
Dorothy				1		
Dunstan				1		
Edmund	1					
Edward the Confessor		1	1			
Edward the Martyr	1					
Erasmus				2		
Faith		1				
Francis	1	1				
Gabriel			1			
George	1	1	1	1	2	
James the Great	2			1		
Jerome				1		
Jesus, Name of			1		1*	2
John the Baptist	2	1	2	1	1	
John the Evangelist	1					
Katherine	2		3	3		
Kerrian	1					
Laurence	1					
Leonard	1					

Table 1 Continued

Cult name	Church/religious house	Free-standing chapel	Altar and image	Image alone	Guild	Liturgical cult
Loye		1	1			
Margaret	1					
Martin	1		2			
Mary Magdalene	1					
Mary the Virgin	9	8	6	8	2	3
Michael	1	2	2	2		
Nicholas	1					
Olave (Olaf)	1					
Pancras	1					
Paul	1					
Peter Martyr			1			
Peter the Apostle		1				
Petroc	1					
Radegund		1				
Roche	1					
Sidwell	1					
Simon and Jude		1				
Stephen	1					
Sythe					1*	
Thomas Becket	1	1	4			
Thomas the Apostle	1					
Trinity – see Christ						
Ursula and Virgins	1					
Walter of Cowick				1		

* Including an altar and image.

surroundings decorated with the monogram IHS. Mary's image stood at the south end of every high altar, and was often placed in the nave of the church as well so that it could be easily accessed by worshippers. Her cult took different forms. During the later Middle Ages devotion to her Assumption became popular, referring to her alleged ascension to heaven which was celebrated on 15 August. This day was specially observed at the Castle Chapel, dedicated to Mary, and presumably at the chapels of St Mary Mincinglake and of Tuckers Hall in Fore Street, which honoured the Assumption. Other people venerated her as Our Lady of Pity: holding the dead body of Christ. There were images of this in the Dominican Friary, outside the Charnel Chapel, and perhaps in other places. By 1514 St David's church had a special cult of its own, 'Our Lady of Rougemont', a formula (Our Lady with a special local association) suggestive of a miracle-working image that drew pilgrims or was intended to do so.[154]

Occasionally we encounter less prominent saints. St Mary Major had an altar of St Apollonia, patroness of toothache, St Kerrian and St Petroc images of St Erasmus, patron of intestinal disorders, and Holy Trinity an altar of St Loye, patron of smiths and farriers. Dunstan occurs at All Hallows (Goldsmith Street) and Dorothy at St Petroc. These may have attracted devotees in search of remedies or those who regarded the saint as the patron of their craft. St Sidwell's church contained a shrine enclosing the alleged body of Sidwell, and Cowick Priory the remains of Walter of Cowick who was not canonised but locally venerated as a saint. We have already noticed the arrival in Exeter of new saint-cults of the later Middle Ages in the chapels erected to Anne and Roche. There was another image of Anne at St Kerrian. A third new saint, Sythe, an Italian woman who was patroness of servants and approached for assistance in finding lost objects, had a statue and guild in St Petroc. In 1505–6 the wardens of that church paid for the insertion of liturgical material into a breviary for two new church feasts: the Visitation of the Virgin Mary on 2 July and the Transfiguration of Jesus on 6 August.

The calendar of each church and chapel followed that of the Church in general by observing the passing of the Church year: the festivals of Christmas, Easter, Whitsuntide, and Trinity Sunday; the penitential seasons of Advent and Lent; and the major saints' days. Each church, and many if not all of the chapels, had other special days peculiar to themselves. One was the patronal festival in honour of the patron saint. Some important saints like Mary and Peter had more than one such day, all of which would have been observed with one of them chosen for particular solemnity. A second feast-day was the dedication festival: the commemoration of the day on which the building had been dedicated by a bishop. Dedication festivals were sometimes changed with the bishop's permission, probably to avoid them clashing with other feast-days in the calendar or to hold them in the more clement months of the year.[155] Further days of local observance were those when obits were held to remember the deaths of wealthy parishioners. Each parish church had a few of these, involving a requiem mass, a probable attendance by family and friends, and sometimes the giving of charity to the poor. On seven days of the year, processions were held outside the church building, these being Palm Sunday, St Mark's Day (25 April), the Rogation days (the Monday, Tuesday, and Wednesday

---

[154] TNA, PROB 11/18/35 (the will of John Chalmore).
[155] Below, pp. 130, 173.

of the sixth week after Easter), Ascension Day (the Thursday of the same week), and Corpus Christi (the second Thursday after Pentecost or Whitsunday). The processions involved the clergy and the parishioners. On Palm Sunday they went round the outside of the church building, if possible, but on the other days along the streets and perhaps to the parish boundaries. On the Rogation days the congregations of the Exeter churches may have joined together in going out of the city to hear mass and a sermon at one of the suburban churches or chapels. This gave them the opportunity to pray for God's blessing on the crops and for the expulsion of the powers of evil from the land.[156]

The Parish Churches and the Laity, 1300–1530

Much of the maintenance of worship in the parish churches fell on the shoulders of the adult laity. They were required to pay tithes and offerings to make a stipend for the rector, but he was responsible only for the upkeep of the chancel, and not always all of that, as well as for one or two of the service-books. The rest of the church maintenance and the provision of ornaments, vestments, materials for services, images, seating, and most of the service-books were additional burdens on the parishioners. Each church had a 'store' or fund which was financed through money raising and donations. Some city churches owned tenements or rents which had been given to them in the past and provided a useful and regular income. Several possessed indulgences providing remission of penance to those who supported the church in any way, but these were generally granted by bishops who could only award a remission of forty days: a poor attraction in the crowded and inflated world of papal indulgences. In 1287 Bishop Quinil ordered all church stores to pay an annual tithe or tenth to the incumbent as a contribution to chancel repairs, but this rule seems to have been neglected in later centuries.[157] However, in 1522 Cardinal Wolsey came up with the idea of taxing the stores for the benefit of the crown, and instituted enquiries into their values. This may have caused local people to reduce or conceal what they possessed, so the following figures need to be treated with caution. St Martin admitted to having £6, St Mary Arches £5, St Mary Major and St Pancras £4, Tuckers Hall chapel £3 6s. 8d., All Hallows Goldsmith Street £2 16s., St Petroc £2, St David £1 6s. 8d., and St Paul £1. St Kerrian alleged that it had only 18s., St Olave 2s. 4½d., and St George 1s. 8d., while St John Bow and St Stephen returned themselves at nil.[158]

---

[156] On Rogationtide processions and their activities, see Nicholas Orme, 'Parish Processions in Medieval and Tudor Cornwall', *Journal of the Royal Institution of Cornwall* (2011), 73–82.
[157] *Councils & Synods II*, ed. Powicke and Cheney, ii, 1053.
[158] *Tudor Exeter*, ed. Rowe, 7–30.

English churches of the later Middle Ages commonly included groups of parishioners who banded together for devotional activities. The simplest of these formed round the store or endowment of an image. Those who venerated the image contributed small sums of money (or cows, sheep, and bees) to maintain it and sometimes to boost the finances of the church as a whole. Such a store needed a warden or two to administer the funds, but need not have involved any social intercourse. Next there was the 'company', to use a modern term, consisting of a group of people defined by gender or age. Churches in the South-West of England frequently had three such companies: the wives, young men, and maidens. It has been suggested that they came into existence because church affairs were generally run by wealthy adult men, while the companies supported social and devotional activities by other kinds of parishioners. Little is recorded about them in Exeter, and it is not clear whether this reflects their absence or their failure to generate records. We hear of maidens raising money for Holy Trinity, however, and there seem to have been several groups of young men. In July 1510 the city chamber forbade them to keep the 'riot' of Robin Hood in their parish church unless it was on the holy day of the church (the day of the patron saint or the dedication of the building), or on some other well-established day.[159] Robin Hood plays and pageants raised money, and no doubt this practice had become abused.

The third kind of grouping was a guild, also known as a fraternity. This was more formal than a company or a store, and would be likely to have elected wardens in charge, ordinances that governed its membership and activities, and more assets in terms of monetary contributions or endowments. Guilds were less common in the South-West than the other parish organisations, and even parishes containing small towns, like Ashburton, often had only a single guild which probably brought together the powerful men of the community, with their wives as associate members. Exeter, as we have seen, came to possess the civic guild of St George and six craft guilds by the Reformation, variously functioning in their own chapels, a monastery, and perhaps (in the case of the skinners) a parish church. Only a few other guilds are recorded: those of Jesus and St Sythe in St Petroc, St George in Holy Trinity, St Mary in St Thomas, and perhaps St Roche based at the hospital of that name. Again this may reflect shortage of evidence, but it is noteworthy that references to guilds are rare in the surviving churchwardens' accounts from pre-Reformation Exeter, in taxation records of the early sixteenth century, and in wills, so that they may not have been very common.[160] The small size of the Exeter parishes may have prevented the growth of sub-groups within them, while the civic and craft guilds provided

---

[159] ECA, Chamber Act Book 1 f. 13v.
[160] None is mentioned in *Tudor Exeter*, ed. Rowe.

other opportunities for the wealthier and their wives to join together for company and worship.

The people of Exeter also involved themselves with their churches, chapels, and religious houses in individual ways, varying from devotion (which could take many different forms) to the avoidance of religious duties as far as possible or even hostility towards them. While everyone had a parish church after 1222 and was expected to attend its services at least occasionally, it was possible to vary this attendance with devotions to one or more of the saints of the church or visits to images or services at the cathedral and the religious houses, especially the friaries and the hospital of St John. Wills of Exeter citizens and their wives illustrate their preferences in giving charity. Money was often bestowed on the poor, sometimes distinguished as the disabled, prisoners, poor scholars, or people in almshouses. Alternatively it might be given for the maintenance of church buildings, church lights, the friaries, or the bridges in the city and the surrounding area. Some Exeter people became clergy, chiefly men, although there are likely to have been a few local women in the nunnery of Polsloe. An occasional woman who did not become a nun adopted a similar way of life as a vowess or anchoress. Vowesses were women, usually widows, who took a vow of celibacy before the bishop but otherwise remained in their own houses. Anna Crugge was one such in the parish of St Kerrian in 1522.[161] Anchoresses retired to cells or small houses, while remaining sufficiently in contact with the world to receive visitors and almsgivers. An unnamed woman of this kind built a cell near Exe Bridge and lived there between 1244 and 1249, obstructing the roadway in a manner that caused the city authorities to complain to the king's justices.[162] Another such person, Alice Bernard, dwelt in a house in St Leonard's churchyard from 1397 until at least the 1420s, while Alice Buttes did so at the hospital of St John in the 1530s.[163]

Personal tastes also counted when people died. Everyone (except for monks, friars, and nuns) was required to have a funeral at the cathedral, but this might be as simple or elaborate as they or their families wished or could afford. Burial for most people also took place in the cathedral cemetery, but the wealthy expressed their higher status by gaining permission for a grave in a parish church, a religious house, or the cemetery belonging to such a house. The friaries encouraged this practice from an early date, and a large number of local knights, gentry, and citizens acquired tombs within their churches. Smaller numbers of outsiders found resting places

---

[161] Ibid., 12.
[162] Hoskins, *Two Thousand Years*, 30–1.
[163] Below, pp. 115, 126.

inside the cathedral and the priories of Cowick and St Nicholas. These were chiefly knights, gentry, and their wives rather than citizens. Citizens by themselves dominated the burials in the hospital of St John and the parish churches. Mayor Thomas Hunt, John Kelly, and Mayor John Symon and his wife Alison, for example, were all laid to rest (or wished to be) in St Petroc.[164]

Commemoration mattered to those who prepared to die. They wished their names to be remembered and prayers to be said for their souls. Tombstones helped in this way with their dates of death and Latin inscriptions *Orate pro anima* ('Pray for the soul of . . .') and *cuius anime propicietur Deus* ('on whose soul may God have mercy'). But the wealthy demanded more formal prayers, preferably by the clergy. In religious houses a text called the 'martyrology' was read out in the chapter house each morning, giving notice of the liturgical material and festivals of saints that would be observed next day. The twelfth-century martyrology of Exeter Cathedral was also used to record the names of local people, who doubtless made a donation for the purpose so that their names would be read out and prayed for on the appropriate day.[165] Other religious houses followed this practice, and in 1520 William Crugge, citizen and former mayor of Exeter, left sums of 10*s*. to the clergy of St John, St Nicholas, and the two friaries to have his name inscribed in their martyrologies, with similar mentions and prayers.[166] Guilds kept lists of members' names to be recited at mass in church, and the list survives that belonged to the guild of Kalendars, ranging in date from the twelfth to the early fourteenth centuries.[167] The names are arranged under months, and were doubtless announced during the guild mass at the beginning of the appropriate month. By the fifteenth century parish churches commonly had a similar document called a bede-roll which was read out by the clergyman during mass on Sundays, with a request that the names should be prayed for. A small fee or offering was required to have one's name inscribed, less costly than in the religious houses since Crugge bequeathed 20*d*. to each parish church in the city to have his name put on to its bede-roll. The fee meant that bede-rolls included people of at least moderate wealth, not the poor majority, although they concluded by praying for 'the faithful departed' in general.

Those with substantial wealth could have themselves remembered with more ritual. They could endow an 'obit' or 'anniversary' by leaving cash or a regular payment from property of a couple of shillings to fund a requiem mass each year on the date

---

[164] Lepine and Orme, *Death and Memory*, 80–1, 104.
[165] Ibid., 250–8.
[166] TNA, PROB 11/19/407.
[167] Lepine and Orme, *Death and Memory*, 263–71.

of their death. Many of these were founded at the cathedral and probably at the friaries (whose records do not survive), as well as in each of the parish churches. Those with yet more money to spend could buy an 'annual' or celebration of masses for one or more years by a chantry chaplain.[168] This cost far more than an obit, in view of the £4 or £5 per annum that such chaplains asked to be paid, and perhaps an additional fee to a city rector to allow the chaplain to function at an altar in his church. Annuals are often mentioned in the wills of wealthy Exeter clergy and citizens, providing a living for a few local priests who engaged in this task. Up to the Black Death, when there was a large supply of clergy willing to work for low wages, there may have been about a dozen such priests at work in Exeter, but thereafter the number was smaller. A taxation list of about 1490 lists sixteen chaplains in Exeter, from whom we need to deduct curates, leaving perhaps eight temporary chantry priests.[169] The taxation of 1522 includes five priests in fourteen parishes who may have been similarly employed; if we take into account six missing parishes, a total of eight looks likely again.[170] A third list of 1540–1, when the Reformation was beginning to take hold, records only six priests in the city other than rectors and curates.[171]

The most expensive memorial was a perpetual chantry. This involved making an endowment of property to pay a chaplain for ever, setting up a governing body to supervise the property and appoint the chaplain, and finding a rector willing to let the chaplain say mass in his church. Most of the perpetual chantries in Exeter were located at the cathedral, where several bishops, cathedral clergy, and knights transferred properties to support thirty-three permanent priests between the thirteenth and the sixteenth centuries. In practice permanency was not always achieved in the long term because endowments declined. Chantries had to be joined together, and there were never more than twenty-one priests at a time.[172] Few perpetual chantries appear to have been founded in the Exeter parish churches.[173]

---

[168] On the work of chantry priests, see Roger Bowers, 'Liturgy and Music in the Role of the Chantry Priest', *Journal of the British Archaeological Association*, 164 (2011), 130–56.
[169] Lambeth Palace Library, MS 721 f. 63r.
[170] *Tudor Exeter*, ed. Rowe, 7–30.
[171] Rose-Troup, Frances. 'Lists Relating to Persons Ejected from Religious Houses', *Devon and Cornwall Notes and Queries*, 17 (1932–3), 82.
[172] Orme, *The Minor Clergy of Exeter Cathedral: Biographies*, 304–8.
[173] No obvious documents are to be found in the *List of Inquisitions Ad Quod Damnum Preserved in the Public Record Office*, 2 vols, Public Record Office, Lists and Indexes, 17, 22 (London, 1904–6) or as charters in the *Calendar of Patent Rolls*, documents that usually accompanied permanent endowment for a religious purpose, although the official process was sometimes ignored or circumvented.

The medieval church of St Edmund on Exe Bridge before its rebuilding in 1833–4, wedged in between houses.

One was planned in St Olave in 1310, but most of the evidence relates to the early sixteenth century. In 1546–8 when such chantries were investigated by the crown with an eye to their dissolution, there were no more than three in Exeter: one each in the churches of St Edmund, St Martin, and St Mary Arches, along with four analogous priests of the shoemakers' and weavers' guilds, Exe Bridge Chapel, and Wynard's Almshouse.[174]

Exeter's religious character may be summarised as resembling a dozen or more major towns in England in having a dominant religious house (the cathedral) and several smaller ones including two friaries. Its distinctiveness lay in the imbalance between the cathedral, with its burial rights, and the large number of small parish

---

[174] Nicholas Orme, 'The Dissolution of the Chantries in Devon, 1546–8', *Devonshire Association Transactions*, 111 (1979), 106–7.

churches. This meant that people's loyalties were divided. They belonged to a parish church by virtue of where they lived, but it could not claim the whole of their allegiance when they died. Unless they made other arrangements, they had to be buried in the cathedral cemetery, and when the wealthy arranged to have graves elsewhere they were more likely to choose the friaries or the hospital of St John than their parish church. Nevertheless the parish churches were not insignificant in the religious life of the city. Several proclaimed the status of their owners or supporters: St Mary Arches and St Stephen that of the bishop, St John Bow that of Plympton Priory, and St Petroc and St Sidwell that of their wealthy citizen parishioners. Some of the rich who chose to be buried in a religious house were still moved to make donations to their parish church and its cults or to endow an obit or an annual of masses there. As the gazetteer in this book makes clear, the churches grew in respect of acquiring aisles, altars, roodscreens, images, vestments, and organs, and had their individual calendars of worship. Three, St Mary Major, St Petroc, and Holy Trinity, seem to have been particularly ambitious in their activities, but even the others were remarkably varied in their devotions and most of them tenacious in their survival down to the Reformation and for long afterwards.

The Reformation

The foundations of the later Middle Ages offset the losses of the thirteenth and fourteenth centuries, and raised the number of public or semi-public religious buildings in the city of Exeter, its associated parishes of Heavitree and Topsham, and the independent parish of Cowick to about forty-eight by 1530. Eight of these were religious houses: the cathedral, St Nicholas, Cowick, Polsloe, St Mary Marsh, the Dominican and Franciscan friaries, and the hospital of St John. The priory of St James had become defunct between 1428 and 1445 but, as we have seen, its church continued as a chapel with regular or occasional services until at least the end of the fifteenth century. The other hospitals and almshouses are not counted here as religious houses because they were small residential foundations chiefly for lay people and some had no place of worship. Twenty-one places of worship were parish churches, and two others (St David and St Sidwell), although chapels-of-ease to Heavitree, had most of the characteristics of parish churches. Seventeen were chapels, variously attached to the castle, the leper hospital, almshouses, the premises of a guild, or free-standing and existing in their own right. There were also private chapels, notably that of the bishop and the cathedral dean and canons, and there are three institutions whose existence is enigmatic. The chapel of St Mary attached to the leper hospital of St Mary Magdalene is not mentioned after the thirteenth century, that of St Mary Mincinglake after 1489, and that of St Roche after 1521, leaving it uncertain whether they still operated by the Reformation.

That series of events destroyed the rich and diverse religious culture of the later Middle Ages. The first foundation to disappear was St Nicholas Priory which was closed by royal commissioners in September 1536. It was followed by the two friaries in September 1538 and by the remaining monasteries (Cowick, St Mary Marsh, and Polsloe) in February and March 1539, along with the hospital of St John. The latter, like such institutions elsewhere, was treated as a monastery rather than a hospital because it had a staff of monastic clergy. Once closed, the churches of the houses were demolished except for the chancel of St John which was eventually turned into a chapel for the mayor. Their cloister buildings were converted to secular uses. The Dominican Friary became Bedford House, the residence of the earls of Bedford, and St Nicholas Priory the house of a merchant. The urban properties of the houses were sold to lay people, and the city became less obviously religious in its landscape, its employment, and its tenurial relationships. Only the cathedral escaped total destruction and even kept its property and privileges within the city, although here too there were some substantial changes. The chantry priests or annuellars were abolished in 1548, their house was turned to other purposes, and the vicars choral were turned from twenty priests into eight (later four) priests and twelve laymen. The Cathedral Close, which had hitherto been an enclave for clergy, began to be invaded by lay residents, as the spectacular merchant's house known as 'Mol's Coffee House' (built in the 1590s) bears eloquent witness.

The parish churches and their clergy survived the Reformation. In 1545 an act of Parliament allowed the union of churches in towns when their incomes were worth less than £6 per annum, but no advantage was taken of this in Exeter where the churches and parishes remained unchanged until the period of the Commonwealth.[175] The chapels, on the other hand, disappeared almost wholly. The reforms to the Church of England that took place under Henry VIII and Edward VI did not formally abolish them, but various contextual changes made it impossible for them to continue. In 1536 papal indulgences were prohibited, and two years later the veneration of images and shrines was forbidden, making it difficult for chapels to collect donations from worshippers or to honour religious cults. In 1548 the second Chantry Act abolished religious guilds and chantries and gave their assets to the crown. This removed the chaplains who had operated on Exe Bridge and in the Guildhall, Wynard's Almshouse, and the shoemakers' chapel of Christchurch.[176] In the following year the new *Book of Common Prayer* of 1549

---

[175] *The Statutes of the Realm, from Magna Carta to the end of the Reign of Queen Anne*, 11 vols (London, Record Commission, 1810–28), iii, 1013–14.

[176] L. S. Snell, *The Chantry Certificates for Devon and the City of Exeter* (Exeter, 1960); Orme, 'Dissolution of the Chantries', 75–123.

restricted the celebration of mass, now called holy communion, to public services in parish churches and large chapels-of-ease, ruling out celebrations in private chapels and even in semi-public ones like the Guildhall Chapel. When the antiquary John Leland visited Devon in 1542, he noted certain chapels already 'neglected' or 'profaned', and that must have been true of those in Exeter by about 1550.[177] The Charnel Chapel was probably dismantled completely at about that time like its counterpart at St Paul's Cathedral, because of its association with prayers for the dead.[178] Even so a handful of chapels survived, largely in private use. They included the Castle Chapel, the almshouse chapels of St Katherine and Wynard's, St Anne (which found fresh life as the chapel of a later almshouse), St Michael (within the deanery), and perhaps the building that became the chapel of Livery Dole if it was brought to that site from elsewhere.

The Reformation thus reduced very greatly the number of places of public worship in Exeter, as it did throughout England. By about 1560 there were only the cathedral, twenty-one parish churches, and two chapels-of-ease. Within each church the worship was reduced and simplified. There were no longer any altars, daily masses, images, cults of saints, or antiphons, and the cathedral alone had daily services. All other churches provided only morning and evening prayer on Sundays and festivals, with rare celebrations of communion. People remained obliged to attend services in their parish churches, and all these services were uniform, so it made no difference where one worshipped except for the sermon one might hear when preaching developed after the Reformation. For a long time only the cathedral offered a different kind of service with choral accompaniments. But this restricted diet of worship was to last for merely a hundred years. By the 1640s, new religious sects were emerging, and after a period of persecution, the Toleration Act of 1689 would allow some of them to found their own meeting houses. In the long history of the Church in England, it is the simplicity of the Reformation that stands out as the exception, rather than the variety of the Middle Ages and the most recent centuries.

---

[177] John Leland, *The Itinerary of John Leland*, ed. L. Toulmin Smith, 5 vols (London, 1907–10), i, 169, 173, 240.
[178] Orme, 'The Charnel Chapel of Exeter Cathedral', 169.

Gazetteer of Religious Houses, Churches, and Chapels in Exeter, 400–1550

The word 'St' is ignored in the alphabetical order.

St Alexius

Founded *c*.1170 by William fitz Ralph (or Prodom) behind St Nicholas Priory on part of the land known as *Irlesbery*, the enclosure or residence of Earls Godwin and Harold in the eleventh century (ECA, ED/SN/2; ECA, Book 53A f. 58r; Oliver, *Monasticon*, 302). The exact location is not recorded. In view of its name it included a chapel dedicated to St Alexius, a fifth-century nobleman who became a beggar and hermit. The dedication is an unusual one, but an altar to the saint was consecrated at St Albans before 1119 and versions of a Life of the saint in French verse were popular from the eleventh to the thirteenth centuries. The hospital was staffed by a body of brothers who formed a corporation with its own seal (p. 37). Being inside the city walls, albeit in a peripheral location, it must have cared for the sick or travellers, not lepers, and may have been under the control or at least the influence of the city government, since it was united with the hospital of St John in 1238–9, which had similar functions. The motive for the union may have been to use the site to accommodate the Franciscan Friary (p. 101), which was established in that area at about the same time (Orme and Webster, *The English Hospital*, 231–3). HER ref. ECC11074. Approximate location SX 9163 9246.

All Hallows (1) Goldsmith Street

The chapel of All Saints recorded in 1177×1184 probably refers to this church (Barlow, *English Episcopal Acta XI*, 87); it first appears for certain *c*.1214 as a chapel in Peter de Palerna's list (D&C 2513). It did not belong to the cathedral in 1194×1204 (Barlow, *English Episcopal Acta XII*, 172–4), which suggests that it was already in the patronage of lay people as it was by 1309, when the first recorded rector was instituted (*Reg. Stapeldon*, 215). The church stood on the eastern side of Goldsmith Street at the junction with the High Street. It was probably made a parish church in 1222, but in 1291 the rector's income was one of those deemed 'scarcely sufficient to maintain a chaplain' (*Reg. Bronescombe*, ed. Hingeston-Randolph, 451). In 1522 the income was valued at £10 (Rowe, *Tudor Exeter*, 11) but in 1535 at £6 4s. 0d. (*Valor Ecclesiasticus*, ii, 316). In 1548 there were three endowed obit masses in the church (Orme, 'Dissolution of the Chantries', 106).

In 1449 Nicholas Attehole or Hole, an Exeter freeman, bequeathed a field called *Bovecliff* in St David parish to finance lights, among other things, to burn before the images of the Virgin Mary and St Dunstan in the church (Reed, 'Allhallows Church', 605–6). John Yeo in his will of 1528 gave two more fields in Teignmouth for the church's repair and ornamentation (ibid., 605). An inventory of the church's ornaments and vestments survives from 1552, which mentions a chancel, altar, roodloft, tower (which had required work on it in 1546), belfry, and three bells (Cresswell, *Edwardian Inventories*, 10–15). The building is depicted on Hooker's and Hogenberg's plan of Exeter, 1587 (Hooker, *Isca*), Sherwood's map of the 1630s (Sherwood), and (with an outline plan) on the Chamber Maps of 1756×60 (ECA, Book 58/13). It consisted of an aisleless nave, a narrow chancel containing an aumbry and piscina, an entrance at the south-west, and a tower (illustration, p. 37). The tower was built or repaired in 1546; this occupied the south-west corner of the nave, but was removed in 1822. The church was closed in 1905 and demolished in the following year. There are detailed accounts of the church and its post-medieval monuments in Cresswell, 7–13 with photograph, and Reed, 'Allhallows Church', 581–616. HER ref. ECC11022. Location SX 9200 9267.

All Hallows (2) on-the-Wall (or Walls)

First mentioned for certain in 1194×1204 as a chapel in the patronage of the cathedral (Barlow, *English Episcopal Acta XII*, 172–4). The location was at the west end of Fore Street next to the city wall. The chapel was probably made a parish church in 1222; in later times the parish extended northwards alongside the city wall towards the Snail Tower. The parish was in a poor district although it had a few wealthy inhabitants, three of whom were buried in St John hospital (Lepine and Orme, *Death and Memory*, 40–1). In 1291 the rector's income was one of those deemed 'scarcely sufficient to maintain a chaplain' (*Reg. Bronescombe*, ed. Hingeston-

Randolph, 451). Even in 1535 the income was one of the poorest in the city, at £5 4s. 8d. (*Valor Ecclesiasticus*, ii, 317), in spite of which the church paid a pension of 1s. 8d. to the cathedral in c.1265, 3d. in 1408 (D&C 3721, 3642), and 2s. in 1535. Meanwhile in 1443 and 1448 Bishop Lacy granted indulgences for contributors to the building, repair, and maintenance of the church, because it was either being rebuilt or simply in need of conservation (*Reg. Lacy*, ed. Dunstan, ii, 279; iii, 1). An inventory of the church's ornaments and vestments survives from 1552, which refers to a steeple [i.e. tower] and two bells (Cresswell, *Edwardian Inventories*, 15–17).

The church tower was a substantial one which is shown appearing behind the city wall on Hooker's and Hogenberg's map of Exeter, 1587 (Hooker, *Isca*); Robert Sherwood's map, 1630s (Sherwood); W. Schellinks's drawing of Exe Bridge, 1662 (Hoskins, *Two Thousand Years*, plate 4); and S. and N. Buck, *South West Prospect of Exeter*, 1736. The building was ruined during the Civil War and not restored although the parish remained in being as an area and an organisation. A ground plan of the church in its ruined state is included on the Chamber Maps of 1756×60. They show it as a small oblong on an east–west axis with an opening at the east end and a semi-circular projection at the west end, the latter being separated from the walls by a small gap. The church is usually described as *super muros* in Latin documents, but *super* may mean 'against' as well as 'upon' the walls. The oblong pointed up Fore Street, and there was an open space to north and south (ECA, Book 58/9, 15). By that time the ruins may have consisted of the tower and all or part of the nave, the tower perhaps standing above the west end of the nave as was common in Exeter, with the projection representing its staircase, while the chancel may have extended into Fore Street. In 1770 the ruins were removed to allow the connection of Fore Street with New Bridge Street and Exe Bridge. A new church with the same name was built in Bartholomew Street in 1843–5, closed in 1938, and demolished in 1950 (Cresswell, 13–14). HER refs ECC11023, 11161. Location SX 9169 9229.

St Andrew – see Cowick, Priory of St Andrew

St Anne

The chapel of St Anne was built a year or so before the summer of 1418 as a votive chapel to a saint whose popularity was growing in England generally and in Devon in particular (Orme, 'Church and Chapel', 89). It stood beyond the East Gate of the city at the junction of the old roads to Tiverton and Polsloe, now Old Tiverton Road and Blackboy Road. This was a good location to attract worship and offerings from passing travellers. In a legal case in the mayor's court in January 1419, John Wygwar, a chantry priest of the cathedral, claimed that he built the chapel in honour of St Anne and All Saints with contributions of money from the earl of Devon and other lords. He added that the dean and chapter of the cathedral, who were rectors of the surrounding parish of Heavitree and therefore owned the right to the offerings made in the chapel, granted him the offerings from the time of the chapel's construction. This situation changed when, according to Wygwar, William Billeford arranged a clandestine marriage in the chapel on 21 August 1418 between John Gascoigne and a woman named Mabilla. On this becoming known, the celebration of mass in the chapel was suspended until the following 1 November, through which, Wygwar claimed, he lost offerings to the value of £10 (ECA, MCR 6–7 Hen V m. 17d).

Billeford defended himself in the court, but did not produce a satisfactory explanation of his conduct, making it appear that Wygwar was the injured party, albeit that the latter's estimate of the value of the lost offerings was greatly exaggerated. This view is supported by the fact that the bishop licensed the celebration of mass in the chapel 'newly constructed' on 2 November 1418, in effect a relicensing, which he would hardly have done if Wygwar was the guilty party (*Reg. Stafford*, 126). After this the chapel seems to have had a quiet existence until the Reformation. Payments from it to the dean and chapter appear in the cathedral's accounts from 1428 to 1502, and range between 3s. 1d. and 10s. 9d. per annum until 1477 when they were standardised at 6s. 8d. (D&C 3750/1–7, 3754). It is possible that the offerings were a little higher than this and that some were applied to the running costs of the chapel, including the payment of chaplains to say occasional masses there, but they are unlikely to have ever been as high as £10 per annum. Exeter Cathedral Library possesses a missal donated to the chapel by John Yott or Hyott, a chantry priest of the cathedral, between 1445 and 1499 (MS 3515; Ker, *Medieval Manuscripts*, ii, 825–7).

The worship in the chapel probably came to an end in 1548–9, but the chapel survived to be used as the place of worship for an almshouse founded alongside it in the late sixteenth century by George and Oliver Mainwaring. It consisted of a two-part building with a west door and two south doors, the latter leading respectively into the nave and chancel (Parker and Collings, 'St Catherine's Almshouses', 128–30). The chapel is depicted as a small building on Hooker's late sixteenth-century maps of St Sidwell's Fee (ECA, Drawer 2; D&C 3530 ff. 37–8) and is still in existence (illustration, p. 179). Photograph of 1906 in Cresswell, 65. HER ref. ECC11097. Location SX 9280 9329.

Annuellars' House

The annuellars or chantry priests of the cathedral came into existence during the thirteenth century. They were endowed by private benefactors, and for most of the time that they existed the cathedral did not provide them with accommodation. Each priest rented his own room or house in the Cathedral Close or elsewhere in the city. In 1528, however, they acquired a common dwelling place in the north-

St George church in 1843: the east end was in South Street, the south walls bordered a lane called George Lane.

west corner of the Cathedral Close, on the right of St Martin's church, largely through the generosity of the cathedral treasurer, John Ryse. This place was known as New Kalendarhay (the original Kalendarhay being the residence of the vicars choral of the cathedral), and took the form of a small quadrangle of houses with its own dining hall. It existed as a community for only twenty years before the chantry priests were abolished in 1548 (Orme, *Exeter Cathedral*, 103–4, 189–90; Parker, *Archaeo-Historical Assessment of 5 The Close*, with reconstruction of the buildings). There was no chapel. The hall and parts of the east side of the quadrangle survive at 5 Cathedral Close. HER ref. ECC11110. Location SX 9212 9267.

Baker's Almshouse

In 1495 William Nordon, citizen of Exeter, bequeathed 13*d*. 'to the poor in the house next to the house of William Baker' (TNA, PROB 11/10/556). Another will-maker, Robert Rawlens in 1503, gave 'to four almshouses that William Baker late made, 6s. 8*d*., half in wood for winter and half in money' (PROB 11/13/487). William Baker was presumably the wealthy Exeter citizen who was a collector of and substantial contributor to a royal tax in 1489 (Rowe, *Tudor Exeter*, 1, 3–4). The later history of this almshouse is not known, and it may simply have been a tenement that was subdivided into four dwellings and let out free of rent. No HER ref. Location: unknown.

St Bartholomew

First mentioned *c.*1214 as a chapel in Peter de Palerna's list (D&C 2513). It did not belong to the cathedral in 1194×1204 (Barlow, *English Episcopal Acta XII*, 172–4), and the patronage is unknown at that time. By the mid fourteenth century it may have belonged to the mayor and chamber of Exeter (ECA, ED/M/434, 454), and certainly did so by 1537 (ECA, Chamber Act Book II f. iir). It stood on the north side of High Street just within the East Gate, separated from the gate by a tenement. The chapel was not made into a parish church in 1222, but seems to have been assigned to the parish of the hospital church of St John which was united to that of St Laurence in 1287. The rector of St Laurence was licensed to celebrate divine service in the chapel in 1424 (*Reg. Lacy*, ed. Dunstan, i, 104). In 1469 part of the East Gate collapsed, badly damaging the chapel, but it was rebuilt by 1481 (ECA, Book 53A f. 20r; Oliver, *Monasticon*, 301). The chapel still existed in 1537 when its altar is mentioned in an inventory of the ornaments of the Guildhall Chapel (ECA, Chamber Act Book II f. iir), but it probably ceased to be used in 1548 or 1549. Further references to its topography survive in ECA, ED/M/592, 729, 842, 850, 880, 891C. HER ref. ECC11058. Location SX 9226 9285.

Bishop's Palace

A chapel existed by 1138×1142 in the bishop's palace, south of the cathedral. At this date it contained an altar dedicated to St Faith (Barlow, *English Episcopal Acta XI*, 41): a female saint popular in France and likely to have been chosen by Bishop Osbern (1072–1103) or his successor William Warelwast (1107–37). A rent of two candles for the chapel is mentioned in 1150–4 (D&C 287). The building would have been used when the bishop was staying in the palace by the chaplains, clerks, and eventually boys of his personal chapel, although for most of the time he lived and they functioned at one of his other Devon manors or at his house in London. There was probably also a resident chaplain in the Exeter chapel. In 1270 Bishop Bronescombe charged the church of Alwington, Devon, with an annual payment of £3 13*s*. 4*d*. to support a chaplain praying for his soul in either the cathedral or the bishop's chapel (*Reg. Bronescombe*, ed. Hingeston-Randolph, 193). The chapel appears to have been chosen for this, since a separate chantry for the bishop was established in the cathedral in the following year (ibid., 279), and by 1381 it was the practice for the rector of St Stephen, Exeter, a church in the gift of the bishop, to have the additional post of serving the chapel and receiving the income of its chantry (*Reg. Brantyngham*, i, 72). This was still the case in 1444–50 (*Reg. Lacy*, ed. Hingeston-Randolph, i, 293; ed. Dunstan, iii, 58).

In 1421 there is a reference to the chapel of St Mary within the bishop's palace (*Reg. Lacy*, ed. Dunstan, i, 48), and ordinations were held in a chapel of the same name in 1509 and 1510 (DHC, Chanter XIII f. 101v). It was possible for ordinations to be held in a small private chapel (see St Mary 10), so that St Mary may have been a separate and more personal oratory of the bishop. Alternatively, it may have been another name for the chapel of St Faith. The latter chapel probably ceased to be used for regular masses in 1548 but may have been revived during the restoration of Catholicism in 1553–9. Thereafter it probably continued in use on an occasional basis, chiefly for private prayer. The building survives, having been much restored by William Butterfield in 1875 but still containing rich Early English details of the early thirteenth century. See also Chanter, *The Bishop's Palace*, 39–53. HER ref. ECC11343. Location SX 9217 9252.

Bonville's Almshouse

Founded by Sir William Bonville, a wealthy landowner in east Devon and Somerset, in 1408 to provide accommodation for twelve poor men and women. The premises of the almshouse consisted of a row of individual dwellings on the south side of Coombe Street, formerly Rock Lane, which branched from South Street opposite Palace Gate. There were probably gardens and the almshouse was endowed with land to provide money for its upkeep and for the giving of a weekly allowance of 7*d*. to each of the almsfolk. The patronage of the almshouse, with the right to appoint the inmates, descended through the Bonville family to that of the Greys, marquesses of Dorset, then to the crown, and finally to the city chamber. No chapel was included, and by 1546 the almsfolk attended services in the church of St Mary Major. Some Exeter historians have identified Bonville's Almshouse with the hospital of St Roche, also in Coombe Street, but this had a chapel and is treated below as a separate foundation (pp. 163–4). The almshouse disappeared in the mid eighteenth century and the former site is shown on the Chamber Maps of 1756×60 (ECA, Book 58/10). For further information, see Orme and Webster, *The English Hospital*, 241–2. HER ref. ECC11094. Location SX 9201 9229.

Castle Chapel

First implied in Domesday Book in 1086, which mentions the canons of the chapel but not the chapel itself. However the chapel, which stood in the inner ward of the castle, was sited close to a Saxon burial ground in use between the ninth and eleventh centuries, containing at least twenty-seven graves (Blaylock et al., *Excavation at Exeter Castle*). The principal place of burial in medieval Exeter was the cemetery of the minster, later the cathedral, and by the twelfth century the cathedral had a monopoly of burials within the city walls. The existence of a burial ground on the castle site points to the likely existence of a nearby church, because burials by this period were usually beside churches, and a church that had some status and independence of the cathedral. The castle was begun by William the Conqueror in 1068, but Dr Robert Higham has suggested that he may have chosen the site because it already belonged to the kings of late Anglo-Saxon England, and that such a site may have had a private church which possessed the privilege of burial rights (Higham, *Anglo-Saxon Devon*, 188; idem, 'Siege of Exeter', 67–106). The minster was itself a royal foundation, and may therefore have been more amenable to granting or tolerating a privilege of this kind.

The Norman Castle Chapel appears to have been founded by Baldwin fitz Gilbert, also known as Baldwin de Meules (died 1090), who was a major landowner in Devon after the Conquest as well as sheriff of the county and castellan of the castle. It must have been a new building rather than a reconstruction of the postulated Anglo-Saxon church, because the footings of its walls cut into the earlier burials, but it was approximately in the same area. Other Norman lords established churches in or near castles within half a century of the Conquest, including Oxford (1074), Pontefract (by 1093), Wallingford (by 1107), and Leicester (1107), the latter of which was also a parish church. The motive of the founders was probably to provide themselves with their own church and clergy rather than to use the local parish churches and their English parish clergy. Normans favoured monks, but it was not possible to accommodate such people in a castle. Canons implied clergy who lived under stricter rules than parish clergy, like canons of cathedrals, and at first such chapel clergy may have been French. Unlike monks they could live either together or in separate accommodation, and operate close to the secular staff and activities of the castle. Baldwin may also have wished to re-establish a church that already existed and perhaps to provide a place of worship for his tenants in Exeter, of whom there were about twenty households (*Domesday Book*, ed. Thorn, 16/1, 58), although it is possible that he also owned the church of St John Bow (p. 118).

The earliest documentary reference in Domesday Book (1086) states that 'the canons of St Mary' held four estates from Baldwin, lying at Ashclyst, Polsloe, Poltimore, and West Clyst, north-east of Exeter, and valued at £2, 10s., 10s., and 15s. respectively (*Domesday Book*, ed. Thorn, 16/89–92). These canons were evidently the clergy of the castle chapel because the estates belonged to their successors in later times. Since the estates had been in several people's hands in 1066, it looks as if they were bestowed on the canons by Baldwin and that he established or re-established the chapel at some date between 1068 and 1086. He was presumably also responsible for giving an estate in Cowick, across Exe Bridge, that came to be known as Hayes (originally *Heghen*), meaning hedges or hedged enclosures. This is not mentioned in the Domesday Survey but Baldwin owned the adjoining manor of Cowick at that date (ibid., 16/106).

The Castle Chapel was Baldwin's private foundation, and therefore distinct from the castle itself which belonged to the king. After his death in 1090 the patronage of the chapel (with the right to appoint the canons) seems to have passed to his sons, the last survivor of whom was Richard fitz Baldwin who died in 1137, and then to Richard's daughter Adeliz, who died in 1142. In that year, according to the annals of Plympton Priory, she gave the chapel to the priory along with other properties (Liebermann, *Ungedruckte Anglo-Normannische Geschichtsquellen*, 29). The grant, which included the 'prebends' or incomes of the canons, was subsequently confirmed by her relative Ranulf Avenel II and by his son William (Bearman, *Charters of the Redvers Family*, 182–3). Despite these grants, the conveyance of the chapel and its property to Plympton did not take effect, and by the beginning of the thirteenth century the patronage was in the hands of the Courtenay family who were Baldwin's heirs through marriage and held his castle of Okehampton with the barony attached. In the early thirteenth century Plympton Priory mounted a legal challenge to Robert de Courtenay (died 1242) for possession of the Castle Chapel and other churches, but agreed to waive its claims in exchange for a grant of land and water rights in Alphington to benefit its cell of St Mary Marsh in that parish (p. 128). The grant was made by Robert between 1219 and 1227 (Powderham, Courtenay Cartulary ff. 134v–5r).

No charter of foundation survives for the chapel. The mention of four estates in 1086 may indicate that there were four clergy from the beginning, styled as canons, but there were certainly four by the thirteenth century. Each canon had a prebend, an endowed benefice, consisting of a piece of land in the area around Broadclyst, and the prebends acquired names based on these lands: Ashclyst (in Broadclyst), Cutton (in Poltimore), Hayes (named from its estate in Cowick), and Carswill(e) (spelt today as Kerswell and also in Broadclyst). Similar prebends were held by the clergy of other Norman castle chapels. Not long after his victory over Plympton, however, Robert de Courtenay granted the prebend of Ashclyst as an endowment to Torre Abbey, probably in 1237 (Barlow, *English Episcopal Acta XII*, 275–6). The grant made the abbey in effect the canon of the prebend, with the right to take its revenues on condition that it arranged for the canon's duties in the chapel to be carried out, and the new arrangement was not to take effect until the resignation or death of the current prebendary (an alternative name for a canon). In fact Torre did not receive the prebend for a long time. The prebend of Ashclyst in 1237 was apparently held by Thomas de Wimundesham. In 1261 the patron of the chapel, who was now Robert's heir Sir John de Courtenay, allowed him to move to the more lucrative prebend of Hayes, but Sir John then nominated a new canon of Ashclyst, William de Stanfere (*Reg. Bronescombe*, ed. Hingeston-Randolph, 139). This prompted Torre to commence a legal action before the king's justices. The action was settled in 1262–3 by a compromise in which Sir John granted property of his at Dolton (Devon) to Torre until the prebend should become vacant (Courtenay

Cartulary ff. 62r–3v). That event had not occurred by the time that Sir John died in 1274 when the Dolton property was seized as one of his assets by the king's escheator (*Cal. Inq. Post Mortem*, ii, 53), but Torre was in possession of the prebend by 1291 (*Reg. Bronescombe*, ed. Hingeston-Randolph, 452).

The chapel is usually described in the earliest documents as a church, partly because there was no clear distinction between churches and chapels until about the mid twelfth century and perhaps because it was a church in the sense of a foundation independent of other churches and with a territory, to wit the area of the castle itself. Later the word 'chapel' tended to be applied to it, probably from the small size of the building and its activities as well as from the recognition that it was not a parish church of a normal kind. In the lack of a foundation charter, it is difficult to ascertain how the building and its clergy were intended to operate. Other castle chapels had a presiding cleric entitled 'dean' or 'provost' but this was not the case at Exeter although, as we shall see, the prebendary of Hayes became in effect the head with a principal role, a house close to the city, and a privileged share of the chapel's property. There is no evidence that the four canons ever acted as a corporate body, taking collective and binding decisions. No chapel seal is recorded and there were apparently no common revenues. Each canon had his own prebend which he administered independently, but the canons were not equal in terms of their incomes or, apparently, of their duties. When church benefices in England were assessed for taxation in 1291, Hayes was the wealthiest prebend with £10, followed by Cutton with £5 13*s*. 4*d*. and Carswill with £2 10*s*., while the former prebend of Ashclyst, now in the hands of Torre, was rated at £2 13*s*. 4*d*. (*Reg. Bronescombe*, ed. Hingeston-Randolph, 452). By 1535, when Henry VIII's government revalued Church incomes in a more stringent way and after values had risen through inflation, Hayes was reckoned to be worth £37 7*s*. 11*d*., Torre's prebend of Ashclyst £12 10*s*. 10¾*d*., Cutton £8 12*s*. 4*d*., and Carswill still only £2 13*s*. 4*d*. (*Valor Ecclesiasticus*, ii, 310, 317, 361).

In 1274–5 the prebendaries were said to be bound to pray for the souls of Hugh de Courtenay (the patron) and the king (*Rotuli Hundredorum*, i, 86), but by the early fifteenth century they had ceased to attend the chapel for this purpose. This is revealed by a petition datable to 1426–7 from the porter of Exeter Castle to the chancellor of England. He explained that the prebendary of Hayes was obliged to provide a chaplain to say divine service in the chapel every day, with free entry and egress to the castle. At the request of the prebendary, Thomas Hendeman, the porter supplied a key to the gate for this purpose, but after a theft of materials from the castle, he changed the lock and key and thereby restricted the access. Hendeman sued him vexatiously in a Church court, causing the porter to ask the chancellor to order Hendeman to show by what right he had access to the chapel (TNA, C 1/8/2). The prebendary of Hayes was still responsible for worship in 1546, but by that time he was merely providing a priest to celebrate mass in the chapel on two days of the week (Snell, *Chantry Certificates*, 16). The only other evidence of a prebendary's duty comes from 1558, when the canon of Carswill was described as having 'the bellringer's office' and acting as clerk-bellringer (*Cal. Patent Rolls 1557–8*, 446). In the thirteenth or fourteenth century, the hospital of St John was responsible for offering half a pound of wax in the chapel on the feast of the Assumption of the Virgin Mary (15 August), which may have been the chief annual festival of the chapel's calendar (ECA Book 53A, p. 37).

It may be that the chapel was planned as, or developed into, a body of one senior cleric (Hayes) with responsibility for worship, assisted by two others (Ashclyst and Cutton), perhaps as priest, deacon, and subdeacon, while Carswill with its low income may have supported a clerk who waited on them. However, long before the scraps of evidence about the work of the chapel, its original function must have been modified. The increasing dissociation between Baldwin's descendants and the castle by the mid twelfth century meant that those who became its patrons, first Adeliz and later the Courtenays, had no use for the chapel as a private church and saw it as an economic resource as much as a religious institution to be safeguarded, hence the attempted grant of the prebends to Plympton and the successful one of Ashclyst to Torre. The determination of the Courtenays to hold on to most of the prebends must have been for purposes of patronage rather than religious worship. When appointments to the prebends begin to be recorded after 1258, they were given as rewards, effectively sinecures, to clergy who had the favour of the Courtenays but who were active in other posts. The fact that the prebendary of Hayes was providing a single chaplain by 1427 indicates that he and his colleagues had ceased to be personally involved with the daily worship of the chapel and that the format of the worship had become very modest in scale.

The prebend of Hayes deserves a further discussion. It belonged to the canon whose estates lay partly in Cowick parish (later St Thomas) and partly near Broadclyst. By 1291 he also enjoyed a pension of £2, later £2 15s. 4d., from the church of Okehampton, paid by the prior of Cowick (*Reg. Bronescombe*, ed. Hingeston-Randolph, 460; BL, Add. MS 49359 f. 92r). Hayes was the name of the Cowick property which lay on either side of Okehampton Street, west of Exe Bridge, since the street was said in 1447 to pass 'through' Hayes (*Reg. Lacy*, ed. Dunstan, ii, 389; see also D&C VC/3219). The estate is sometimes referred to as a park, meaning an enclosed area, or as two parks, 'Great Park' and 'South Park' (R. B. M., 'Hayes Prebend', 46). Hooker's and Hogenberg's map of 1587 shows the area north of Okehampton Street as a partly-fenced piece of uncultivated land, and part of the area south of the street in a similar way (Hooker, *Isca*). The prebend extended at least a little way along Cowick Street to include small tenements with owner-occupiers. Conveyances of some of these tenements in 1292, 1314, and 1323 describe them as lying in the prebend of *La Heghen* or *La Heghes* (BL, Add. Ch. 32988–9;

Grendon's Almshouse, before 1879. The original foundation of c.1400 was a row of ten small houses, to which chimneys and a pentice walkway were probably added later.

TNA, E 40/5526), which evidently had the status of a manor distinct from the manor of Cowick belonging to Cowick Priory, although the prebend lay within the parish of Cowick. The conveyance of 1292 was witnessed by Peter de la Grene 'then bailiff' of Hayes, indicating that the canon employed an agent to look after his property there.

By 1389 the canon had a house on his Cowick estate called Hayes or Hayes Barton, with a chapel in which Bishop Brantingham allowed him to perform divine service or employ other clergy to do so (*Reg. Brantyngham*, ii, 680). The house stood on the north side of Okehampton Street near its junction with Cowick Street and not far from Exe Bridge. It was a moated house, presumably for defence because of its extramural location, and remained in secular use after the Reformation until it was destroyed in 1643 during the Civil War (Ponsford, 'Post-Medieval Britain', 115–16). Hooker's and Hogenberg's map shows it as a substantial walled house and places it further away from Exe Bridge than was the case (Hooker, *Isca*). The canon, if he chose to live there, was in effect one of the wealthiest clergy in the city apart from the canons of the cathedral. The proximity of the estate to Exeter may have caused its value to rise in terms of letting or selling parcels of land, and it also owned a mill on the river (*Valor Ecclesiasticus*, ii, 317).

As has been observed, the chapel was a private not a royal foundation and therefore had no immunity from the authority of the bishop. He approved and instituted the canon-prebendaries, and in 1309 Bishop Stapledon censured the patron of the chapel, Lady Eleanor Courtenay, for allowing one canon to hold two prebends at once (*Reg. Stapeldon*, 155). In 1322 Stapledon made a visitation of the chapel. He noted that divine service was celebrated there every day, but found that the chapel was ruinous, the roof partly uncovered, and the doors broken, which caused him to require repairs to be made (ibid.). The three prebends that survived the grant of the fourth to Torre continued to be filled by the earls of Devon, but when Henry VIII's government made the new valuation of Church incomes in 1535, the three were not even listed together, so detached had they become from the chapel (*Valor Ecclesiasticus*, ii, 310, 317). The Ashclyst estate was still in the hands of Torre Abbey, but after the dissolution of the abbey in 1539 it was purchased from the crown in 1543 by a layman, Thomas Godwyn, who soon sold it on (*Letters and Papers, Henry VIII*, xviii part 2, pp. 58–9).

The chapel next appears in the survey of chantries carried out for Henry in 1546. This gives the dedication as the Trinity, perhaps through confusion with the nearby chapel of Christchurch; other references are always to Mary. The chantry survey mentions only the prebend of Hayes, now valued at £40 13s. 3d., and reports, as has been stated, that the occupant had to provide a priest to celebrate two masses each week in the chapel (Snell, *Chantry Certificates*, 16). The prebendary of Hayes at this time was John Stevyns, doctor of theology and canon of the cathedral, who had held the prebend since 1531 (Emden, *Biographical Register 1501–40*, 540). In 1543 he leased it to Anthony Harvey of Columbjohn for twenty-one years at a rent of £37 7s. 11d., which was legitimate, but on 22 September 1548 he alienated it altogether to the king's servant, Robert Keilway (Oliver, *History of Exeter*, 194–5). That was irregular because a prebendary, like any cleric, was only the tenant for life of his benefice. Normally the patron of the benefice would have vetoed the alienation, and the law would have upheld the patron.

However the context in 1548 was unusual. The previous patron, Henry Courtenay, marquess of Exeter, had forfeited his possessions in 1538 before his execution in the following year. The patronage currently belonged to the child king Edward VI, and Keilway was one of Edward's commissioners for dissolving chantries, religious guilds, free chapels, and collegiate churches, both in Devon and in England generally. Either Keilway persuaded Stevyns to make the alienation, perhaps with the backing of the royal court, or Stevyns sought to profit by giving up his prebend. Much Church property was seized at this time by the crown or its courtiers, and the prebend of Hayes was on the borderline of what might be spared or confiscated. Nevertheless the irregularity of the alienation may have been a problem, because Keilway conveyed the prebend to Edward VI in 1550, and the king then granted it to his servant Nicholas Wadham, esquire (*Cal. Patent Rolls 1549–51*, 292). There was a chance that the alienation might be reversed in 1553 when Edward's successor

Queen Mary restored Henry Courtenay's son Edward as earl of Devon and returned to him much of his ancestral property, including the patronage of the prebends of Hayes and Cutton (*Cal. Patent Rolls 1553–4*, 256). But Courtenay died without heirs in 1556 and Wadham remained in possession. The prebend and its property descended from him by sale or inheritance through several families, until it belonged by the nineteenth century to the Bullers of Downes, Crediton (Oliver, 'Ancient Church', 157–64; *History of Exeter*, 195–6). Unfortunately the exact boundaries of the pre-Reformation prebend cannot be traced with confidence from the Bullers' possessions listed in the tithe award of 1838 (DHC, TA and TM St Thomas, Exeter).

The remaining prebends of Carswill and Cutton survived the Reformation, and prebendaries continued to be appointed to them down to Victorian times (Oliver, 'Ancient Church', 157–64; *History of Exeter*, 200–4). Whether they carried out any duties in the chapel is unknown, despite the reference to the holder of Carswill as the clerk-bellringer in 1558 (*Cal. Patent Rolls 1557–8*, 446). The chapel also endured in a minimal way. It was said to be ruined in the early seventeenth century, but repairs were made in 1683 so that the place might be used for a service and sermon when the quarter-sessions of magistrates were held at the castle. The building was removed only in 1792 after the construction of a new shire hall that included a chapel (Oliver, 'Ancient Church', 157–64; *History of Exeter*, 197). Its earliest depictions are on Hooker's and Hogenberg's map of Exeter, 1587 (Hooker, *Isca*), Hooker's undated drawings of Exeter (ECA, L619) and St Sidwell's fee (D&C 3530 ff. 37–8), and Robert Sherwood's map of Exeter in the 1630s (Sherwood). All represent it as a small detached building, inside and to the right of the castle entrance. John Norden's plan of the castle in 1517 portrays it in a similar form, with a walled enclosure extending from its south side to the castle walls (British Library, Add. MS 6027 ff. 80v–1r). Perhaps the enclosure was a burial ground for castle personnel (since they did not live in a parish) or for prisoners. The chapel appears on the Chamber Maps of 1756×60 as a simple oblong and no enclosure is shown (ECA, Book 58/8).

The only detailed representations of the building are on Hedgeland's model of Exeter in 1824 (Hedgeland) and in an engraving of 1831–2, based on an earlier drawing by R. S. Vidal (Sprake, *Gates*). Both show the building as a low structure comprising a nave with a short narrower chancel, backed by an open space on the south side containing trees. The engraving is the more detailed; it records a narrow round-headed window on the north side of the chancel and a round-headed door on that of the nave which point to the Norman period of architecture. There were small windows on two levels of the nave (a feature also noted by Norden), and the building was surmounted by a small bell-cote towards the west end of the nave (illustration, p. 41). HER ref. ECC11083. Location SX 9213 9296.

Cathedral

Exeter Cathedral is the latest successor of a series of important churches near its site at the centre of the city. The existence of a cemetery containing graves that seem to be Christian in nature in the south-west corner of the Cathedral Close, in what was then the forum or civic centre of Exeter, points to the existence of a nearby church towards the end of the Roman period, perhaps by about AD 400 (Bidwell, *Legionary Bath-House*, 2, 111–13). City life then collapsed for some time, but an eighth-century source states that Wynfrith, the future St Boniface, became a trainee monk in a monastery at Exeter, which would have been in about the 680s. On this and on what follows, see Orme, *Exeter Cathedral*, 1–18. In the eleventh century there were traditions at Exeter of a church foundation in 670, which would harmonise with this other evidence. The next mention of a church is in the 890s, when the Welsh bishop and historian Asser records that King Alfred gave him 'Exeter', meaning a church there and its endowments, probably so that Asser could work as a bishop in Devon and Cornwall. The gift implies that the church at Exeter was already a royal possession. When Alfred's successor, Edward the Elder, decided to establish a permanent bishop in the region in 909, however, he did not place the bishop at Exeter, perhaps wishing to keep the church in royal hands, and established him close outside the city at Crediton.

The Exeter church received further royal patronage from Edward's successor Æthelstan. Charter evidence shows that he visited the city in 932, and a record of the sixteenth century (which cannot have known of this evidence) states that he refounded the church in that year. Records subsequently term the church a 'minster', meaning a church staffed by a body of clergy, in this case 'clerks' who lived separately and might be married, rather than monks. Æthelstan's church has been identified with the remains of an Anglo-Saxon church found beneath the former church of St Mary Major, west of the present cathedral, but there are also indications that point to the possibility of two churches on the minster site, the second of which may have stood further east (Blair and Orme, 'The Anglo-Saxon Minster', 24–6, pp. 7–9). The foundation was stated to be dedicated to Mary and Peter in the mid tenth century, and later references are to one or other or both of these saints, to whom Paul was added by the fourteenth century (Orme, *English Church Dedications*, 159). The minster appears to have possessed a substantial body of endowments in the form of lands and churches in east and south Devon, and Æthelstan gave it a large and impressive collection of relics.

The minster is likely to have had a continuous existence from Æthelstan's time. In 968 King Edgar, who was encouraging the establishment of the monastic life in England, appointed Sideman 'to rule as abbot the monks gathered at Exeter', indicating a plan to make the minster a monastery. Such a plan usually involved introducing monks alongside clerks until the latter died out, but changes of monarchs and Viking invasions probably frustrated this plan, and although there are some possible subsequent mentions of abbots (Knowles et al., *Heads of Religious Houses I*, 48), the foundation seems to have remained largely one of clerks until the mid eleventh century. In 1046 Leofric became bishop of Crediton, and agreed a plan with the king, Edward the Confessor, by which the king would give up his patronage of the minster and make it available to become the seat of the bishop rather than Crediton. Accordingly in 1050, with papal permission, the Exeter minster became the cathedral of a diocese embracing the whole of Devon and Cornwall.

Leofric wished the clergy of his new cathedral to live strict lives in common premises, not in the seclusion of monks but as 'canons' able to carry out duties in the world. This wish was not effective in the long term, and the canons reverted to living in individual houses, although observing celibacy. There were eventually twenty-four canons, and by the thirteenth century a hierarchy of dignitaries emerged so that the cathedral was headed by a dean, accompanied by a precentor in charge of music, a chancellor responsible for secretarial tasks and education, a treasurer who looked after the portable goods of the church, a subdean who acted as confessor to the clergy, and the four archdeacons of the diocese. Most of these dignitaries were also canons, and of the canons who were not dignitaries, some resided in Exeter while others did not. Other groups of clergy emerged during the twelfth and thirteenth centuries. A body of vicars choral, originally twenty-four in number, later reduced to twenty, acted as assistants to the canons and deputised for them performing the daily services. Twelve adolescent clerks known as 'secondaries' and fourteen choristers also took part in the services and did other tasks in the church. Finally a group of privately funded chantry priests known as 'annuellars' celebrated masses in the cathedral for the souls of the dead, and joined in saying the services. Their number reached twenty-one in the early fourteenth century, declined to about a dozen after the Black Death of 1349, and rose again to eighteen by the reign of Henry VIII.

Leofric's cathedral occupied the building or buildings of the Anglo-Saxon minster. A new cathedral was begun in 1114, probably at the instance of Bishop William Warelwast, on the site of the present cathedral nave. It began to be used in 1133 and was completed towards the end of the twelfth century, but the church on the site of St Mary Major was also rebuilt in that century, presumably as a secondary building. In turn a third and larger cathedral was begun in the 1270s, occupying the space of its predecessor but extending further eastwards. This building was completed in the 1340s, with the addition of cloisters towards the end of the century. The Close around the cathedral contained a number of parish churches and chapels, which are examined elsewhere in this work, and houses for the canons, some and perhaps all of which had chapels (p. 162). In 1387 Bishop Brantingham financed residential buildings for the vicars choral in Kalendarhay, and an attempt was made by Bishop Stafford to establish a common building for the annuellars in 1410. The latter project was not successful, and they did not acquire their own premises until 1528, just before the Reformation.

The green space that now surrounds the cathedral on its north and west sides was the principal burial ground of the city until 1637. Around the edges of the green were roads, and beyond them a ring of houses forming the Cathedral Close. On the north and south sides of the cathedral the houses were those of the cathedral canons, eventually accompanied by the communal dwellings of the vicars choral (south) and the annuellars (north). The west side of the Close contained only the backs of buildings in the High Street, so that the dwellers within the area were solely clergy and their male servants. In 1286 seven gates were erected across the lanes leading into the Close, and these were locked at night. Within the Close there were seven chapels by the early thirteenth century (St Martin, St Mary Major, St Mary Minor, St Michael, St Peter Minor, St Petroc, and SS Simon and Jude), three of which became long-term parish churches. Other religious objects installed during the later Middle Ages included the Charnel Chapel (p. 84) above the crypt where loose bones were stored, a probable cross on a stepped plinth which served as a Christian emblem and was visited during the celebrations of Palm Sunday, an image of Our Lady of Pity near the Charnel Chapel, and a statue of the Saviour on the north wall of St Mary Major. A more utilitarian object was a round building near the north-west corner of the cathedral which housed the water conduit of the dwellers in the Close.

The history of the cathedral is too large a topic to be covered here. There is an outline history by Hope, Lloyd, and Erskine, *Exeter Cathedral*; a liturgical and social history (with discussion of saint cults) by Orme, *Exeter Cathedral*, with a detailed bibliography; a relevant constitutional study of cathedrals by Edwards, *The English Secular Cathedrals*; a study of the medieval canons by Lepine, *A Brotherhood of Canons*; and two of the minor clergy by Orme, *The Minor Clergy* and *The Minor Clergy: Biographies*. Works on the buildings of the annuellars and vicars choral are listed in the present book under their entries. HER ref. ECC11214. Location SX 9211 9255.

St Catherine's Well

The 1806 edition of Alexander Jenkins's *History of Exeter* (348) refers to a tradition that 'an ancient chapel dedicated to St Catharine' stood at the meeting point of Paris Street and Heavitree Road. No vestige of it then survived except for 'the name of an adjoining well . . . which in ancient writings is termed St Catharine's Well'. The site lay in the parish of Heavitree, but no such place is mentioned in a list of chapels in the parish in 1401 (*Reg. Stafford*, 126) or in the records of the cathedral which, in the fifteenth century, appropriated the offerings made to chapels within the parish. A chapel therefore looks unlikely, unless it was an early sixteenth-century foundation. A well is easier to envisage, since wells were not licensed or necessarily recorded, and such a well might have included a stone image to a saint: presumably in this case St Katherine of Alexandria. More evidence is desirable. No HER ref. Approximate location SX 9275 9282.

Catherine – see also Katherine

Charnel Chapel

Established early in 1286 when John of Exeter alias Picot, treasurer of the cathedral, received royal permission to grant property to maintain two chaplains in 'the chapel of St Edward the King in the cemetery of St Peter of Exeter next to the minster of St Peter' (TNA, C 143/10/10; *Cal. Patent Rolls 1281–92*, 222). The chapel should not be confused with a reference of *c.*1214 to a chapel of St Edward in the city, identical with the church of St Mary Steps (p. 137; Rose-Troup, *Lost Chapels*, 19–20, 34–7). Its foundation was linked with John's claim to be dean of the cathedral which led to a bitter dispute with the bishop: a dispute that resulted in the murder of one of the bishop's leading supporters, the cathedral precentor Walter of Lechlade, in 1283. Edward I came to Exeter in person to supervise the trial of the alleged murderers during Christmas 1285, and John, who was implicated in the murder, had to resign both his claim to the deanery and his post as treasurer. A tradition of the sixteenth century states that he built the chapel, and he certainly promised an endowment towards it, probably as part of his penance. The choice of dedication, confirmed by a document of the mid fourteenth century (Owen, *John Lydford's Book*, 106), was evidently a compliment to the king, since the saint was Edward the Confessor after whom Edward I was named (Orme, 'The Charnel Chapel', 164–5). Some historians have been puzzled by a reference in a cathedral inventory of 1506 to 'the chapel of St Edmund above the charnel in the cemetery' (Oliver, *Lives of the Bishops*, 375). Edmund is probably a mistake for Edward by the original writer or, more likely, a misreading of the text by its transcriber, George Oliver, because he confused the Charnel Chapel with the chapel of St Edmund at the west end of the cathedral. Since the original text has been lost, the truth cannot be ascertained.

Charnel chapels were founded in several cities and towns from about the thirteenth century as a response to growing populations and the frequent need to make new graves in already crowded churchyards. Bones exposed in this process were gathered and kept in a crypt or cellar, and a chapel was sometimes placed above the crypt. The Exeter Charnel Chapel lay north of St Mary Major and west of the west front of the cathedral. No depiction of it survives, and it had disappeared by the time

Heavitree church in 1840 before Victorian rebuilding. A substantial structure, it included tower, chancel, nave, and two aisles.

that John Hooker made his maps of Exeter and the Cathedral Close in the late sixteenth century. Excavations in the 1970s, however, suggest that it was a low building, facing east and measuring at least 12 metres (39½ feet) by 6.5 metres (21 feet) externally. Beneath the chapel was the crypt, accessed from the west by a flight of steps. This still contained many bones, some of them sorted into groups of arms, legs, and skulls (Henderson and Bidwell, 'The Saxon Minster', 151, 168–9). By the sixteenth century the chapel had two exterior features as well. One was an image of Our Lady of Pity (the Virgin Mary weeping as she holds the dead body of Jesus across her lap) attached to the chapel or near it. In 1495 William Nordon requested burial in the cathedral cemetery 'next to the charnel house before the image of the Blessed Mary of Pity' (TNA, PROB 11/10/556), and Robert Browne in 1513 similarly asked to be buried in the cemetery 'before the image of Our Lady of Pity' (PROB 11/17/376). The other feature was an outdoor pulpit from which a preacher could address an open-air congregation. This was memorably used by Hugh Latimer to preach in favour of the Reformation in 1534 (Orme, *Exeter Cathedral*, 194).

It is not clear that John of Exeter's promised endowment of two chaplains was ever effective. The first reference to a cleric operating in the chapel occurs in 1322 when Bishop Walter Stapledon endowed a chantry priest to serve there (*Reg. Stapeldon*, 148, 374–6). After the Black Death priests seem to have been appointed only intermittently, and in 1508 Bishop Oldham gave the duty of saying a daily mass in the chapel to the vicars choral of the cathedral. The chapel was used from time to time for other purposes. From 1426 to 1431 the Exeter craft of skinners came there for mass on the day of Corpus Christi, although there is no subsequent reference to their presence. From at least 1451 the vicars choral used the chapel for a monthly mass 'of benefactors', which was probably a continuation of the 'kalendar mass' once held by the guild of Kalendars at the beginning of each month; this guild transferred its property and activities to the vicars choral during the fourteenth century (p. 120). It is possible that the chapel of St Mary 'in the cemetery', mentioned from 1510 to 1515 as a place where ordinations of clergy were held, refers to the Charnel Chapel (p. 141). More certainly the chapel was used in the 1530s and 1540s for holding the lectures on theology or canon law which the cathedral was required to provide from time to time. The cathedral chancellor, Robert Tregonwell (1537–43), and the subdean, Nicholas Weston (1539–47), are both recorded as givers of these lectures (Orme, 'The Charnel Chapel', 166–9).

There is an inventory of the chapel ornaments in 1506 (Oliver, *Lives of the Bishops*, 375), and in 1514 John Chalmore, an Exeter citizen, gave 20*d*. in his will for the repair of the charnel house (TNA, PROB 11/18/35). The chapel still existed in 1543 when the antiquary John Leland visited Exeter and noticed its presence (Leland, *Itinerary*, i, 228). It probably ceased to be used in 1548 when masses for the dead came to an end in England, and it seems to have been demolished soon afterwards like its counterpart at St Paul's Cathedral, London, which is recorded as being destroyed in that same year. The disuse of the small chapels within the cathedral meant that there was no need to hold activities such as lectures in the Charnel Chapel, and the chapel's association with prayers for the dead and the cult of the Virgin Mary would have made it obnoxious to Reformers such as the dean of the cathedral, Simon Heynes. The building was dismantled to ground level, and the crypt filled with rubble including pottery of the mid sixteenth century (Orme, 'The Charnel Chapel', 169). HER ref. ECC11051. Location SX 9201 9257.

Christchurch

First mentioned with a distinct date in 1194×1204 as the chapel of *Crystyschurch*, when it belonged to the cathedral (Barlow, *English Episcopal Acta XII*, 172–4). It was built, probably in the twelfth century, by a certain Algar who was regarded as a 'brother' or supporter of the cathedral, where his death was annually commemorated

(Lepine and Orme, *Death and Memory*, 251). Presumably he gave it to the cathedral. The chapel stood in Christchurch Lane, later known as Musgrave's Alley, off the north side of High Street and is referred to as the chapel of Holy Trinity in Peter de Palerna's list of c.1214 (D&C 2513) and other documents, which has led to an erroneous belief that there were two distinct chapels in the same location (Rose-Troup, *Lost Chapels*, 37–9, 41–2, 53). In fact other churches and chapels dedicated to the Holy Trinity in medieval England were known as Christchurch (notably in Bristol and London), so the dedication here was probably also to the Trinity. The popular use of 'Christchurch' seems to have arisen because it was easier to imagine Christ than the Trinity and also helped to distinguish the chapel from the parish church of Holy Trinity.

The chapel does not appear to have been made a parish church in 1222. In 1343 an inquisition was held to establish its status, at which witnesses said that it was in the parish of St Laurence, not parochial but dependent upon the cathedral, and not dedicated or consecrated. The remark about dedication and consecration is not significant, the same being sometimes said about parish churches, and the witnesses went on to observe that 'Sir Henry Caperoun, chaplain in the same chapel, has sometimes celebrated and until now celebrates divine service by special licence . . . of the bishop of Exeter', and that the dean and chapter received the offerings in the chapel (D&C 3672, pp. 368–70). Small sums of money from the chapel are occasionally mentioned in the cathedral's financial accounts (D&C 3750/1–7; 3754; 3773 ff. 23v, 70v). One such sum of 6s. was offered on the feast of the Holy Trinity in 1401 (D&C 3773 f. 54v). In 1344 Richard Braylegh, dean of the cathedral, built new premises for the High School (p. 109), the chief grammar school of Exeter in the lane near the chapel, but without affecting its operations (Orme, *Education in the West of England*, 47–8).

In 1423 the dean and chapter recorded that they had given a sum of £1 6s. 8d. (two marks) to the 'brothers of the fraternity of the Holy Trinity of the chapel of Christchurch' as a contribution to the new erection of the chancel of the chapel which the brothers were carrying out at their own expense. Despite this gift, the wardens of the fraternity, 'that is to say the shoemakers', had cut down trees without permission that were growing in a garden there, but on the wardens submitting themselves to the dean and chapter, no penalty was exacted on condition that they did not fell other trees without authorisation (D&C 3550 f. 133r/152r). The garden is also mentioned in 1445 (ECA, ED/M/784). The fraternity was evidently the guild of the city shoemakers, who must have gained the cathedral's consent at about this time to use the chapel for their religious services and possibly even their meetings, and took the chapel's alternative name of Holy Trinity as their own name. In 1546 the chantry certificates of Henry VIII called the chapel itself 'Holy Trinity' and stated that the shoemakers had an income of £6 19s. 4d. per annum, of which they paid

£1 as rent to the dean and chapter and the rest (or perhaps most of it) to a priest praying for their members (Snell, *Chantry Certificates*, 12). In 1548 the income was valued at only £3 (Orme, 'Dissolution of the Chantries', 94, 107). The dissolution of the chantries in that year must have put an end to the shoemakers' services and to the functioning of the building as a chapel. HER ref. ECC11036. Location SX 9211 9278.

St Clair

First mentioned in 1430 when the cathedral 'excrescence accounts' mention 'the offerings at the image of St *Clarus* . . . in the box in the chapel next to the church of St Leonard' (D&C 3750/2). Later references in cathedral records include one of 1439 to 'the chapel of St *Clarus* outside the South Gate of Exeter in the parish of Heavitree' (D&C 2737) and another of 1458 to 'the chapel of St *Clarus* near *Bockerell* in the parish of Heavitree' (D&C 3750/3). Taken together these records indicate that the chapel stood in Matford Lane, not far from St Leonard church and close to a tenement known as Buckerell, now commemorated by the Buckerell Lodge Hotel. In later times a well in the lane (still extant and known as Parker's Well) was reputed to be good for curing eye complaints (Polwhele, *History of Devonshire*, i, 16; Dymond, *History of the Parish of St Leonard*, 20). It is probable that the chapel adjoined the well. There were three male saints named Clair (Latin *Clarus*), meaning 'clear', and all were patrons of cures of diseases of the eyes (Orme, 'Medieval Chapels of Heavitree', 125–6). The offerings in the chapel appear in cathedral accounts from 1430 to 1502, since they belonged to the cathedral canons as rectors of the parish of Heavitree. The sums of money ranged from 2*d*. to 7*s*. 1*d*. (deductions may have been previously made for the running costs of the chapel), and were eventually standardised at 6*s*. 8*d*. or 7*s*. (D&C 3750/2–7, 3754).

The Victorian historians George Oliver and W. Harding seem to have known only one of these references, that of 1439, on the basis of which they conjectured that the chapel was that of the almshouse of Livery Dole on Heavitree Road and that the saint was the female Clare, companion of Francis of Assisi. In fact this almshouse was not founded until about the 1590s, and its chapel may well have been rebuilt from the materials of a chapel elsewhere (Orme, 'Medieval Chapels of Heavitree', 121–3, 127–8). The cathedral documents undoubtedly refer to a different saint and chapel in Matford Lane, which probably continued in use until about 1538–49 when all such chapels lost their ability to function. No HER ref. Near Parker's Well, HER ref. ECC11580. Location SX 9276 9180.

St Clement

First mentioned in 1194×1204 as a chapel in the patronage of the cathedral (Barlow, *English Episcopal Acta XII*, 172–4), and confirmed in the cathedral's possession by Bishop Brewer in 1225 (ibid., 224–5). It is not included in Peter de Palerna's list *c*.1214 (D&C 2513). The chapel was located near the River Exe (BL, Cotton MS Vitellius D.ix f. 68r; *Reg. Bronescombe*, ed. Hingeston-Randolph, 2–3). It lay down a lane off the former main road from Exeter to Crediton (now St David's Hill), known as 'St Clement's Lane' by the fourteenth century (BL, Cotton MS Vitellius D.ix f. 143r–v), which followed a similar trajectory to the present day St Clement's Lane. The site of the chapel, 'St Clement's Meadow', is depicted on the Chamber Maps of 1756×60, now covered by St David's Station, on low-lying ground separated from the River Exe by a narrower drainage channel (ECA, Book 58/1). The chapel lay within the parish of Heavitree, and in 1401 Bishop Stafford ruled that the offerings made there belonged to the vicar of the parish, but he did not make the vicar responsible for its upkeep (*Reg. Stafford*, 126).

The purpose of the chapel is not clear. It lay off rather than beside the main road and was not therefore passed by travellers unless they turned off the road, and there was no river crossing or ferry at this point. It may have been visited by a few local people living at Taddiford, but the pastoral needs of the area were provided by St David nearby, which was a recognised chapel-of-ease. Perhaps it was simply a place of devotion to St Clement, the first-century bishop of Rome, who was widely venerated in England. Even the economy of the chapel is obscure because the award of the offerings to the vicar of Heavitree means that they do not appear in the accounts of the cathedral like those of some other chapels in that parish. The last reliable reference to the chapel occurs in the churchwardens' accounts of St Petroc in 1537, when money was paid for carrying timber from the building, possibly because it was being dismantled (DHC, Exeter, St Petrock, PW 3). In 1573 it was described as 'the late chapel' (ibid.). HER ref. ECC11043. Approximate location SX 9110 9361.

Cowick, Priory of St Andrew

Baldwin fitz Gilbert, alias Baldwin de Meules (died 1090), sheriff of Devon, was endowed by William the Conqueror with extensive lands and churches in Devon, including the manors of Cowick and Exwick (*Domesday Book*, ed. Thorn, 16/106–9). His son William fitz Baldwin gave these and other properties to the abbey of Bec-Hellouin in Normandy between 1090 and 1096 (Morgan, *English Lands of Bec*, 11), after which the abbey founded the priory of St Andrew, Cowick, as a daughter house. The date of foundation is not known, but a monk of Cowick named Regenold is mentioned in about the 1120s or 1130s (Yeo, *Monks of Cowick*, 6), and the priory was certainly in being by 1137. It was subject to Bec whose abbot appointed its priors, these being usually French until the middle of the fifteenth century as were most or many of the monks, and Cowick paid an annual sum of £12 to Bec in token of its subjection (Morgan, *English Lands of Bec*, 21). At the same time the priory was independent in terms of administering its property in England, rather than being a totally dependent cell as it became after 1462. It was also firmly under the control of the bishops of Exeter, who instituted the priors after their appointment. The patronage of the priory passed to the descendants of Baldwin fitz Gilbert, and belonged by the end of the twelfth century to the Courtenay family, later earls of Devon. The perquisites of the patrons were the right to exercise influence over the priory's affairs, to be received on visits, and to be buried in the priory church if they requested.

The priory was located north-east of the buildings called Cowick Barton (now an inn) in Cowick Lane. A large stone coffin and some burials indicate the site of the chancel or choir of the church (Yeo, 'Where was Cowick Priory?', 321–6; Allan et al., 'Site of Cowick Priory', 135–40). The monastery was staffed by a prior and five monks up to the fourteenth century (Morgan, *English Lands of Bec*, 122). The church, dedicated to St Andrew, was originally both a monastic church where monks said daily services and the parish church of the parish of Cowick, now known as St Thomas; the church of St Thomas (p. 169) was originally a chapel within the parish. The choir or chancel of the priory church may have been used by the monks and the nave by the parishioners. A cemetery lay outside the priory gate in which at first parishioners were buried, adjoined by a chapel of St Michael (p. 144). There was a priory estate or demesne, in effect a home farm, extending over the fields beside the priory and on the opposite side of Cowick Lane (illustration, p. 20). These fields were still free of tithe in 1838 (DHC, TA and TM St Thomas, Exeter). The monastery's endowments also included the manors of Christow, Cowick, and Exwick with some smaller properties, as well as the churches of Christow, Cowick (nowadays St Thomas, Exeter), Meath, Okehampton, Oldridge, Spreyton, and Whimple. The monks appointed the clergy of these churches and took tithes of grain or pensions of money from their revenues. The (under-)estimated income from the land holdings was said to be £16 5s. 8d. in 1291, and that of the churches £26 8s. 8d., giving an approximate value of £42 (*Reg. Bronescombe*, ed. Hingeston-Randolph, 452, 454–5, 463). A more accurate valuation of the priory in 1294 reckoned its income to be £53 18s. 8d. (Morgan, *English Lands of Bec*, 121).

By the fourteenth century priories controlled from France were regarded as 'alien priories' and the English kings took control of their finances in war time to prevent them sending money abroad that might help the war efforts of the French kings. 'Keepers' or 'farmers' were appointed for such priories, who were expected to maintain the monks and their buildings but had the right to appropriate surplus revenues. The economy of Cowick at the end of the century is recorded in a statement drawn up by the prior, William Esterpeny, in 1394 and preserved in a register of the Courtenay family. He estimated the revenues of the priory as £85 8s. 8d. of which the manor of Cowick (presumably including Exwick) produced £44 10s., the church of Cowick £7 3s. 4d., the manor of Christow £11 6s. 8d., Okehampton and Halstock £1 10s., the church and land at Spreyton £5 14s., Hawkwell £1 10s., the church and land at Whimple £1 12s. 8d., land at Woolverstone 15s., the church and land at Oldridge £1 17s., and land at *La Fenne* and *Calwylynche* 5s. each. Out of this the prior was obliged to pay £12 to the king during the time of war plus various ecclesiastical pensions and dues, amounting to a total of £19 1s. 6d. which left him with £66 7s. (BL, Add. MS 49359 f. 92r).

The priors of Cowick continued to come from France in all or most cases, but in 1378 Parliament ordered foreign monks to leave England unless they were priors of houses, making it difficult to staff a priory like Cowick. It may have had very few monks at times thereafter, since although the prior received the king's permission to import monks from Bec in 1410 and 1412, there was only one monk beside the prior in 1429 and only three in 1446 when they elected the last French prior, Robert de Rouen (Yeo, *Monks of Cowick*, 19). Nevertheless the priory was not without achievements in the early fifteenth century. In 1412 the monks built a new church of St Thomas in Cowick Street (p. 171), and this became the parish church of Cowick with a new cemetery, although some parishioners continued to be buried at the priory site. And as late as 1451 substantial work was done on the priory's church of Spreyton. An inscription still to be seen there states that those responsible included the prior, Robert of Rouen; the vicar, Henry le Maygne, a native of Normandy; and Richard Talbot, the lord of the manor.

Meanwhile in 1414 Parliament authorised the suppression of alien priories without monks other than a prior, and although this was not always implemented, it undermined the legal status of the houses that continued. In 1451 Henry VI granted the priory and its endowments to his new foundation of Eton College. Prior Robert resigned, and he and the remaining monks presumably returned to Bec. For over ten years there were no monks on the site, and the church is said to have been used to house animals: perhaps only the nave of the church, because it was unusual to close religious buildings altogether (compare St James Priory). In 1461, however, Henry VI was replaced by Edward IV. John Dynyngton, the abbot of Tavistock, was a supporter of Edward and managed to gain a royal grant in 1462 transferring Cowick and its possessions from Eton to Tavistock. In the following year the abbot sent two monks and a chaplain to re-establish worship and life in the priory. From now onwards the priory was a cell of Tavistock Abbey and managed from there, although the monk in charge continued to be called the prior and to have two or three companions. In 1517 Tavistock secured a papal grant of exemption from the

The church of St John Bow, Fore Street, 1864. The bow that supported the chancel is clearly visible to the left of the tower.

authority of the bishop of Exeter, and this consequently applied to Cowick as well until the dissolution of the monasteries (Oliver, *Monasticon*, 95–6, 103–4; *Letters and Papers, Henry VIII*, iii part 1, p. 153).

More is known of the priory's buildings and activities in the fifteenth century, thanks to the survival of some of its archives from this period among those of the Russell family, dukes of Bedford. The shape of the church is not recorded but would have included a chancel or choir and nave, and perhaps aisles or transepts or both. There was an image of Jesus with a crucifix, presumably on a roodscreen, and a shrine to the priory's own saint, Walter of Cowick. This man, probably one of the twelfth-century priors, was venerated although not officially canonised, and was said to have made a journey to hell or purgatory (Orme, 'Saint Walter of Cowick', 1–7). The church possessed tiled floors, a clock, and a tower with bells; a few of the titles survive as does the coffin mentioned above (Allan et al., 'Site of Cowick Priory', 138–9). It also contained the tombs of Sir Hugh Courtenay (d. 1292), his son Hugh, first earl of Devon (d. 1340), and their wives (Lepine and Orme, *Death and Memory*, 61–2), although later members of the family chose to be buried elsewhere. In 1300 the Courtenays secured a grant of indulgences from four bishops at Rome (it was the year of the papal jubilee) for those who prayed for the soul of Sir Hugh by saying the Paternoster and the Ave Maria (BL, Add. Ch. 13913). Besides the church the priory included a cloister, chapter house, parlour, hall for entertaining guests and servants, and 'earl's chamber' presumably for the use of the Courtenay earls of Devon, although they also had accommodation at the Dominican Friary. The priory was surrounded by walls and approached through a gateway, probably from Cowick Lane.

The priory's ancient possessions were revalued in 1535 by which time they were managed by Tavistock Abbey. The manor of Christow was reckoned to be worth £18 2s. 10d. per annum, and that of Cowick with Exwick and other minor properties £78 16s. 7¼d. Of the churches, the income from Okehampton was valued at £10 13s. 4d., Christow at £8, Spreyton at £7, Meath at £2, Whimple at £1 6s. 8d., and Cowick (which had absorbed Oldridge) at £2 4s. 5d. after deducting a salary of £6 paid to the vicar of St Thomas. The total revenues from the priory's ancient possessions were therefore about £128 (*Valor Ecclesiasticus*, ii, 382–4). Being a cell of Tavistock and no longer an independent community, Cowick was exempt from the closure of religious houses worth less than £200 per annum in 1536, and it survived until the suppression of all the monasteries in Devon in the early spring of 1539. The prior and his companions were ordered to report to Tavistock Abbey where they joined in signing the surrender of the house on 3 March (*Letters and Papers, Henry VIII*, xiv part 1, p. 172). The site and buildings (like those of Tavistock) were granted to John Lord Russell, later earl of Bedford, on 4 July 1539 (ibid., pp. 585–6).

Further information will be found in Yeo, *Monks of Cowick*. The priors of Cowick are listed in Knowles et al., *Heads of Religious Houses I*, 101–2; Smith and London, *Heads of Religious Houses II*, 153–4; and Smith, *Heads of Religious Houses III*, 170–2. HER ref. MDV15171. Location SX 9093 9114.

Crosses, Standing

Standing crosses of various sizes were erected widely in medieval England, from at least Anglo-Saxon times. Large ones, elevated on a pyramid of steps, often stood in town centres or market places. In the late sixteenth century Exeter had a covered water conduit at its principal cross-road rather than a high cross like Bristol (Hooker, *Isca*), but Celia Fiennes referred to a 'very fine market cross' at an unidentified place in the late seventeenth century (Fiennes, *Journeys*, 248). Elevated crosses were usually to be found in churchyards, where they were sometimes known as 'palm crosses' because they were decorated and visited during the celebration of mass on Palm Sunday. Salisbury Cathedral had one outside the west front of the building (Dickinson, *Missale*, 262; Tatton-Brown and Crook, *Salisbury Cathedral*, 111), and it is likely that Exeter Cathedral (which followed much of Salisbury's practices) reproduced this feature. The Franciscan Friary in Holloway Street certainly possessed one

(Little and Easterling, *Franciscans and Dominicans*, 15–16), and the other extramural churches such as St Sidwell probably did so. Small crosses were placed along some roads or on open land where they acted as guides for travellers, indicators of boundaries, or marks of places where bearers rested while bringing the dead from outlying places to the parish church. By the sixteenth century it seems to have been common for people to say the Paternoster (Lord's Prayer) when they passed by them (Orme, *Church in Devon*, 125–7). The association of crosses with Latin worship led to their disparagement after the Reformation, and many of the larger ones were removed, especially from churchyards. If there was one in the cathedral cemetery, it had been dismantled by the time that John Hooker made his plans of the area in the sixteenth century. In contrast smaller roadside and field crosses were often left untouched through being useful markers or too unobtrusive to attract attention.

At least three medieval crosses survive in Exeter, completely or in part. The oldest is the tenth- or eleventh-century Anglo-Saxon cross shaft found in the ruins of the medieval Exe Bridge and preserved in the Royal Albert Memorial Museum. It may be identical with a 'broken cross' outside the West Gate mentioned in 1316–17 (Cramp, *Corpus of Anglo-Saxon Stone Sculpture, VII*, 86–7). A fragment of a later-medieval cross, a shaft surmounted by a double tau cross, is now remounted in Cowick Street, having been moved from a previous location in the vicinity (Phillips, 'Ancient Stone Crosses', 323; HER ref. MDV17808, Location SX 9098 9170)). A granite cross, also of the later Middle Ages, formerly stood to the west of St Loye's chapel and is now resited on the south side (Phillips, 'Ancient Stone Crosses', 323; HER ref. MDV17810, Location SX 9461 9195). Other crosses are recorded in documents or place-names. Scarlett's Cross, first mentioned in the late sixteenth century (ECA, Drawer 2), stood at one of the northern approaches to Exeter at the junction of Old Tiverton Road with Mount Pleasant Road and Rosebarn Lane (HER ref. MDV 18262, Location SX 9311 9388). Little John's Cross, so called in 1573, formerly occupied a similar place on the west side of the city, where Dunsford Hill intersected with Barley Lane and Little John's Cross Hill (Phillips, 'Ancient Stone Crosses', 323). This cross gave name to Crossmead, an adjoining field later occupied by a Victorian house and a university hall of residence. The names of these two latter crosses may be linked with Robin Hood plays and fund-raising activities, popular in the sixteenth century.

St Cuthbert

First mentioned in 1194×1204 as a chapel in the patronage of the cathedral (Barlow, *English Episcopal Acta XII*, 172–4) and as a chapel in Peter de Palerna's list *c*.1214 (D&C 2513). It was described in 1285 as *supra* the North Gate of the city of Exeter (D&C 2111). The Latin word may mean 'above', 'beyond', or 'against', but the fact that there were chapels at ground level very close to the East and South Gates suggests that St Cuthbert may have been in a similar position, perhaps inside the North Gate on the west side and facing east. The street that went west from inside the gate, now Bartholomew Street East, is termed in 1259 'the back street lying between the church of St Cuthbert and the church of the Friars Minor [Franciscans]' (ECA, ED/M/90). Baldwin, 'chaplain of St Cuthbert', and his successor Robert are mentioned in the 1210s and 1219–20 respectively (BL, Cotton MS Vitellius D.ix f. 70r; ECA, ED/M/22). The chapel was probably made a parish church in 1222, and it is likely that the parish territory covered the area around the north end of North Street and the adjacent parts of Bartholomew Street and Paul Street. A tenement in the parish near the city wall, probably in Bartholomew Street, is mentioned in the 1260s (BL, Cotton MS Vitellius D.ix ff. 118v–19r). The income of the church was evidently small, and although John de Doulys, a local layman, bequeathed an annual rent in 1267 to maintain a light in the building (Lepine and Orme, *Death and Memory*, 144), the church and parish were united by Bishop Quinil on 13 March 1285 to those of St Paul a little further north-east (D&C 2111). It is not known whether the church continued in use after this, or when it disappeared. HER ref. ECC11042. Approximate location SX 9178 9266.

St David

First mentioned in 1194×1204 as a chapel in the patronage of the cathedral (Barlow, *English Episcopal Acta XII*, 172–4), but not included in Peter de Palerna's list *c*.1214 (D&C 2513). Its location was near that of its modern successor, but a little closer to St David's Hill (the old road to Crediton) from which it was accessed. By 1225 when Bishop Brewer confirmed its possession by the cathedral, it was again described as a 'chapel' and was presumably already within the parish that was eventually called Heavitree (Barlow, *English Episcopal Acta XII*, 224–5). In later times St David had its own sub-parish within Heavitree, which was probably the case in the later Middle Ages (Orme, 'Medieval Chapels of Heavitree', 122). The sub-parish covered the area from the north walls of the city up to Stoke Woods, and also included a narrow corridor outside the east and south sides of the city walls as far as the middle of Southernhay (illustration, p. 15). By 1454 the chapel possessed a burial ground like the other extramural churches of St Leonard and St Sidwell (ECA, DD 3204), so when Bishop Veysey licensed his suffragan bishop to consecrate the chapel and cemetery of St David in 1541, this must have been a reconsecration rather than a new initiative, perhaps related to the building of the aisle mentioned below (DHC, Chanter XV f. 108v). In 1401 the vicar of Heavitree received the offerings in the chapel but was responsible for bearing the burdens arising from the same (*Reg. Stafford*, 126), burdens that probably involved paying a clergyman to serve the chapel. A 'curate' is mentioned in 1448 and a 'parish chaplain' in 1450, and similar clergy are likely to have existed much earlier (*Reg. Lacy*, ed. Dunstan, iii, 16, 58). They would have received the usual stipends of chaplains, but these do not appear in records. In 1548 there were two endowed obits in the church (Orme, 'Dissolution of the Chantries', 106). An inventory of the church's ornaments and vestments survives from 1552, when it possessed four bells (Cresswell, *Edwardian Inventories*, 17–20).

Hooker's and Hogenberg's map of Exeter, 1587, shows the chapel with a battlemented tower but does not include the rest of the building (Hooker, *Isca*), and Robert Sherwood's map of 1632–3 depicts it only as a brick-shape with a west tower (Sherwood). The Chamber Maps of 1756×60 contain an outline and elevation of the building (second illustration, p. 180). These suggest that the chapel originally consisted of a short chancel, a wider longer nave, and a battlemented west tower. A north aisle was added later, extending the whole length of the building and therefore probably incorporating an eastern chapel north of the chancel (ECA, Book 58/2). Such a chapel could well have been a Lady chapel, and if so may relate to a bequest by John Chalmore in 1514 of 12*d.* to 'Our Lady of *Rugmound* in St David's church' (TNA, PROB 11/18/35), meaning an image of the Virgin Mary associated with the hill of Rougemont which lay in the sub-parish. Images named after a place were often real or intended objects of pilgrimage, like Our Lady of Walsingham, and the name may even hint at associations with Henry of Richmond, Henry VII, who visited Exeter in 1497. By the early nineteenth century the tower contained four bells and the building was said to lack a chancel (Jenkins, *History of Exeter*, 353). This observation may indicate the removal of the roodscreen that formerly divided the chancel from the nave. The medieval chapel was rebuilt in 1816, and the new building was replaced by the present, third church on the site in 1897 (Cresswell, 16–25). HER refs ECC11044, 11557. Location SX 9147 9308.

Dominican Friary

First mentioned in 1232 when King Henry III allowed the Dominican friars (also known as Black Friars and Friars Preachers) to take stone for their church from a quarry by the castle (*Cal. Close Rolls 1231–4*, 101). Because the church was being built, the friars probably arrived in Exeter in that year or a little before. In 1441 Bishop Lacy claimed to be 'patron and founder' of the friary, implying that his predecessor William Brewer (1224–44) may have played a part in allowing the friars to establish themselves in the city (*Reg. Lacy*, ed. Dunstan, ii, 241). They built their church and ancillary buildings down a lane to the south-east of what was later known as Catherine Street behind and parallel with High Street. A lane led eastwards from the street towards the friary, protected by a substantial gateway at the street end. The lane led from this gateway to an outer courtyard from which one could enter the west end of the church or pass through a second gateway into an inner

St Laurence church, High Street, from a photograph of 1906. The church was bombed in 1942 and later demolished.

courtyard to reach the domestic buildings of the friary (illustration, p. 51). There was also a cemetery between the church and Catherine Street. Friars were not subject to the authority of local bishops, and the Dominican site was a privileged area or 'peculiar jurisdiction' outside the diocese. The privilege survived the disappearance of the friars, and the friary site retained its special status outside any parish, known as Bedford Precinct, down to the twentieth century. The privileges of the Dominican Order conflicted with the claims of the cathedral clergy that all funerals of people in Exeter other than monks, friars, and nuns should be held in the cathedral, and that they should not be buried in the cemeteries of religious houses without permission. This led to a lengthy dispute when the cathedral clergy seized the body of Sir Henry de Ralegh, a knight who had died in the Dominican Friary in 1301, and gave it a funeral and burial despite the protests of the friars (Lepine and Orme, *Death and Memory*, 12–13; Orme, *Exeter Cathedral*, 20).

The friary church was dedicated by Bishop Bronescombe in 1259 (*Reg. Bronescombe*, ed. Hingeston-Randolph, 67). In its fully developed form, by the end of the Middle Ages, the building consisted of a long narrow choir or chancel, a nave of the same width, and narrow aisles on both the north and south sides of the nave, each about four metres wide (illustration, p. 51). A 'steeple', probably a turret, stood above the roof of the church perhaps at the junction of the nave and choir, and contained two bells. When an inventory of the friary's possessions was made in 1538, the list of rooms in which they were housed included a vestry and a 'high sextry' or sacristy, both doubtless attached to the church (TNA, E 36/115, pp. 119–21). There was also eventually a small building parallel with and attached to the north side of the north aisle. This appears to have been a chapel rather than a vestry because it contained a small number of graves, hinting at the private chapel of a wealthy family. The church was probably dedicated to the Virgin Mary and St Dominic and contained, as well as the high altar in the choir, some lesser altars in the rest of the church. One altar was dedicated to St John the Baptist and the Salutation of the Virgin Mary, and another to St Peter the Martyr, an Italian Dominican murdered in 1252. There were also images of St George and Our Lady of Pity. Excavations of the site of the friary church have revealed a series of coloured tiling schemes on the floors as well as fragments of stone furnishings such as tombs, pulpit, screens, or piscinas.

The excavations uncovered large numbers of graves within the church, the occupants of which were probably local gentry, merchants, and their wives who paid for the privilege through donations or fees. The gentry included Oliver Dinham (1299) and his wife Isabel (1300), substantial landowners in Devon, Cornwall, and elsewhere; Sir William and Lady Eleanor Martyn (before 1329); and Sir John and Lady Jane Dinham mentioned (1458 and 1497). The head of a thirteenth-century knight from an effigy tomb in the church is now conserved in the Royal Albert Memorial Museum, Exeter (first illustration, p. 181). Burials of worthies of the city included those of Richard Seler, mayor of Exeter (1344), Thomas and Elizabeth Calwoodleigh and their son (before 1480), John Colshill (1518), and his brother Peter who had died earlier. People with the highest status were given the holiest and most valued sites in the church. Oliver and Isabel Dinham were placed at the south-east end of the chancel near the high altar, and Peter Colshill in front of the image of St George (Lepine and Orme, *Death and Memory*, 64). Philip Budwyke asked to be buried before Our Lady of Pity in 1499 (TNA, PROB 11/12/285).

The domestic buildings of the friary stood on the south side of the church and were grouped around a cloister. An inventory of 1538 describes the cloister as containing a washing place and mentions the frater or dining room, kitchen, buttery, library, and hall – the latter of which would be used for entertaining guests and feeding any lay servants. The friary also included a suite of rooms to house the Courtenay earls of Devon during visits to Exeter. There is no reliable evidence as to the number of friars in the community, which must have fluctuated in any case. At its height it may have reached thirty or more, but there were only fifteen when the house was dissolved in 1538. This event took place on 15 September 1538 (*Letters and Papers, Henry VIII*, xiii part 2, p. 139). The site of the friary, including the church, steeple, and churchyard, were granted by the crown in 1539 to John Lord Russell, later first earl of Bedford, a prominent royal servant and courtier, who turned the buildings into a dwelling for himself (ibid., xiv part 1, p. 586).

More detailed histories of the friary can be found in Little and Easterling, *The Franciscans and Dominicans of Exeter*, and Orme, 'The Dominican Friars of Exeter' which also contains a list of priors of the house. An archaeological report on the friary will also appear. HER ref. ECC11059. Location SX 9225 9271.

St Edmund

The chapel of St Edmund was built at the same time as the building or rebuilding of Exe Bridge in the late twelfth century, apparently to act as a bridge chapel and perhaps in part to collect donations from travellers. Gregory, 'chaplain of the bridge of Exeter', witnessed a charter of Bishop Marshal of Exeter in 1196 (Barlow, *English Episcopal Acta XII*, 184). The building is first named as a chapel dedicated to St Edmund in Peter de Palerna's list, *c.*1214 (D&C 2513). It was not a cathedral possession in 1194×1204 (Barlow, *English Episcopal Acta XII*, 172–4) and probably belonged to the city authorities from its foundation, as was certainly the case by 1265 (*Reg. Bronescombe*, ed. Hingeston-Randolph, 140). It stood on the north side of the bridge resting upon the second and third arches from the eastern or Exeter end (Brown, *Exe Bridge*). St Edmund was probably made a parish church in 1222 and in later times its parish covered the islands of Bonhay and Exe Island. The benefice was described in 1259 as poor (*Reg. Bronescombe*, ed. Hingeston-Randolph, 140) and in 1291 as scarcely sufficient to support a chaplain (ibid., 451), but in due course the church benefited from the development of the islands and in 1535 the rector's income was estimated at £10 16s. 8d. (*Valor Ecclesiasticus*, ii, 317). A pension of 6d. was paid to the cathedral in that year.

The original church was a simple rectangle measuring 18.6 by 5.2 metres, presumably consisting of a nave and chancel, supported on the cutwaters of the bridge and other piers. It was rebuilt in about 1449, since Bishop Lacy granted an indulgence in that year to those contributing to the 'construction, rebuilding, and repair of a new bell tower' at the west end of the church (*Reg. Lacy*, ed. Dunstan, iii, 21). Later still, in about 1500, a north aisle was added to the nave, measuring 12.6 by 3 metres and also raised on piers above the river. In about the 1520s Christine Chapman founded a chantry in the church, very likely based at an altar in this aisle. The chantry was endowed with an income of over £11, supporting a priest with a stipend of £6 (Orme, 'Dissolution of the Chantries', 106). When the chantry was suppressed in 1548, there were also four endowed obits in the church (ibid.). An inventory of the church's ornaments and vestments survives from 1552, including three bells (Cresswell, *Edwardian Inventories*, 20–4).

St Edmund is depicted on Hooker's and Hogenberg's map of Exeter, 1587, as a modest building with a small west tower (Hooker, *Isca*), and its tower appears on W. Schellinks's drawing of Exe Bridge, 1662 (Hoskins, *Two Thousand Years*, plate 4). The north aisle was extended in 1658, and a plan of the church in this form appears on the Chamber Maps of 1756×60 (ECA, Book 58/3). Jenkins (*History of Exeter*, 406–7) confirms the presence of tower, nave, and aisle but does not mention a chancel, perhaps implying (as at St David) that the roodscreen separating it from the nave had been removed by the late eighteenth century. A good engraving of the south elevation of the medieval church survives from 1835. It shows the church alongside the road with houses placed against its west tower and east end, two large nave windows and two smaller chancel windows in the Perpendicular style, with doors to the nave and the chancel (E. I. C., 'Church of St Edmund', 148–50; illustration, p. 62).

The church was entirely rebuilt in 1833–4 (Cresswell, 29) and last used for services in 1968. Most of the fabric was demolished shortly afterwards, and what is left survives as a ruin beside the remains of the old Exe Bridge. The building history and features are fully covered by Stewart Brown, *Exe Bridge*. HER refs ECC11024, 11224. Location SX 9167 9218.

St Edmund – see also Charnel Chapel

St Edward – see Charnel Chapel; St Mary Steps

Eleven Thousand Virgins – see St Roche

Exe Bridge Chapel

Founded and endowed according to tradition by Walter Gervas, who died *c*.1258 (Lepine and Orme, *Death and Memory*, 140–1; Snell, *Chantry Certificates*, 13). The Exe Bridge had been rebuilt in the late twelfth century, and it appears that Walter's father Nicholas was a leading figure in that project. The church of St Edmund (p. 99) was built as part of the new bridge and may have served at first as a bridge chapel to collect alms for the upkeep of the structure. In due course St Edmund became a parish church, probably in 1222, which may have prompted Walter Gervas to build an additional chapel that could commemorate his family and perhaps continue to collect contributions for the bridge. This stood on the south side of the road near the east end of the bridge, opposite St Edmund. Gervas was later said to have endowed a chaplain to serve the chapel, and by 1380 the chaplain was appointed by the mayor and chamber with a stipend of £4. The chapel was then described as dedicated to the Virgin Mary (ECA, ED/M/478, 572, 945, 983). Eventually in 1534 the chaplain's post was combined with that of the Guildhall Chapel, and in 1537 his duties included saying mass in the Exe Bridge Chapel on three days of the week (ECA, Chamber Act Book II f. 35v). In 1546 the income of the chapel was said to be £18 15*s*. (Snell, *Chantry Certificates*, 13) and in 1548 £13 19*s*. 8*d*. (Orme, 'Dissolution of the Chantries', 106). Services in the chapel ceased and the endowment was confiscated in the latter year. The building, however, survived and is recorded on the Chamber Maps of 1756×60 (ECA, Book 58/3); it was demolished in 1833. HER ref. ECC11088. Location SX 9169 9218.

St Faith – see Bishop's Palace

St Francis – see Franciscan Friary; St Mary (9) and St Francis

Franciscan Friary

First recorded in 1240, when the friars of the Franciscan Order (also known as Friars Minor and Grey Friars) received a grant of property next to their house from the city hospital of St John the Baptist (ECA, ED/SJ/2). It is likely that the house had been in existence for a year or two, since other friars, the Dominicans, were in Exeter by 1232. The Franciscans may have taken over the site of the hospital of St Alexius which was united to that of St John in 1238–9, perhaps to allow the friars to use the buildings (see St Alexius). Both hospital and friary lay in the region behind St Nicholas Priory, where the friars' original church and buildings occupied the area later known as Frerenhay or Friernhay surrounded on the north and west by the city walls and on the south and east by Bartholomew Street. The friars appear to have occupied the eastern three-fifths of this area, roughly equivalent to what later became St Bartholomew's churchyard and is now an open space. The western two-fifths consisted of private houses (ECA, Book 58/9). The site was constricted and had drainage problems, causing the Franciscans to resolve at the end of the thirteenth century to move to a new location outside and to the east of the South Gate of the city: on the south-west side of what is nowadays Holloway Street. The relocation was being planned by 1291, the property in the area was being acquired in the 1290s, and the new house was probably opened between about 1303 and 1307, in the latter of which there is a reference to the 'old site' (ECA, ED/M/206). The church in Frerenhay, or part of the church, continued to exist for much of the later Middle Ages as a chapel, dedicated to St Mary and St Francis (p. 140).

The new site of the friary was an extensive piece of land stretching from Holloway Street downhill to the River Exe. It was entered from the street via a gateway, and the church and buildings stood at the top of the site, a little south-east of the gateway. A small part of the church was excavated in 1973, revealing the north end of a transept or chapel. The church was probably dedicated like its predecessor to Mary and Francis; the suggestion that it was named after John the Baptist (Little and Easterling, *Franciscans and Dominicans*, 19) is based on a misunderstanding of Hale and Ellacombe, *Accounts*, 30. Franciscan churches generally consisted of a long nave, sometimes with aisles, ending in an east wall. Beyond this would be a transverse passage, a further wall, and a long narrow chancel or choir where the friars said their daily services. The church roof at Exeter was topped by a steeple containing three bells, the word 'steeple' denoting any kind of tower and perhaps a turret in this case. The high or principal altar would stand at the east end of the choir; the altar at Exeter had a carved retable behind it, and in 1510 there was an image of St Francis on one side of the altar, when Lady Katherine Huddesfeld asked to be buried in front of it (TNA, PROB 11/18/20). An image of the Virgin Mary doubtless stood on the other side. The church contained at least two other altars, and the will of Thomas Parker mentions an image of the Virgin in the nave in 1506 (PROB 11/15/639).

The church acquired a chapel by 1442 through a benefaction by William Wynard, the founder of Wynard's Almshouse nearby (PROB 11/1/181). This was either an enclosure within the main walls of the church or an extension from them, and may be identical with the chapel or transept projecting from the north side of the church detected in 1974. The latter contained stone-lined burials and a tiled floor. Like all friaries, the Franciscan church provided space for the tombs of important people who had supported the house with favour and money. Only ten names of such people are known at present, a smaller number with fewer high-ranking individuals

St Leonard church, c.1830; it has since been rebuilt twice. The setting was still rural at that date.

than those who obtained a grave in the Dominican Friary. The two most superior were widows of knights: Lady Katherine Arundell (died 1479) and Lady Katherine Huddesfeld (died 1514), the latter of whom left money for a friar to say mass for her before the high altar for seven years (PROB 11/18/20). The other eight were prosperous Exeter men or their wives, including two Wynards and John Taylour, who died in about 1500. The ledger stone above the latter's grave was discovered during the excavation of the friary site, and contains an inscription describing him as a tin merchant.

The domestic buildings stood on the south side of the church and were arranged around a courtyard or cloister. In 1442 William Wynard bequeathed the friars 100 marks (£66 13s. 4d.) with which to build a new cloister (PROB 11/1/181). An inventory of 1538 mentions a kitchen and buttery (TNA, E 36/115, pp. 111–12), and there would have been a frater (refectory), dorter (dormitory), lecture room, library (or at least book store), and other buildings, as well as a chapter house which existed by 1383 (ECA, ED/M/496, 956). The friary contained enough accommodation to house important visitors and their servants, either in a special suite or in rooms vacated by the friars. Casual mentions of such people in city records, when entertainment was provided for them, include Sir Philip and Sir Peter Courtenay in 1391, Sir John Fortescue in 1433, and Sir Richard Rivers in 1451 (Little and Easterling, *Franciscans and Dominicans*, 25). On at least three occasions, in 1413, 1426, and between 1532 and 1538, the lord admiral of England held his court at the friary to adjudicate maritime matters (ibid., 24–5; TNA, C 1/717/23). Outside the church and cloister was the churchyard or cemetery, part of which, containing both male and female burials, was found at the Holloway Street end of the site in 1976–7.

Evidence about the size of the community is elusive, as is often the case with friars since they do not appear in taxation records as do other kinds of clergy, due to their vow of poverty. There may have been thirty or more friars in the late thirteenth century, but by 1538 there were only ten or eleven, although this followed some losses and doubtless a falling away of support. Friars, unlike monks, did not remain in a single house throughout their careers, and the Exeter friary would have sent its members away for periods to study in other houses while receiving student friars from elsewhere (Exeter was a study centre for Franciscan friaries in western England), graduates from universities, and even trainee recruits from other countries. Friars from Germany, the Netherlands, and Ireland are recorded in the early fifteenth century. The friary was dissolved on 15 September 1538, the same day as the Dominican Friary. In 1541 its site was leased for twenty-one years to John Hull of Larkbeare, esquire, whose house stood a little way from the friary down Holloway Street (TNA, E 315/214 f. 83v). Two years later the site was sold in a parcel of former religious properties to Humphrey Colles of Barton (Somerset), subject to Hull's lease (*Letters and Papers, Henry VIII*, xviii part 1, pp. 196, 198). There is a map of the site in the 1630s, after the demolition of the church (Sherwood).

More detailed histories of the friary can be found in Little and Easterling, *The Franciscans and Dominicans of Exeter*, and Orme, 'The Franciscan Friars of Exeter' which also contains a list of priors of the house. First site references: see below, p. 140. Second site: HER ref. ECC11102. Location SX 9215 9217.

St George

The church existed by the eleventh century in view of the presence of Anglo-Saxon masonry in the church fabric (Fox, *Roman Exeter*, 25–9). It is recorded as a chapel in Peter de Palerna's list of *c*.1214 (D&C 2513) and Ellis, 'chaplain of St George', occurs in 1228–9 (ECA, ED/M/38). The building stood on the west side of South Street opposite the entrance to the Cathedral Close called Little Stile. It did not belong to the cathedral in 1194×1204 (Barlow, *English Episcopal Acta XII*, 172–4), and was probably then in lay patronage as it was in 1328, the date of the first recorded institution of a rector (*Reg. Grandisson*, iii, 1267). In 1410 the patronage passed to the crown (*Reg. Stafford*, 97–8, 171). The chapel was probably made a parish church in 1222; in later centuries the parish stretched westwards down the south side of Smythen Street. The benefice was one of the less poor in the city in 1291, although it was rated at only 2*s*. (*Reg. Bronescombe*, ed. Hingeston-Randolph, 451). In 1522 it was valued at £10 (Rowe, *Tudor Exeter*, 27) and in 1535 at £9 13*s*. 8*d*. (*Valor Ecclesiasticus*, ii, 317).

Like some other city churches, St George was enlarged in the course of time. In *c*.1330 the city authorities granted the rector a piece of land on the south side of the chancel, 16 feet long and 11 wide (4.9 by 3.4 metres). The grant was made in honour of God, St Mary, St George, and All Saints, which was probably the full dedication of the church (ECA, ED/M/301), and this extended the church to a lane on its south side called George Lane. In 1425 Henry Hull of Exeter bequeathed 20*s*. towards mending the bells of St George (ECA, 48/13/10/11), and in 1449 Bishop Lacy granted an indulgence of forty days to contributors towards the construction of the 'new work' of the church, indicating that building work was in progress at the time (*Reg. Lacy*, ed. Dunstan, iii, 35). In 1472 Richard Geffrey left money to fund a chaplain to celebrate mass for his soul for two years (MCR 16–17 Edw IV m. 9d), and William Obley for an obit in 1505 (MCR 2–3 Hen VIII m. 26d). Five years later a yeoman named William Doun provided in his will for the permanent endowment of a mass in honour of the Name of Jesus to be held in the church every Friday (ECA, ED/M/964). In 1522 Henry Radway bequeathed 12*d*. to the store or endowment of this cult and the same amount to the store of St Martin in the church (MCR 14–15 Hen VIII m. 6). Doun's endowment still existed at the dissolution of the chantries in 1548 (Orme, 'Dissolution of the Chantries', 107). An inventory of the church's ornaments and vestments survives from 1552, when it possessed four bells (Cresswell, *Edwardian Inventories*, 24–8).

The church appears on Hooker's and Hogenberg's map of Exeter, 1587, as a tower surmounted by four tall pinnacles (Hooker, *Isca*), similarly on a manuscript map of Exeter by Hooker (ECA, L619), and on Robert Sherwood's map of the 1630s (Sherwood). On the Chamber Maps of 1756×60 the building appears as comprising a chancel facing South Street, a nave behind the chancel, a shorter south aisle beside the nave (presumably on the extended site of *c*.1330), and the tower occupying the west end of the south aisle. The church had entrances from George Lane and South Street (ECA, Book 58/14; Jenkins, *History of Exeter*, 387; Hedgeland). There is a good drawing by George Townsend, 1843 (Townsend, *Sketches*, 1; illustration, p. 71). St George was demolished in 1843 and its parish joined with St John Bow, but a fragment of the early masonry is preserved in the ruins of the hall of the vicars choral on the opposite side of South Street. HER refs ECC11025, 11201. Location SX 9195 9250.

St George and St John the Baptist – see Guildhall Chapel

Godshouse – see Wynard's Almshouse

Grendon's Almshouse

Founded by Simon Grendon, citizen and mayor of Exeter (died 1411), in or shortly before 1399. This was the earliest almshouse to be founded in Exeter as distinct from a hospital. It was located on the south-east side of Preston Street, about a hundred yards from its junction with South Street, and consisted of a row of ten houses which became known as the 'Ten Cells'. The Chamber Maps of 1756×60 show a plan of the houses with a garden and a privy lying behind them (ECA, Book 58/15), and the front elevation is recorded in a drawing of 1879. By that date the houses were fronted by an enclosed walkway with a door and window for each house, allowing interior access between each house as well as a personal outer entrance. Presumably behind the walkway there were interior doors to the houses, each of which had a lower storey and an upper one lit by a dormer window; there were also chimneys by that time (Crocker, *Sketches*, plate 18; illustration, p. 78). The almshouse was supervised by a warden, who was appointed by the city council and nominated the inmates. These seem originally to have been men and women, but two later references of the fifteenth century mention 'men' and one of the seventeenth 'women'. Grendon provided little by way of endowment, and the almsfolk seem to have depended on charity rather than on receiving weekly allowances like those of Bonville's Almshouse. There was no chapel, and the inmates worshipped in the church of St Mary Major as did the people of Bonville's. Grendon's Almshouse was moved to Grendon Road in about 1879, and still exists (Orme and Webster, *The English Hospital*, 240–1). HER ref. ECC11095. Location SX 9192 9237.

Guildhall Chapel

A chapel was added to the Guildhall, the civic building of Exeter, as part of a reconstruction of the premises in 1483–5. The chapel was described as 'newly built' in 1486 and occupied the part of the first floor at the front of the building that now forms the lord mayor's parlour; it contained a screen and therefore consisted of an antechapel and sanctuary (Blaylock, 'Exeter Guildhall', 134–5). By 1499 there was a fraternity or guild of brothers and sisters of St George and St John the Baptist, probably chiefly made up of the twenty-four members of the city chamber and their wives or widows, whose dedication was also that of the chapel (Lloyd Parry, *Exeter Guildhall*, 21–9). The chapel was formally licensed by the archbishop of Canterbury in 1531 (ECA, ED/M/1022). In 1533 the chamber resolved that each of the twenty-four should be a member of the guild and pay 4*d*. a year to its funds (ECA, Chamber Act Book II f. 32v). The choice of George reflected his growing popularity as patron saint of England during the fifteenth century; the Baptist may have been a tribute to the wool trade or to the hospital of St John which was a popular church with the Exeter citizens.

A priest was employed in the chapel from at least 1487, perhaps in part through John Kelly's bequest in 1486 of a tenement to maintain a chaplain celebrating divine service there (MCR 3–4 Hen VIII m. 10d; ECA, ED/M/941). In 1496 the crown pardoned the chamber for having acquired without licence the manor of Awliscombe through the gift of Thomas Calwoodleigh, esquire, and permitted the income of the manor to be used for relieving the poor and maintaining a chaplain in the chapel (*Cal. Patent Rolls 1494–1509*, 74; ECA, ED/AWL/55). William Ayssh was appointed chaplain in 1512 with an annuity of £3 13s. 4d. and the promise of succession to the chapel on Exe Bridge (ECA, ED/M/983), although he did not gain the latter until 1534. In 1537 his duties were defined as saying mass in the Bridge chapel on three days of the week and in the Guildhall Chapel every Monday (the principal day of chamber business) (ECA, Chamber Act Book II f. 35v). Endowments for prayers were given by John Kelly as above, Richard Turner in 1491 (ECA, ED/M/914), and William Wilford in 1511 (ED/M/980). A list of ornaments in the chapel survives from 1537 (ECA, Chamber Act Book II f. iir); it probably ceased to be used in 1548 or 1549. HER ref. ECC11098. Location SX 9198 9264.

Hayes – see Castle Chapel

Heavitree, St Michael

First mentioned in 1153 as a church dedicated to St Michael, the property of the cathedral (DHC, Chanter 1001; Oliver, *Lives of the Bishops*, 18–20). In 1194×1204, however, it is described as a chapel in a list of the cathedral's churches in Exeter, showing that it was regarded as subject to the cathedral like the chapels within the city (Barlow, *English Episcopal Acta XII*, 172–4). The site was the modern one, a little south of Heavitree Road. St Michael was probably made a parish church in 1222, and was confirmed in the possession of the cathedral by Bishop Brewer three years later (ibid., 224–5). Its parish stretched around the north and east of Exeter and may represent the rural part of the ancient parish of the minster, later the cathedral (illustration, p. 15). The chapels of St David and St Sidwell lay within the parish and were technically chapels-of-ease, subject to the parish church and its clergy, although they acquired sub-parishes for which they were responsible. These sub-parishes belonged to the rural deanery of Exeter, but the rest of the parish constituted a peculiar jurisdiction of the cathedral, which meant that it did not come under the normal administration of the diocese. The cathedral chapter appointed the clergyman, who was a vicar not a rector because the cathedral appropriated the tithes of grain that normally belonged to a rector.

A visitation of the parish was made by two canons of the cathedral in 1281. It listed the ornaments, vestments, and books of the church, stated that there were twelve acres of glebe, and estimated the value of the tithes of grain received by the cathedral as £13 6s. 8d. and the income of the vicar as £4 (D&C 3672A). The latter figure is likely to be incomplete because the 'Taxation of Pope Nicholas' in 1291, which was under-assessed, gave the cathedral's revenues as £10 and the vicar's as £5 (*Reg. Bronescombe*, ed. Hingeston-Randolph, 465). In 1401 it was stated that the vicar had the right to receive all tithes other than those of grain, together with the profits of the twelve-acre glebe and all offerings made in the parish church and the chapels of St David, St Sidwell, St Clement, and St Loye within the parish. In return, he had to bear the burdens of Heavitree, St David, and St Sidwell, meaning the payment of chaplains to serve the latter two places and probably a share in the upkeep of all three chancels (*Reg. Stafford*, 126). Three other chapels – St Anne, St Clair, and St Mary Mincinglake – were subsequently established in the parish, but the offerings made in them were appropriated by the cathedral. By 1535 the tithes of grain were worth only £6 13s. 4d. while the vicar's revenues had risen to the substantial sum of £34 3s. 2d. (*Valor Ecclesiasticus*, ii, 293, 317), perhaps reflecting the replacement of agriculture in the parish by market gardening and suburban development.

The medieval church possessed a chancel and nave, the latter having north and south aisles separated by arcades of four bays (Jenkins, *History of Exeter*, 441; Oliver, *Ecclesiastical Antiquities*, i, 43–50). Three engravings of the building survive from c.1840–2 (Somers Cocks, *Devon Prints*, nos. 1145, 1147–8), that of Augustus de Niceville, 1840, being reproduced here (illustration, p. 85). In 1840 George Oliver recorded several gravestones of the pre-Reformation period: John Ford (no date), John Vener (1527), John Legh, priest (probably early sixteenth century), Hugh Legh (1536), and Alice and Elizabeth Uphome (no date). Oliver noted that the former roodscreen, panelled with paintings of saints, had been removed by this date, but parts in fact survive painted with saints and sibyls. The body of the church was rebuilt in 1844–6, incorporating but heightening the late-medieval aisles, and the tower was replaced in 1887 (Cresswell, 32–47). HER ref. MDV18320. Location SX 9376 9226.

High School

The High School was not a religious house, church, or chapel, but may claim an entry here, as the almshouses do, in order to complete the list of religious institutions in medieval Exeter. It was the principal school in the city and the only one (apart from the song school for the choristers of the cathedral) that had official recognition. The name means 'chief school', implying that it was not the only one, and there must have been a number of others, mainly private and concerned with the teaching of reading. It was not a cathedral school, since it was supervised by the archdeacon of Exeter and was situated in the city rather than the Cathedral Close, but some of its masters were former cathedral clergy and it taught some of the adolescent clerks who served there. In the thirteenth century the school was located in Smythen Street, close to Preston Street which was associated with the priests of the city, but in 1344 the cathedral dean, Richard Braylegh, built a new schoolroom and a dwelling house for the master in Musgrave's Alley off High Street, close to the chapel of Christchurch (p. 86). It is not known if the school used the chapel for worship, and during the fifteenth century the chapel became the home of the guild of shoemakers.

The business of the High School was to teach Latin grammar to boys. Its size is not known but may have extended to over a hundred pupils, aged chiefly between ten and eighteen. Boys are known to have attended it from the city and from other places in Devon, not only to study for careers in the Church but to acquire the literary skills required of gentry, merchants, and secretarial clerks. Fees were charged and boys from a distance had to board in private houses, but Bishop Stapledon planned a scheme which Bishop Grandisson implemented in 1332 by which twelve poor scholars were given free board and lodging in the hospital of St John while they attended the school (Orme, *Education in the West of England*, 46–55). The number of these scholars fell to nine after the Black Death, but remained at this level until the hospital was closed in 1539. Three manuscripts survive which preserve Latin texts and exercises that were written at the school during the mid fifteenth century. They include passages of composition that make numerous references to school work and to everyday life in Exeter (Orme, *English School Exercises*, 108–76). The school survived the Reformation, and died out only in the eighteenth century. No HER ref. Location SX 9217 9278.

Holy Trinity – see Trinity, Holy

St James (1) Priory

In 1086 a woman named Alveva is mentioned as holding a small property called *Jacobscherche* which she had held in 1066 (*Domesday Book*, ed. Thorn, 52/50). The name of the property was taken from a church of St James, lying east of St Leonard church in the parish of Heavitree, and Alveva may have owned the church as well as the estate by 1066, as later owners did. The status of the church in this early period is uncertain, since 'church' may mean any of what were later differentiated as a religious house, parish church, or chapel, but its likely function is that of a private estate chapel or a place of devotion to St James, and perhaps both. In the early 1140s the church and estate belonged to Walter son of Wulward, a tenant of Baldwin de Redvers who had recently been created earl of Devon by the Empress

St Loye chapel in 1839 in another rural location. It probably originated as a chapel linked with a nearby substantial house.

Matilda. At Baldwin's request, Walter transferred the estate and church, now described as the 'chapel' of St James, to the Cluniac monks of the priory of St Martin-des-Champs, Paris, while Baldwin gave other properties to St Martin to endow a cell or daughter house of monks at the chapel (Bearman, *Charters*, 75–7). The foundation of the cell began in or shortly before the year 1141 when grants to it by Baldwin were confirmed by Matilda (*Regesta Regum Anglo-Normannorum*, iii, 241–2), and he himself issued further charters of endowment in 1143–6 (Bearman, *Charters*, 74–8; Barlow, *English Episcopal Acta XI*, 32–4). Cluniac monks from France had taken possession of the chapel, or were expected to do so, by 18 October 1143 when the prior of St Martin agreed with the canons of Exeter Cathedral that he would hold the chapel from them in perpetuity and that the territory of the monastery would pay tithes to the cathedral (which owned the adjoining parish of Heavitree). In return the canons allowed the monks to have a cemetery for their own use on condition that they did not bury parishioners of Heavitree or receive them as monks without the consent of the canons (D&C 2074).

The priory lay beside the River Exe, south of the Topsham Road, from which it was reached by a lane called St James Lane, approximately opposite Barrack Road. The site was not large and the priory, as we shall see, was only modestly endowed. Little is known about the priory church except that in 1486 it possessed a chancel (King's College, SJP/180) and therefore presumably a nave, and that in the early thirteenth century a local benefactor named Richard fitz Walter granted the priory land and moveable property in return for the right to be buried in the church in front of the altar of St Mary (SJP/45). This altar may have been at the east end of the nave, if nave and chancel were divided by a wall as was common in monastic churches. Carved stones from the site now preserved in the Royal Albert Memorial Museum, Exeter, come from an open twelfth-century cloister arcade and a doorway of the same date; they are enriched with crude stone heads. Earl Baldwin gave the priory the wealthy church of Tiverton as its principal endowment, together with some woodland at Cotley in Dunsford and half the tithes of his fishery at Topsham (Bearman, *Charters*, 77–8), but his son Earl Richard I repented of the gift of Tiverton and reduced it to half of that church (ibid., 93–5; Orme 'Early History of Tiverton Church'). During the thirteenth century the priory's share was further diminished so that by 1291 it held only a quarter of the income of the church. The monks acquired a few other small properties, chiefly near the priory in the area south-west of the city, but the loss of most of their Tiverton revenues impoverished their foundation and in 1291 their income was estimated at no more than £9 9s. per annum, although perhaps double that in practice (*Reg. Bronescombe*, ed. Hingeston-Randolph, 454, 473).

The historian George Oliver (*Monasticon*, 191) averred that the monastery was intended to support a prior and four monks. This may be speculative, and by the late thirteenth century there was only a prior and one monk (Duckett, *Visitations*, 25–6). The priors and probably most of the monks were usually French until the second half of the fourteenth century. By this time the Hundred Years War between the kings of England and France had led the former to take control of the lands of French monasteries in England and the cells that stood on them. These cells, which had come to be known as 'alien' or foreign priories, were not closed but their surplus revenues were confiscated and it became difficult for their French mother houses to appoint priors. Those of St James were usually Englishmen from 1363 onwards. In 1378 Parliament ordered all foreign monks to leave England unless they were priors of houses, causing a crisis of recruitment in small houses like St James which could not afford to recruit and train Englishmen. St James limped on with a series of English priors, assisted by a single Cluniac monk as late as 1346 (TNA, E 199/8/8), but very likely as time went on with only a hired English chaplain. The crown put the priory's endowments into the hands of a series of 'keepers' or 'farmers' (lessees) who administered them and took the surplus revenues.

In 1414 a statute of Parliament ordered the abolition of small alien priories staffed only by a prior without monks. Nonetheless the Cluniac Order was anxious to preserve St James, and in 1419 Thomas Dene, subprior of Lenton Priory (Notts.), was instituted as prior. Dene was a substantial figure. He was appointed as vicar-general of St Martin-des-Champs in England (Smith, *Heads of Religious Houses III*,

237), held a visitation of Barnstaple Priory, and commissioned a fine silver seal the matrix of which survives in the Royal Albert Memorial Museum (Cherry, 'The Silver Seal', 138–9). But his position was impossible. He took over the responsibility of keeper, which obliged him to pay an annual rent of £16 to the crown, leaving him an inadequate surplus revenue. In 1427–8 he was accused of selling the priory's woods and of failing to maintain services in the priory church, in the first case evidently to raise money and in the second because he had no fellow monk and could not afford to hire a chaplain (TNA, E 106/12/27). He was still in office in 1428 and probably in the following year, when the priory sponsored a cleric for ordination for the last time (*Reg. Lacy*, ed. Dunstan, iv, 123–6), but after that date we hear only of other keepers and farmers, and there was probably no monk left. In 1438 the priory was leased for life to John Delabere, high almoner of Henry VI (*Cal. Patent Rolls 1436–41*, 151) and in February 1445 it was granted outright to Henry's new foundation of King's College, Cambridge, to take effect when Delabere died (*Parliament Rolls*, xi, 1447). That event took place in or soon after 1460. One can therefore say only that the monastery ceased to be served by a monk at some date between 1428 and 1445, and probably nearer the former than the latter.

After the decease of the priory the church, or part of it, remained in use: in effect as a chapel in Heavitree parish. King's College leased the priory's properties to a 'farmer' whose accounts record expenditure on repairs to the 'chapel' of St James in 1466, the 'church' in 1467, the 'church' in 1471, the 'chancel' in 1486, and the 'chapel' in 1499; there is a further possible reference to the 'chapel' in 1504 (SJP/169, 176–7, 179–81). The mention of the chancel may but need not indicate that only that part of the church remained in use. An inventory of the goods in the chapel survives from the second half of the fifteenth century. It lists two vestments, a chalice, a missal, and an unbound quire with material for services on St James's festival (SJP/92). This suggests that masses were sometimes celebrated and the day of the patron saint still observed. The farmer was also required to bear the expense of paying a priest to celebrate mass in the chapel, praying for the king and the priory's benefactors (King's College, KCAR/3/3/1/1/1 ff. 66v–67r). The likelihood is that the chapel remained in being, with at least occasional services, until the period 1538–48 when chapels in England began to be closed and private masses were discontinued. The site of the priory and its property, however, did not come within the compass of the dissolutions of the monasteries and chantries between 1536 and 1548, and they remained in the possession of King's College down to modern times, the priory buildings being rented out to a private tenant. In the eighteenth century there was a house on the site known as 'The Old Abbey' (ECA, Book 58/17).

The priors of St James are listed in Knowles et al., *Heads of Religious Houses I*, 118; Smith and London, *Heads of Religious Houses II*, 228–9; and Smith, *Heads of Religious Houses III*, 237. There are fuller accounts of the priory in Orme, 'St James Priory' and 'The Early History of Tiverton Church'. HER ref. MDV15172. Location SX 9309 9099.

St James (2) Parish Church

First mentioned in 1194×1204 as a chapel in the patronage of the cathedral (Barlow, *English Episcopal Acta XII*, 172–4) and also as a chapel in Peter de Palerna's list *c*.1214 (D&C 2513). It stood on the north-east corner of the junction of Palace Gate with South Street; in later times the church site formed part of the parish of Holy Trinity with which St James was eventually united. Roger, 'clerk of St James', presumably the parish clerk, witnessed a deed in the early thirteenth century (D&C 228). The chapel was probably made a parish church in 1222, and the first recorded institution of an incumbent is in 1313 (*Reg. Stapeldon*, 215). A rental of *c*.1265 states that the church paid a due of 10*d*. to the cathedral chapter (D&C 3721). In about 1258 Walter Gervas bequeathed an annual rent of 5*s*. to burn before 'the body of Christ' in the church: either the reserved sacrament or the statue of Christ on the roodscreen (Lepine and Orme, *Death and Memory*, 141), and in or after the 1220s Robert de Malmysbury granted a tenement to the chapter to augment the food and maintenance of the priest and to support a candle at the altar of the Virgin Mary in the church (D&C 3672, pp. 397–9). An annual payment of 16*d*. to St James appears in the cathedral obit accounts from 1305 (Lepine and Orme, *Death and Memory*, 280).

These records imply that the benefice and parish were impoverished as early as the thirteenth century. To judge from the parish boundaries of later centuries, that of James was probably limited to the church and a small block of territory on the opposite side of South Street. In 1291 the rector was not taxed 'because of poverty' (*Reg. Bronescombe*, ed. Hingeston-Randolph, 451), and a rental of about 1308 records the church's payment to the chapter as 'nothing, on account of poverty' (D&C 3722). In 1336 the bishop gave the church *in commendam* (i.e. as a provisional appointment) to a chantry priest of the cathedral, a sign that the benefice itself was too poor to support a priest (*Reg. Grandisson*, ii, 811), and in 1350 he gave it in a similar manner to the rector of Holy Trinity (ibid., iii, 1404). This probably brought about a union between the two churches and benefices, although mention of a tenement opposite St James in 1359 may indicate that the building was still extant (ECA, ED/M/411). No further institutions of rectors are recorded, however, until 1384 when Archbishop Courtenay, while making a visitation of Exeter diocese, appointed John Cobthorne (Lambeth Palace Library, Reg. Courtenay f. 107r). This appointment probably had little or no effect, since although two deeds of 1387 and 1388 mention the church as a location (ECA, MCR 11–12 Ric II mm. 6, 50), a third of 1387 refers to 'a waste place in which the church of St James was formerly built in South Street' (ECA, ED/M/518). A fourth deed of 1403 describes a tenement 'opposite the old church of St James, now fallen down' (MCR 4 Hen IV m. 31). The parish was joined to that of Holy Trinity, although no formal act of union is recorded. HER ref. ECC11037. Location SX 9206 9239.

St John (1) Hospital

First mentioned in 1184×1185 when Henry II confirmed its property, suggesting that it was founded earlier than this but at an unknown date (Rowe and Cochlin, 'Evidence of St John's Hospital', 211–13). Its site was just inside the East Gate of the city on the south side of High Street. The hospital was refounded and apparently rebuilt between 1224 and 1235 by Gilbert and John, the sons of Walter Long, of whom John was warden of the hospital. The dedication of the foundation was in honour of God, Mary, John the Baptist, and All Saints. In 1238–9 it absorbed the endowments of the hospital of St Alexius. Up to this time it was at least partly under the patronage of the city authorities, but in 1244 Bishop Brewer came to an agreement with the mayor and citizens that he should have the sole patronage of St John in return for conveying to them sole patronage over the hospital of St Mary Magdalene (Barlow, *English Episcopal Acta XII*, 237). This agreement may have been an adjustment of rival claims over both hospitals, but probably also reflected the wish of the bishop to control an institution that was in part a small religious house of clergy.

From this date onwards the bishop appointed a warden to supervise the hospital, who was a cleric and often a canon of the cathedral. The resident head of the institution under the warden was the master or prior, also a cleric. He was accompanied by brothers and at first by sisters, who presumably lived a religious life and probably provided lodgings for travellers and an infirmary for sick or infirm people other than lepers. The hospital chapel appears to have been made a parish church in 1222 with a parish extending over part of the neighbourhood including the chapel of St Bartholomew. In 1287, however, Bishop Quinil united the parish of St John with that of St Laurence, while at the same time removing the hospital from the parish and making it an independent area subject only to the bishop (ECA, Book 53A f. 8v). The hospital was engaged in building works in 1307–10 when the executors of Bishop Bitton gave the brothers and sisters £20 for the purpose (Hale and Ellacombe, *Account*, 30), but its community life seems to have declined in the early fourteenth century when the sisters cease to be mentioned. Bishop Grandisson (1327–69) claimed that he found only one professed brother and few infirm people (*Reg. Grandisson*, ii, 1125), and he did much to reform the hospital. In 1329 he gave it the grain tithes of the church of Holne so that the clergy might be augmented to comprise a prior and four priest brothers. In 1332 he added the grain tithes of Yarcombe to complete a scheme planned by Bishop Stapledon to support twelve (later nine) scholars in the hospital who were studying in the city High School. In 1351 he consecrated the nave and an area near the church to serve for burials, and in 1354 he confirmed the right of the hospital to bury its own members. Hitherto these had been taken to the cathedral cemetery. He also allowed the burial of other people, subject to the rights of the cathedral, and either ordered or confirmed that the brothers should live according to the Rule of St Augustine (*Reg. Grandisson*, i, 483; ii, 666–9, 1106–7, 1125).

After the Black Death when Church incomes fell and costs rose, the hospital's staff declined again to consist of the prior and two priest-brothers in charge of twelve poor male inmates (probably almsmen in effect) and nine boy scholars. The community was now largely confined to men, including one or two private boarders, servants, and servants at a grange called *Rokysdoune* which presumably acted as a farm supplying the priory (will of William Reygny, TNA, PROB 11/20/186). There was one woman, however, by the 1530s: an anchoress named Alice Buttes who would have lived in an enclosed space. The prior and brothers possessed a number of books, and during the fifteenth century they caused a cartulary to be compiled, containing the charters of their properties (mostly tenements within the city) as well as local antiquarian information (ECA, Book 53A; Davis, *Medieval Cartularies*, 45). When the incomes of religious houses were calculated for taxation in 1535, St John was rated at £102 12*s*. 9*d*., of which about £84 came from property in Exeter and elsewhere while about £18 was produced by the tithes of the three churches belonging to the priory: Holne, Yarnscombe, and St Laurence in Exeter, the latter an acquisition from Merton Priory (*Valor Ecclesiasticus*, ii, 314). Four years later the hospital was classified as a religious house and its three remaining clergy were required to surrender themselves and their possessions to the king on 20 February 1539 (*Letters and Papers, Henry VIII*, xiv part 1, p. 127). The clergy were granted pensions and the twelve poor men (whose names are recorded) received allowances of 5*d*. per week (TNA, SC 6/HenVIII/7300 m. 24d). On 29 April 1540 the church, churchyard, and anchoress's house were granted to Thomas Carew of Bickleigh (*Letters and Papers, Henry VIII*, xv, p. 299).

Some details of the layout of the hospital may be gathered from documents and a map. The chief documents are Grandisson's interventions and a burial list of about 146 people, mostly outsiders, who had graves in the hospital up to the 1530s (Lepine and Orme, *Death and Memory*, 39–43). The map is one of the Chamber Maps of 1756×60 (ECA, Book 58/13), which records much of the footprint of the medieval buildings (second illustration, p. 181). The church stood alongside High Street with the chancel or choir towards East Gate. It is possible that the chancel was the original church while the nave was the infirmary for the sick, since hospitals were often constructed with a chapel and infirmary on an east–west axis so that the sick in their beds could watch the mass at the high altar. This conjecture is perhaps supported by Grandisson's consecration of the nave in 1351; if so, the infirmary became the nave at that time and was itself removed to another location. The chancel contained the high altar of St John the Baptist, a stall for the prior and doubtless others for the brothers, with a high cross or rood and therefore a roodscreen that separated the chancel from the nave. There was a chapel of the Trinity and side altars dedicated to Jesus, Katherine, and Thomas Becket in the chancel or nave, with appropriate images. An image of St Michael is mentioned in 1505 when William Obley asked to be buried in front of it (MCR 2–3 Hen VIII m. 26). Mention of a door at the west end of the church, presumably in the north wall of the nave, suggests that this was the entry point for members of the public.

South of the church was a courtyard surrounded by a cloister of four walks or three omitting the north walk. One south door in the chancel communicated with this cloister and another with the dormitory of the brothers, the latter being probably on the first floor of the east range of the cloister. Grandisson's permission for burials extended to 'the church of the hospital, a certain area within the enclosure of the same contiguous to the aforesaid church, together with the interior ambit of the said church, with part of the cloister and the chapter house'. The 'interior ambit' seems to have been the cloister walks and the 'certain area' perhaps the open plot within them, which may have abutted the south side of the church. The 'part of the cloister' (if cloister in the sense of cloister buildings) may have been an alley leading off one of the walks. The chapter house is likely to have stood in the east range, and space in the cloister buildings would have been needed for a prior's chamber, a refectory for the brothers, and a library or book-cupboard. South of the cloister lay the buildings housing others than the clergy, arranged along alleys and accessed from the High Street via a lane to the west of the church, probably with a gatehouse at some point. These buildings must have included the infirmary, a kitchen, a hall for feeding visitors and inmates (unless they were admitted to the clergy's refectory), and lodgings for servants and the poor scholars. During the later Middle Ages the infirmary is likely to have been divided into or replaced by small rooms, a common development in hospitals as these institutions increasingly catered for long-term almsmen rather than the sick. South of the outer buildings was an open space which served as gardens in the eighteenth century.

Following Grandisson's permission for the burial of outsiders (after their funerals had been held at the cathedral), the hospital church became a popular choice for that purpose among the wealthier members of local society. The burial list includes the names of Sir John Hille, justice of the king's bench; members of gentry families such as Lercedekne, Ralegh, and Speke; numerous leading citizens and their wives (including mayors John Talbot and William Obley); and some local clergy. The later parts of the list indicate the locations of the graves, showing that most of these people were buried in the chancel or the nave, with a few of the hospital's own clergy having interments in the chapter house. The cloisters are not mentioned, but since the list is largely restricted to outsiders it may be that almsmen, scholars, and servants were laid to rest there or within the cloister garth (Lepine and Orme, *Death and Memory*, 39–43). Some citizens who asked for burial in the hospital in their wills gave money for the celebration of obit masses in their memory. This was the

St Mary Arches, one of the earliest aisled churches in Exeter, very likely reflecting an ownership of the church by the bishop of Exeter.

case with William Hodell in 1400 (BL, Add. Ch. 27580), Richard Baker in 1484 (to be held every 28 March) (BL, Add. Ch. 27631; MCR 2 Ric III to 1 Hen VII m. 18d), and William Obley in 1505 (MCR 2–3 Hen VIII m. 26).

At the end of the sixteenth century the premises came into the possession of the city authorities and the institution was refounded in 1630 as a school and an orphanage. The chancel was made into the mayor's chapel, the nave was divided into two storeys, and a new entrance to the courtyard was opened between the nave and the chancel. The medieval and post-medieval buildings were demolished in the second half of the nineteenth century. Further details of the history of the medieval hospital will be found in Orme and Webster, *The English Hospital*, 233–9. HER ref. ECC11058. Location SX 9226 9279.

St John (2) Bow

First mentioned in 1160×1187 as a 'church' in relation to a piece of property lying next to it (ECA, ED/SN/4), but in practice a chapel like the others in the city. The building stood on the south side of Fore Street at its junction with John Street, opposite and a little higher than Tuckers Hall, and was known by 1291 as St John 'of the arches' (*de Arcubus* in Latin) and later 'St John Bow' to differentiate it from the hospital of St John (*Reg. Bronescombe*, ed. Hingeston-Randolph, 451). It was not a possession of the cathedral in 1194×1204 (Barlow, *English Episcopal Acta XII*, 172–4), suggesting that it was either in lay hands or already belonged to Plympton Priory as it did by 1291. Very likely it was donated to Plympton by Adeliz (died 1142), daughter of the leading Devon landowner Richard fitz Baldwin, son of Baldwin fitz Gilbert, or her relative Ranulf Avenel II, both of whom gave the priory other churches in and near Exeter in the twelfth century (Bearman, *Charters*, 182). If so it may formerly have been the church of Baldwin fitz Gilbert and his family for their tenants in the city.

St John is named as a chapel in Peter de Palerna's grant in *c*.1214 (D&C 2513) and was probably made a parish church in 1222, but Plympton took all the tithes and offerings, paying a chaplain to do duty for a small stipend (compare Topsham, pp. 172–3). In consequence the clergy of the church were not instituted as rectors, like those of most of the other city churches, and few of their names are known. In 1291 it was said that the church could scarcely support a chaplain due to its poverty, although the prior of Plympton took revenues estimated at 20*s*. (*Reg. Bronescombe*, ed. Hingeston-Randolph, 451–2). It paid a pension of 6*d*. to the cathedral in 1408 (D&C 3642). In 1421 the church's income was valued at £5 6*s*. 8*d*. (Oliver, *Monasticon*, 143), in 1522 at £10 (Rowe, *Tudor Exeter*, 29), and in 1535 at £9 19*s*. 2½*d*. (*Valor Ecclesiasticus*, ii, 377), these sums being appropriated by Plympton which continued to serve the church through a canon of Plympton or a hired chaplain. A canon is mentioned in this role in 1454, no doubt based at the Plympton's dependent priory of St Mary Marsh in Alphington parish (*Reg. Lacy*, ed. Dunstan, iii, 198).

Churchwardens' accounts survive in a broken series, the earliest being one of 1413 (DHC, DD 36765). They raise the question as to which St John was the patron saint of the church. The use of the term 'St John Bow' implies the Baptist, to distinguish the church from the hospital dedicated to him, and the Baptist is named as the church saint in a deed of the thirteenth century (BL, Cotton MS Vitellius D.ix f. 74v–75r). The regular appearances in the accounts of the feast of the Nativity of St John the Baptist (24 June) also suggest that this was the patronal festival (e.g. DD 36768). However there are references to a feast of St John the Evangelist in 1509 (DD 36769), to an image of the same saint in 1510 (ibid.), and most conclusively to the church of St John the Evangelist in 1508 (ECA, ED/BC/6) so it appears that the church was originally dedicated to the Baptist but subsequently to the Evangelist or to both St Johns. The accounts also mention the font, Easter sepulchre, and bells in 1421 (DD 36765), an altar of St Katherine in 1431 (DD 36766), a Lady chapel in 1477 and an image of the Virgin Mary in 1488 (DD 36768), an image of St Michael in 1505 (ibid.), the high cross (i.e. rood) in 1509 (DD 36769), an image of St James in 1518 (ibid.), the aisle of St Michael in 1530 (ibid.), and various obits. By 1548 the church had two endowed obits (Orme, 'Dissolution of the Chantries', 107). In 1521 the city chamber agreed that the wardens and parishioners might have ground on which to build an ambulatory in return for a rent of 12*d*. (ECA, Chamber Act Book II f. 29v). An inventory of the church's ornaments and vestments survives from 1552, when it possessed three bells and a clock (Cresswell, *Edwardian Inventories*, 28–34).

The church, like most of the others in Exeter, underwent various changes during the Middle Ages but these are difficult to describe and date in view of its disappearance. It probably began as a simple chancel and nave which were possibly enlarged in the thirteenth or early fourteenth century with narrow nave aisles and more certainly by an extension of the chancel eastwards across the bow. Later still a south chapel was built, and a tower was inserted north of the chancel and east of the nave. The reasons for postulating nave aisles are the references to the aisle of St Michael and the altar of St Katherine, while the south chapel may have been designed as a Lady chapel to hold the altar of Mary. Moreover the use of the term *de Arcubus* in 1291 must refer to the existence of either the bow or aisles of arches like St Mary Arches by that date (*Reg. Bronescombe*, ed. Hingeston-Randolph, 451). The construction of a comparatively ambitious building, comparable with St Mary Arches and St Stephen, would also fit with the facts that Plympton Priory was a wealthy foundation and owned some fifty tenements in Exeter in later times (Oliver, *Monasticon*, 142–3), whose tenants may have attended the church before the parochial system was established in 1222. The building would have been the obvious place to hold the manorial court of the priory's property in Exeter.

St John is depicted on Hooker's and Hogenberg's map of Exeter, 1587, with a tower surmounted by four tall pinnacles (Hooker, *Isca*), on Robert Sherwood's map of the 1630s (Sherwood), and (with an outline of the plan) on the Chamber Maps of 1756×60 (ECA, Book 58/15). The church was partly rebuilt and extended southwards in 1791, lost the 'bow' and most of the chancel in 1863, was declared redundant in 1934, and was partly demolished in 1937–8, the tower and shell of the church surviving until 1957. Other evidence of the building is recorded by Jenkins, *History of Exeter*, 399–400; Hedgeland; drawings by Edward Ashworth, 1864 (illustration, p. 92), and H. Besley, 1887; and Cresswell, 66–73; while a ground plan of the church at the time of its closure is shown in Everett, 'St John's Church', 176–7. HER refs ECC11050, 11344. Location SX 9179 9239.

Kalendars, Guild of

The guild of Kalendars was the chief religious guild in Exeter, or one of the chief, during the twelfth and thirteenth centuries. It is first mentioned in about 1200, when it appears to have joined with another 'guild of twenty brethren' to make an agreement with the canons of the cathedral. By the agreement the guilds surrendered to the canons their rights in the chapels of St Paul and St Peter the Little in return for permission to function in the chapel of St Mary Major (Orme, 'Kalendar Brethren', 153–4). Since the guild of Kalendars held property near St Paul, that may have been their chapel where they worshipped, while the guild of twenty may have been linked with St Peter the Little. The motive of the guilds may have been to improve their profile by moving to what was then one of the principal chapels of the city in a prominent position beside the cathedral.

The Kalendars' guild was named from its practice of meeting on or near the first day of the month (*kalendae* in Latin) to attend a mass with intercessions for the souls of the members. The names of those who had died in that particular month were read out, and the list of names survives as it was at about the beginning of the fourteenth century (Lepine and Orme, *Death and Memory*, 263–71). There were guilds with similar names in Bristol and Winchester; in Exeter the members seem to have been wealthy citizens and their wives together with a few cathedral canons and rather more members of the local parish clergy. The term 'brothers and sisters' occurs in a deed of 1279–80 (D&C VC/3074). From 1200 onwards the Kalendars seem to have dominated the federation, and the guild of twenty is no longer mentioned under that title. The Kalendars acquired some modest pieces of property in the city and had their own seal to authenticate documents. They must have used their rents or subscribed money to pay for clergy to celebrate their monthly masses, and may have acted as a friendly society, supporting members who were ill, infirm, or in need. The guild gave its name to the lane called Kalendarhay which led from near the west front of the cathedral towards South Street (but did not originally join with that street). This lane probably got its name from an adjoining piece of land likely to have been an outlying part of the great cathedral cemetery that was reserved as a burial ground for members of the guild (Orme, 'Kalendar Brethren', 156–9).

The guild still functioned in 1336 but between then and 1382 it transferred its property to the vicars choral of the cathedral. They took over the duty of saying the kalendar masses, and the guild appears to have withered away. This may have reflected competition from the city parish churches, to which citizens were increasingly drawn for religious and social activities. It may be presumed that the property transferred to the vicars included the land at Kalendarhay, and that this explains why the residential buildings of the vicars choral were built there at the initiative of Bishop Brantingham in the 1380s. The vicars continued to say the monthly masses until at least 1545 and probably until masses for the dead became unlawful in 1549, as well as keeping some of the Kalendars' records (ibid., 158–60). A surviving 'obit book' of the vicars includes a liturgical office for receiving new brothers and sisters, a bidding prayer to be read at the kalendar masses with requests for prayers for the living and dead of the guild, and the list of names to be prayed for (D&C 3675). No HER ref. Location of Kalendarhay SX 9199 9252.

St Katherine's (Catherine's) Almshouse

Founded *c.*1450 by John Stevens, canon of Exeter Cathedral and rector of Blackawton, for twelve or thirteen poor men, preferably servants of the cathedral clergy. The almshouse gave its name to Catherine Street, north of the Cathedral Close, where the ruins of the buildings are preserved (first illustration, p. 182). They include a chapel (comprising a larger chancel and smaller nave, with an additional room above), a communal kitchen, and individual cells for inmates arranged not in a quadrangle but along a narrow twisting courtyard. The chapel is described as dedicated to Our Lady in one early document, but the hospital is named as St Katherine in an endorsement of the founder's will, drawn up in 1457: perhaps the dedication was to both saints. The founder provided little endowment other than the house next to the almshouse and the room above the chapel, both of which were rented out, and the cathedral gave each of the almsfolk 4*d.* per quarter. Beyond that they must have depended on charity, and occasional bequests were made to them in wills (e.g. William Reygny, 1519, TNA, PROB 11/20/186). There is no evidence that the chapel ever had a salaried chaplain, and in 1546 the almsfolk were said to attend services in the nearby church of St Stephen. The almshouse survived the Reformation but the buildings were ruined by bombing in 1942. Its history is outlined in Orme and Webster, *The English Hospital*, 244–5, and there is a detailed archaeological description in Parker and Collings, 'St Catherine's Almshouses', 75–205. HER ref. ECC11091. Location SX 9215 9269.

St Katherine – see also St Catherine's Well; Polsloe Priory

St Kerrian

First mentioned in 1177×1184 as *capellam sancti Kerani* (Barlow, *English Episcopal Acta XI*, 87). It belonged to the cathedral by 1194×1204 (Barlow, *English Episcopal Acta XII*, 172–4), and stood about halfway along North Street on the east side, next to a lane called St *Kerien's* Lane in 1242–3 (ECA, ED/M/51) and later Trichay Street, which went eastwards to St Pancras church. It is also mentioned as a chapel in Peter de Palerna's list, *c.*1214 (D&C 2513). The building was probably made a parish church in 1222. In 1291 the rector's income was valued at 6*s.* 8*d.* (*Reg. Bronescombe*, ed. Hingeston-Randolph, 451) and in 1535 at £5 18*s.* 4*d.* (*Valor Ecclesiasticus*, ii, 316). A pension of 6*d.* was paid to the cathedral in *c.*1265 and 1408 (D&C 3721, 3642), and of 2*s.* in 1535.

A saint called *Kyeranus* appears in a litany of Exeter Cathedral in the late eleventh century (Lapidge, *Anglo-Saxon Litanies*, 198), and in the cathedral's twelfth-century martyrology where his feast day is 5 March (D&C 3518 f. 5v). Other cathedral calendars list the commemoration of *Keranus* on the same day (*Ordinale Exon*, ed. Dalton and Doble, i, pp. xxii–iii, 16, 216, 344). The saint of the church is *Keranus* or *Kyeranus* in Latin documents, with Kerrian as the local vernacular pronunciation. These name-forms are close to that of the Irish saint Ciarán of Saighir, and it is not impossible that St Kerrian chapel was named after him as a result of trading links between Exeter and Ireland. However the Cornish St Piran, a distinct saint, was also identified with Ciarán. A Latin life of him was written, based on Ciarán's, and he was given the same feast day, 5 March. Piran was probably better known in Exeter, due to its links with Cornwall, and the cathedral owned his chief church, Perranzabuloe, by about 1160 (Barlow, *English Episcopal Acta XI*, 46). Later he shared the dedication of an altar in the cathedral. It may well be that Piran was the inspiration for the Kerrian dedication, albeit believed (as Piran usually was) to be identical with Ciarán. In practice it made little difference, because in England the written Lives of the two saints were similar and their feast-day identical (Orme, *Saints of Cornwall*, 160, 220–3).

Although the church was small, it was situated in a wealthy part of the city and bequests to it occur in wills. John de Doulys gave a rent of 2*s*. per annum to the lights of the church in 1257 (Lepine and Orme, *Death and Memory*, 144); John Hamond bequeathed money for a priest to celebrate mass for six months in the church in 1474 (MCR 16–17 Edw IV m. 32d); and William Cremell established an obit in 1483 (MCR 1–2 Ric III m. 28d). By 1548 the church possessed four endowed obits and an endowment for a candle before the image of St Christopher (Orme, 'Dissolution of the Chantries', 109). The church's moveable possessions are listed in two early inventories. The first, in 1417, contains a good example of the array of vestments, ornaments, and books likely to have been possessed by any of the city churches before the Reformation. It mentions the high altar and includes enough altar cloths and linen to have furnished two small side altars, which may have been placed near the high altar. There are references to images of the Trinity, the Virgin Mary, her Assumption to heaven, and SS Anne, Christopher, Erasmus, and John the Baptist (Whitley, 'An Inventory', 309–18). A shorter inventory of the church's ornaments and vestments after the Reformation exists from 1552, when the church possessed two bells (Cresswell, *Edwardian Inventories*, 34–7).

The church consisted of a nave and a short narrower chancel, and was entered from the west end in North Street. The earliest representation of the church is on Hooker's and Hogenberg's map of Exeter in 1587. This shows a battlemented tower at the west end, consisting of two identical stages (may the upper one be a correction of the height?) with a small turret centred above the tower (Hooker, *Isca*); another rather indistinct image appears on Robert Sherwood's map of the 1630s (Sherwood). A more accurate elevation on the Chamber Maps of 1756×60 depicts the west front of the church as one unit with a central door, a large gothic window above the door, partly blocked at the bottom, a gable, and a bell turret with two openings (ECA, Book 58/12, 14; second illustration, p. 182). Hedgeland's model of Exeter (1824) likewise portrays a western facade of a single unit topped by the bell turret. The church had a house on its south side but would have been lighted from its east and west ends and possibly from part of the north wall. In 1350 the rector received permission from the mayor and chamber of Exeter to erect a house on the north side next to the church, presumably as his residence. It was built on Trichay Street which thereby became a cul-de-sac. The condition was made that the city authorities should have the right of entering the building by a key in time of war or whenever the need or use of the city should demand it (ECA, ED/M/388), and the rector paid a ground-rent of 8*d*. per annum to the city (Hooker, *Description*, iii, 752). Hedgeland's model is not accurate in showing this house, which he replaces by two larger houses and shifts Trichay Street to a more northerly line. St Kerrian church was disused for most of the nineteenth century and was demolished in 1873. No other painting or photograph of it has yet been discovered. HER ref. ECC11041. Location SX 9186 9263.

St Laurence

Domesday Book mentions an unnamed 'church' in Exeter which belonged to King Edward the Confessor in 1066 and to Robert count of Mortain in 1086 (*Domesday Book*, ed. Thorn, 15/1). The historian O. J. Reichel identified this church with St Laurence: it is not clear on what grounds (*VCH Devon*, i, 446). However St Laurence is first recorded *c*.1202 as belonging to the French abbey of Ste-Marie-du-Val in Normandy (Oliver, *History of Exeter*, 157). This abbey was endowed with property in Devon and Cornwall by Goscelin or Joscelin de Pomeroy, lord of Berry Pomeroy, who flourished 1114–23 (Sanders, *English Baronies*, 106–7; *Documents Preserved in France*, ed. Round, 536–7; Orme, *History of the County of Cornwall*, ii, 278–9). Goscelin's father Ralph de Pomeroy was a major landowner in Devon in 1086, and his possessions included six houses in Exeter (*Domesday Book*, ed. Thorn, 34/58). It is therefore likely that Goscelin or another member of his family owned and then granted what was then technically the chapel of St Laurence to the abbey, and in 1268 his descendant Henry (V) de Pomeroy acknowledged the possession of the church by Merton Priory which had acquired it from the abbey by that date (Rowe, *Cornwall Feet of Fines*, i, 150–1). In the account of St Stephen (pp. 166–7), it is argued that the count of Mortain's church is more likely to have been that church.

St Laurence therefore probably existed by the 1120s, but it cannot yet be dated before that period. The record of it in *c*.1202 is followed by its inclusion in Peter de Palerna's list of chapels *c*.1214 (D&C 2513) and the mention of Robert, 'chaplain of St Laurence', in 1211–12 (ECA, ED/M/15). The building was situated on the north side of High

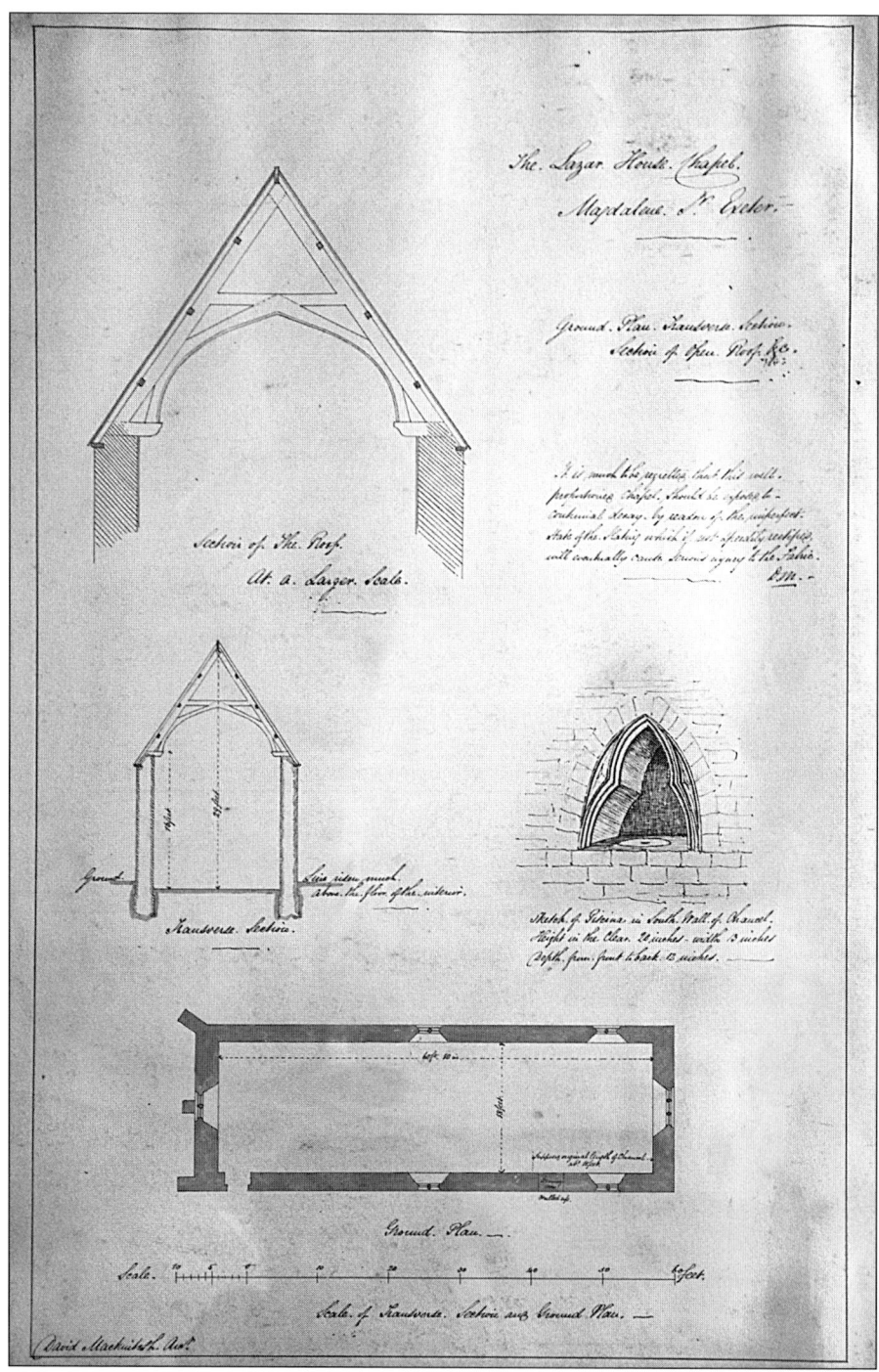

The chapel of St Mary Magdalene Hospital. Plan and detail of the roof and piscina before demolition in 1851.

Street, a little to the west of Castle Lane (later Castle Street). In 1267 St Marie-du-Val transferred its properties in England to Merton Priory, Surrey, including a 'moiety' or half-share of the church of St Laurence (BL, Cotton MS Cleopatra C.vii f. 148r; Heales, *Records of Merton Priory*, 148; D&C 2099). However when institutions of rectors are recorded, which is not until 1338, Merton Priory is named as the sole patron (*Reg. Grandisson*, iii, 1322). St Laurence was probably made a parish church in 1222 and the parish was enlarged with the parish of the hospital of St John (excluding the hospital premises) in 1287 (ECA, Book 53A f. 8v). The enlargement brought with it the chapel of St Bartholomew by the East Gate. Despite this, the benefice income was rated at 'nothing, because of poverty' in 1291 (*Reg. Bronescombe*, ed. Hingeston-Randolph, 451), and at only £7 16s. in 1535. In the latter year the church was said to be appropriated to the hospital of St John, although an annual pension of £1 6s. 8d. was paid to Merton Priory. A small sum of 6s. 8d. per annum was reckoned to arise from offerings to the images of St Laurence and St Bartholomew, the latter presumably in the chapel (*Valor Ecclesiasticus*, ii, 314). There were two endowed obits in the church in 1548 (Orme, 'Dissolution of the Chantries', 107). An inventory of the church's ornaments and vestments survives from 1552, when the church possessed three bells, a pair of organs, and a mantle for the image of Our Lady (Cresswell, *Edwardian Inventories*, 37–41).

St Laurence is depicted on Hooker's and Hogenberg's map of Exeter, 1587, with a battlemented tower (Hooker, *Isca*), on Robert Sherwood's map of the 1630s (Sherwood), and (with an outline of the plan) on the Chamber Maps of 1756×60. It consisted of a chancel with a north chapel, a nave, a south-west tower partly in the nave and partly projecting southwards from it, and an entrance porch east of the tower (ECA, Book 58/13). In 1519 the merchant Richard Hewet paid 6s. 8d. for a grave in the chancel alongside that of his wife (TNA, PROB 11/19/330). A. W. Everett, who examined the church before its demolition, suggested that part of the east wall was perhaps Anglo-Saxon, that the church was largely rebuilt in the fifteenth century, and the south wall again in 1674. He also drew attention to a crocketted niche and shelf for an image at the north end of the east wall, which evidently stood in the chapel and suggested its status as a Lady chapel (compare the reference to Our Lady above), but no firm documentary evidence survives about the chapel's dedication (Everett, 'St. Lawrence Church', 314–16). The church was partly rebuilt in 1674 but portions of the roodscreen survived until the twentieth century (Stabb, *Old Devon Churches*, ii, 74, plate 77). Photograph of the exterior, 1906, in Cresswell, 75; illustration, p. 97. The building was gutted by fire in the air raids of 1942 and never restored, the ruins being removed in 1946. See also Cresswell, 74–9, and Francis, *Lost Churches*, 44–6. HER refs ECC11017, 11196. Location SX 9216 9279.

St Leonard

First alluded to in about 1146×1149 when a woman named Avice of St Leonard gave a small endowment of land nearby to the priory of St James (Bearman, *Charters*, 77–8), and specifically mentioned as a chapel in 1177×1184 (Barlow, *English Episcopal Acta XI*, 81, 86). It was not a cathedral possession in 1194×1204 (Barlow, *English Episcopal Acta XII*, 172–4) and was probably then in lay patronage, as it was by 1348 when the patronage was disputed between the earl of Devon and William de Boyecote, the former winning the dispute (*Reg. Grandisson*, ii, 1049). St Leonard probably originated as the church of a small private estate, as did St James, neither of which could become parish churches because they lay within the rural part of the parish of the cathedral. It is called a chapel in the reference of 1177×1184 and in Peter de Palerna's list *c*.1214 (D&C 2513) but was probably made a parish church in 1222 along with the major chapels of the city. The parish covered only a modest area between the River Exe and Magdalen Road, and the rector's income was valued at no more than 6*s*. 8*d*. in 1291 (*Reg. Bronescombe*, ed. Hingeston-Randolph, 451). This was still merely £4 19*s*. 4*d*. in 1535 (*Valor Ecclesiasticus*, ii, 317). The church paid a pension of 3*d*. to the cathedral in 1408 (D&C 3642), and 1*s*. in 1535 in token of its dependent status. In 1426 Bishop Lacy ratified an agreement between the cathedral canons (rectors of the adjoining parish of Heavitree) and the rector of St Leonard by which the cathedral was awarded the tithes of two acres of *Spyceryspark* near Topsham Road (the rector having the rest), of four acres of *Lowdysparke* nearest the Exe (the two higher acres being shared between it and the rector), and of the whole meadow called *Pryourysmede* (*Reg. Lacy*, ed. Dunstan, i, 172–5). The parish belonged to the rural deanery of Exeter but it was not included in the city and county of Exeter established in 1537, and so no inventory of the church's ornaments and vestments survives from 1552 as in the other city parishes (Cresswell, *Edwardian Inventories*).

The medieval church occupied part of its present site on Topsham Road, well outside the city walls, and possessed a cemetery like the other extramural churches by 1397 when Bishop Stafford commissioned a canon of the cathedral to enclose a woman named Alice Bernard as an anchorite 'in a house in the cemetery of the parish church of St Leonard' (*Reg. Stafford*, 20, 99). Bequests to her, usually under the name of 'the anchorite of St Leonard', occur in local wills down to 1436 (ibid., 379–80, 393–4, 413; *Reg. Lacy*, ed. Dunstan, iv, 4, 7, 25, 32). In 1447 Bishop Lacy appointed the cathedral precentor to examine Christine Holby, an Augustinian canoness from Ireland, who wished to live as an anchoress in a cell in the churchyard, to enquire into her means of support, and to enclose her if appropriate. A month later the bishop issued an indulgence to all who gave her assistance (*Reg. Lacy*, ed. Dunstan, ii, 394–6, 403). The churchyard was in a far more rural situation than it is today, and therefore suitable for an anchorite who sought quiet yet closeness to a city from which she could receive alms and visitors.

The church is shown on Hooker's and Hogenberg's map of Exeter, 1587, as a small building with a western bell turret (Hooker, *Isca*). The dimensions are said to have been internally only 28 by 15 feet (8.5 by 4.6 metres), and there was no tower but the turret (Exeter, St Leonard, 1862A/PW 113). Oliver described the church in 1840 as having consisted of a chancel and nave, with a raftered roof until ceilings were installed in 1732 (*Ecclesiastical Antiquities*, i, 162–7). An engraving of the church was published in 1831–2 (Sprake, *Gates*), and there is a drawing of about the same period (illustration, p. 103). The bishop gave permission to demolish the building in 1831 and a new church was consecrated two years later but this building was itself replaced in 1876. HER refs ECC11049, 11143. Location SX 9244 9191.

Livery Dole Almshouse

This almshouse was not founded until about the 1590s, when it was equipped with a chapel of late-medieval character: either new and modelled on a chapel of that period or rebuilt with materials taken from some other chapel site. References in cathedral documents to the different chapel of St Clair in Matford Lane were misinterpreted by the Victorian historians George Oliver and W. Harding as relating to the chapel of Livery Dole, and they also misunderstood the saint as the female St Clare (p. 88). There is no evidence that the Livery Dole chapel existed before the almshouse or that it was ever dedicated to St Clare (Orme, 'Medieval Chapels of Heavitree', 121–3, 127–8). HER ref. MDV15880. Location SX 9356 9245.

St Loye

First mentioned in records on 1 April 1387 when Bishop Brantingham licensed Henry and Joan Tirelle to have divine service celebrated in their presence in the chapel of St Loye [*Eligius*] within their house of Wonford in the parish of Heavitree, especially on the morrow of Trinity Sunday (*Reg. Brantyngham*, ii, 636–7). That date implies that the chapel was consecrated, dedicated, or first used on 25 June 1386 which was both the feast-day of the translation of St Loye and the morrow of Trinity Sunday. The documentary evidence, however, does not accord with parts of the surviving fabric, such as the lancet windows and the use of local sandstone rubble, which point to construction during the thirteenth or early fourteenth centuries (Worthy, *Suburbs*, 18–26; Lega-Weekes, 'Saint Loye's, 361; Everett, 'St Loye's Chapel, 62–5; Falla, *Heavitree*, 40–1; John Allan, private information). It is rare to find documentary references to chapels or licences for them before the fourteenth century, so that such a chronology is acceptable in which case St Loye originated as an earlier domestic chapel, a more public devotional chapel, or both.

The chapel stood, and its remains survive, in Rifford Road. There are early descriptions of it in Jenkins, *History of Exeter*, 438, George Oliver, *Ecclesiastical Antiquities*, i, 44–5 (with engraving, illustration, p. 110), and Worthy, *Suburbs*, 18–26. Engravings of it were made in 1839 and *c*.1840 (Somers Cocks, *Devon Prints*, nos 1143–4). It seems to have been more than a wholly private building by 1401, since the offerings made there were then stated to belong to the vicar of Heavitree, although by implication he was not responsible for the staffing or upkeep (*Reg. Stafford*, 126). As at most such chapels, its worship probably declined or ended at the Reformation, and by 1607 part of it was let as a dwelling house (Falla, *Heavitree*, 40–1). HER ref. MDV16822. Location SX 9459 9194.

St Lucy's Lane

The lane called Friernhay, leading north from the lower end of Fore Street, was also known as St Lucy's Lane in the seventeenth century (Hoskins, *Exeter in the Seventeenth Century*, end map). I have not found any documentary evidence of a chapel of the saint in the vicinity, and wonder if the name is an allusion to the darkness of the lane, St Lucy's day (13 December) being regarded as the shortest day of the year in the Julian calendar. No HER ref. Location SX 9173 9244.

St Margaret – see Topsham, St Margaret

Marsh, Priory of St Mary

Founded in Alphington parish in 1142, according to the annals of Plympton Priory, as the result of gifts of property to Plympton by Adeliz (died 1142), daughter of the leading Devon landowner Richard fitz Baldwin, son of Baldwin fitz Gilbert. The cemetery of the priory was consecrated by Bishop Robert Warelwast on 19 May in that year (Liebermann, *Ungedruckte Anglo-Normannische Geschichtsquellen*, 29; Fizzard, *Plympton Priory*, 62–4). Adeliz also granted to Plympton the Castle Chapel in Exeter, but this grant did not take effect and by the early thirteenth century the patronage of the chapel was in the hands of Robert de Courtenay who had inherited much of the property of Baldwin's family. Plympton complained about this to Pope Honorius III (1216–27), who appointed judges delegate to hear the case, and a compromise was reached that included the priory of Marsh. Between 1219 and 1227 Robert de Courtenay restored to Plympton twenty-one acres of land in his marshland in Alphington, which he acknowledged as their ancient right, and added a further thirty acres together with the promise of a flow of water from Alphington across his land and that of his men for the domestic uses of the priory. In return Plympton abandoned its claim to the Castle Chapel and certain other churches (Powderham, Courtenay Cartulary ff. 134v–5r).

The priory of Marsh was dedicated to the Virgin Mary and was known as St Mary of [the] Marsh; its site and property were also known as Marescombe. It was a dependent cell of Plympton under the full authority of that house, and as such a small community of Augustinian canons. The priory did not lie within Exeter, strictly speaking, but in the parish of Alphington and it is included here because its site is now within the city. The suggested location is at SX 9226 9088. In 1841 the tithe map shows this site as linked by a lane to the road from Exe Bridge to Alphington. At its inner end the lane crossed a stream (very likely the flow of water mentioned by Courtenay) towards an entrance into a field called Barn Field. Outside this entrance, the lane turned at right-angles to continue onwards to a small farm named Marsh Barton (DHC, Alphington TA and TM). A map in the archives of Powderham Castle shows, near Barn Field, a long building called 'Marsh Barn' with a square courtyard on its south side (HER ref. MDV17271). A document of 1689 refers to 'the hall of the said barton of Marsh now turned into a barn' (DHC, DD 38034). It looks as though the priory was close to the later farm, which was perhaps originally its home farm, but no features of the monastery buildings now remain above ground.

The canons of St Mary Marsh consisted of a prior and one or two companions who maintained daily services in the priory church and supervised the nearby property of Plympton Priory, including the church of St John Bow (Exeter) and about sixty-four tenements in the city and in the parishes of Alphington and Heavitree. In 1421 the value of the tenements was estimated at £21 10s. 1d. per annum plus £5 6s. 8d. from the church of St John Bow (Oliver, *Monasticon*, 142–3), and in 1535 at £28 8s. 11d. plus £9 17s. 2½d. from St John Bow (*Valor Ecclesiasticus*, ii, 375, 377). In 1445 an agreement was drawn up between Plympton Priory and the rector of Alphington to define their respective rights over St Mary Marsh. The lands of the priory were to pay tithes to the rector, except for one acre which presumably represented the enclosure and gardens of the canons. The priory buildings included an inner court which accommodated domestic servants (and no doubt premises for the canons) and an outer court with further servants who were probably agricultural labourers. Servants in the inner court were to attend Alphington church for confession and Easter communion unless they were ill, in which case they could receive these sacraments from the prior of the cell. They also had the right to be buried in the cemetery of the priory, which presumably also contained the graves of such canons as died there unless they were interred in the priory church. Servants in the outer court, whether ill or not, were to receive all sacraments from the rector of Alphington and to be buried in his church (*Reg. Lacy*, ed. Dunstan, iii, 296–9). Previous to this in 1409, there is a reference to the priory hall: presumably used for feeding servants and guests (*Reg. Stafford*, 77). The only three surviving names of the priors are listed in Smith, *Heads of Religious Houses III*, 477.

On 16 October 1538 Sir Richard Pollard obtained a lease of St Mary Marsh for ninety-nine years from the prior and canons of Plympton (Youings, *Devon Monastic Lands*, 64–5). It is not clear whether the lease envisaged the closure of the priory, but its community cannot have survived much longer since Plympton was dissolved by the crown on 1 March 1539 and all its possessions came into royal hands (*Letters and Papers, Henry VIII*, xiv part i, p. 168). Pollard's lease was confirmed by the crown, but only for twenty-one years, and the site was sold to James Coffin and Thomas Godwyn on 9 September 1545, subject to the lease (Youings, *Devon Monastic Lands*, 64–5). HER ref. MDV17271. Suggested location as above, SX 9226 9088.

St Martin

Dedicated as a church (*templum*) on 6 July 1065 in honour of Jesus Christ, the Holy Cross, St Mary the mother of Christ, St Martin the bishop, and All Saints, according to notes from an 'old missal' of the church copied into the medieval cartulary of the hospital of St John (ECA, Book 53A f. 26r). The building incorporates masonry from the late Anglo-Saxon period, suggesting (with the dedication evidence) that the church was built or rebuilt in 1065 (Blaylock and Westcott, 'Late Saxon Fabric', 119–22). It has always occupied its present location at the north-west corner of the Cathedral Close beside the entrance to Catherine Street. It was described as a chapel belonging to the cathedral in 1194×1204 (Barlow, *English Episcopal Acta XII*, 172–4) and as a chapel in Peter de Palerna's list *c*.1214 (D&C 2513), before probably becoming a parish church in 1222. The parish consisted chiefly of the block of housing bounded by the Cathedral Close, High Street, and St Martin's Lane. In 1291 the rector's income was described as 'nothing' (*Reg. Bronescombe*, ed. Hingeston-Randolph, 451) and in 1390 there was a proposal to unite the church with those of St Mary Major and St Petroc, but the scheme was abortive (D&C 3550 f. 61r–v/63r–v). In 1522 the rector's income was estimated at £10 (Rowe, *Tudor Exeter*, 9) and in 1535 at £8 14s. 6d. (*Valor Ecclesiasticus*, ii, 316). The church paid a pension of 6d. to the cathedral in *c*.1265 and 1408 (D&C 3721, 3642), and 2s. in 1535.

The hospital cartulary contains other transcripts from the 'old missal' which list names of people commemorated on particular days of the year and, in some cases, their endowments of prayers to be said for them in the city's other churches and chapels (ECA, Book 53A f. 36r; Lepine and Orme, *Death and Memory*, 262). In 1330–1 John le Bole bequeathed a rent worth 12d. to support the lights in the church (ECA, MCR 4–5 Edw III m. 19). In 1409 Bishop Stafford agreed to move the feast of the church's dedication from the original date to the Sunday after the translation of St Thomas Becket (7 July) and granted an indulgence of forty days to those present at services on that day. The change was probably requested because by this time the dedication feast clashed with the octave of the cathedral's important feast of

St Nicholas Priory from the north-west, as reconstructed by Richard Parker. The view suggests a church with two towers and a cloister with other buildings north of the church.

SS Peter and Paul (ECA, Book 53A f. 77v). During the fifteenth century John Bradeworth, a wealthy parishioner, asked to be buried in the church before the altar of the Virgin Mary, established an obit for himself, and made a bequest to the fraternity of Corpus Christi. The location of the fraternity is not specified, but the bequest is listed with others to St Martin church (D&C 2538/2). The Exeter guild of skinners was devoted to Corpus Christi in the early fifteenth century, and it may be that they transferred their meetings to the church from the Charnel Chapel, where they are mentioned up to 1431 (p. 86). By 1548 William Duke had endowed a stipendiary priest (probably a chantry priest) in the church with an income of £6 8s. 8d.; the post and its endowment came to an end in that year, along with endowments for an obit and for wax for the church lights (Orme, 'Dissolution of the Chantries', 107). An inventory of the church's ornaments and vestments survives from 1552, when the church possessed three bells (Cresswell, *Edwardian Inventories*, 41–4).

The church probably originated as a two-part building consisting of chancel and nave. Much rebuilding was done in the fifteenth century when a north tower was added projecting from the nave. The ground floor of the tower forms a small transept which was probably the site of the altar of Mary and hence a Lady chapel. Large west and south windows were added in the nave, one of which contains the arms of Bishop Lacy (1419–55) and those of Courtenay (perhaps for Bishop Courtenay, 1478–87) but there is no evidence that Lacy gave a window, as stated by Cresswell, 86. The building is represented on Hooker's and Hogenberg's map of Exeter, 1587, with a tower topped by four small pinnacles (Hooker, *Isca*); the tower appears on Hooker's undated map of the Cathedral Close (D&C 3530 ff. 59–60) and on Robert Sherwood's map of the 1630s (Sherwood). An outline is shown on the Chamber Maps of 1756×60 (ECA, Book 58/11, 13). The church survives at the present day (illustration, p. 183). See also Cresswell, 86–90 with photograph. HER refs ECC11001, 11109. Location SX 9211 9266.

St Mary (1) Arches

First definitely mentioned as a chapel *c.*1214 in Peter de Palerna's list (D&C 2513), but at least a little older in view of its Norman arcades. Its site was and is on the east side of Mary Arches Street, originally a narrower and more winding street than today. The chapel did not belong to the cathedral in 1194×1204 (Barlow, *English Episcopal Acta XII*, 172–4) but the patronage is not known for certain until 1334 when it was owned by the bishop of Exeter who held it thereafter (*Reg. Grandisson*, iii, 1302). However the pillared arcades in the building, which date from about the second half of the twelfth century (illustration, p. 117), are of an elaborate kind that were unique among the city's chapels when they were built, except perhaps for St Stephen (p. 168). They indicate unusual wealth and ambition, appropriate to the bishops and making likely their ownership of the chapel by about 1200.

St Mary Arches is likely to have been 'the church of the most holy Virgin Mary behind the public [i.e. the principal] street in the city of Exeter' to which Bishop Brewer gave an indulgence in 1231–2 on the day before Trinity Sunday, the anniversary of the dedication of the building (Barlow, *English Episcopal Acta XII*, 237–8). It was probably made a parish church in 1222 but its parish was small and the rector's income in 1291 (when the church is named as 'Mary of the Arches') was stated as scarcely enough to support a chaplain (*Reg. Bronescombe*, ed. Hingeston-Randolph, 451). St Mary Arches paid a pension of 1s. to the cathedral in 1408 (D&C 3642), and in 1535 the rector's revenues were leased in return for a sum of £10 per annum (*Valor Ecclesiasticus*, ii, 316). In 1494 Gervase Luysshant endowed a mass of Our Lady at the high altar every Saturday (Mary's day), to be celebrated between 6.00 a.m. and 7.00 a.m. (DHC, Exeter, St Mary Arches 332A/PF 29–30add). The will of Giles Kyrke in 1546 mentions Our Lady (probably an image) in an aisle of the church (TNA, PROB 11/31/95), and that of John Maynard in the same year refers to the chapel of the Holy Trinity (PROB 11/31/454). In the chantry surveys of 1546–8 the church was credited with an endowed chantry founded by Thomas Andrew, mayor of Exeter (died 1519), for one priest; an endowment for a priest to celebrate a mass of the Name of Jesus every Friday; and an endowed mass in the name of Blessed Mary, presumably that of Luysshant. There were also four endowed obits by 1548 (Orme, 'Dissolution of the Chantries', 107), one of them probably that of William Obley established in 1505 (MCR 2–3 Hen VIII m. 26). An inventory of the church's ornaments and vestments survives from 1552, including an image of Mary and four bells (Cresswell, *Edwardian Inventories*, 45–8).

The church consists of a chancel (probably once longer), a nave with north and south aisles divided by the arcades of four bays, and a small west tower. George Oliver states that the Trinity chapel was in the north aisle (*History of Exeter*, 158), and the Andrew chantry (perhaps a Lady chapel) was undoubtedly in the south aisle where his tomb survives. The tower replaced a larger one that stood further west and is shown on Hooker's and Hogenberg's map of Exeter, 1587, surmounted by a tall spire (Hooker, *Isca*), and in a similar manner on Robert Sherwood's map of the 1630s (Sherwood). A plan of the church, showing the four bays of the arcades, appears on the Chamber Maps of 1756×60 (ECA, Book 58/15). The building still contains the ledger-stone of Alice Blackaller (died 1535), daughter of Thomas Andrew (Cresswell, 91–110). Photographs of the interior in Cresswell, 91, and Stabb, plate 78. It remains in being, but is not used for worship. HER ref. ECC11026. Location SX 9186 9253.

St Mary (2) Major

St Mary Major originated as the church or one of the churches of the ancient minster of Exeter, later the cathedral. As stated in the Introduction, the foundations of a late Anglo-Saxon church excavated on the site of St Mary Major in the 1970s were interpreted as those of a single minster church that became the cathedral in 1050 (Henderson and Bidwell, 'The Saxon Minster', 145–76). Other considerations, however, raise the possibility that the minster and cathedral consisted of two churches. Major Anglo-Saxon minsters and cathedrals were sometimes built in this way, and Exeter may have needed more than one building: St Mary and another yet undiscovered lying further east (pp. 7–9). Domesday Book, 1086, mentions an unnamed 'church' as belonging to the bishop and linked with the forty-seven houses and their inhabitants that he owned in the city – houses that had probably once been the property of the minster (*Domesday Book*, ed. Thorn, 2/1). This church is likely to have been the cathedral, in other words St Mary Major, either because it was the sole church of the minster or because, if there were two, it was the one that provided pastoral services such as funerals for local people and worship for the minster's or bishop's tenants in Exeter (pp. 9, 13–14).

In 1114 the construction of a new cathedral building began on the site of the present cathedral (Bodleian, MS Digby 81 f. 88r; Rose-Troup, *Exeter Vignettes*, 24). The clergy moved into this building in 1133, but a companion church to it was evidently desired because St Mary was retained with most of its Anglo-Saxon fabric and it was provided with an impressive Norman tower that echoed those of the cathedral. There were as yet no parish churches in the city, so the retained church must have been needed to provide some general function on the cathedral site such as a ministry to the laity of Exeter like that which it may have supplied before. During the twelfth century, however, the bishop appears to have moved his tenants from St Mary to St Stephen (p. 14), and St Mary's importance may have ebbed somewhat. By 1194×1204 it is described as a chapel in the patronage of the cathedral clergy, and had evidently come to be regarded as a separate entity from the cathedral itself (Barlow, *English Episcopal Acta XII*, 172–4). Nevertheless it was attractive enough in about 1200 for two religious guilds of the city, the guild of twenty and the guild of Kalendars, to transfer their worship there from two other chapels in Exeter (p. 120).

The reference of 1194×1204 calls it the chapel of St Mary Major, and in Peter de Palerna's list *c*.1214 it appears as the chapel of St Mary the Great (*Magne*) (D&C 2513). 'Major' or 'Great' was meant to distinguish it from the chapel of St Mary Minor or the Little which adjoined it, rather than from the other Mary churches in the city as suggested by Hoskins, 'Early Churches in Exeter', 23. An alternative name was St Mary *de Turre*, 'of the tower' (ECA, 51/1/1/1). The site was opposite the west front of the Norman and present-day cathedrals. The chapel was probably made a parish church in 1222 and its clergy were thereafter called rectors, although the title of vicar is recorded on one occasion in 1284 (*Reg. Bronescombe*, ed. Hingeston-Randolph, 345). Its parish was bigger than was usual within the city walls, including the church itself, Cook Row (the narrow north end of South Street), and a large area of the southern end of the 'West Quarter' between South Street and Fore Street. This parish is sometimes regarded as a remnant of the minster's parish, but that is unlikely because all the city parishes appear to have been formed at the same time in 1222. Those who drew up their boundaries had difficulty giving a parish to St Mary because it was surrounded by other churches. It may have been given the southern end of the 'West Quarter' because some of the bishop's houses were located there (Curtis, *Some Disputes*, 90), or because no church existed nearby with which local people had developed links, and the size of the area may reflect a smaller population. Moreover in about 1285 St Mary Major was united with its neighbour St Mary Minor, and we do not know if the latter had possessed a parish (p. 137). The rector's income was (under-)assessed at 20*s*. per annum in 1291 (*Reg. Bronescombe*, ed. Hingeston-Randolph, 451); it was reckoned to be £20 in 1522 (Rowe, *Tudor Exeter*, 17) and was rated as the wealthiest within the city walls at £15 14*s*. 8*d*. in 1535 (*Valor Ecclesiasticus*, ii, 315–17). It paid an annual pension of 5*s*. to the cathedral in *c*.1265 and 1408 (D&C 3721, 3642), and of 22*s*. in 1535. There was a proposal to unite the churches and parishes of St Mary Major, St Martin, and St Petroc in 1390, but this came to nothing (D&C 3550 f. 61r–v/63r–v).

Much of the Norman tower with the Norman tower arch into the nave survived until the church was demolished in the 1860s. The rest of the building underwent some reconstruction from the twelfth century onwards. Its eastern apse was removed to give it a square east end (a process common in England during the twelfth or thirteenth centuries), and the chancel was reduced in length. Perpendicular window tracery was inserted in the nave, but the alterations did not change the basic shape of the church from comprising a chancel, nave, and large west tower (illustration, p. 184). By the nineteenth century the chancel measured 24 feet 6 inches by 17 feet 8 inches (7.5 by 5.4 metres) together with a small vestry on its south side and a door and porch on the north side. The nave was longer and wider at 63 by 25 feet (19.2 by 7.6 metres) (Ashworth, 'St Mary Major', 24–8). There were no aisles. Bishop Grandisson dedicated the high altar on 6 November 1336, presumably after one of the rebuilding phases (*Reg. Grandisson*, ii, 832). The chancel and nave were divided by a roodscreen decorated with figures of saints, the roodloft being accessed by an externally projecting staircase on the north side of the church. Part of the screen was removed to St Mary Steps in 1865 (Cresswell, 122–4), but two bays were retained in the rebuilt Victorian church of St Mary Major until 1970 (Stabb, *Old Devon Churches*, ii, plate 79) and are now in Offwell church (Devon). In 1268 Walter le Spec gave a tenement to maintain a wax taper burning before the crucifix on Sundays and festivals, presumably on the roodscreen; if so, this is an early indication of such a screen in a church (ECA, 51/1/1/2a). In 1286 another tenement was given to provide 12*d*. towards the church lights (ECA, ED/M/148). An altar of St Thomas Becket in the church is mentioned in 1349 (Lepine and Orme, *Death and Memory*, 166) and one of St Apollonia (patroness of toothache) beneath the tower in 1428 (*Reg. Lacy*, ed. Dunstan, iv, 12). By the early sixteenth century there was a large image of Christ the Saviour on the north exterior of the church; this was removed in about 1538 by Simon Heynes, dean of the cathedral (Orme, *Exeter Cathedral*, 198). A small sculpture of the martyrdom of St Laurence was attached to the outside wall of the chancel above one of the north windows by 1806 (Jenkins, *History of Exeter*, 367); in 1840 George Oliver judged this to have been fixed there 'at a comparatively recent period' (*Ecclesiastical Antiquities*, i, 19–21). There is no written evidence of a cult of St Laurence at the church.

The west tower of the medieval building was a massive structure, which explains why the church was often identified by this feature. Two round stair turrets projected at its outer western corners and the tower eventually acquired a tall spire crowned by a whistling weather-cock. The cock was taken down so as not to disturb Katherine of Aragon during her stay at the nearby deanery in 1501 (ECA, Book 51 f. 330v), and the spire itself was demolished in 1581. Hooker's and Hogenberg's map of Exeter, 1587, shows the church tower without the spire but topped by a flagpole, flag, and turret for access (Hooker, *Isca*). The height of the tower is stressed on

Hooker's undated map of the Cathedral Close (D&C 3530 ff. 59–60), but this height was reduced in 1768. At ground level there was once an entrance through the west wall of the tower, but it was blocked by an adjoining house in the nineteenth century. By that period one entered the church through the north wall of the tower, and turned left to enter the nave. The ground floor housed the font and the altar of St Apollonia. Since the latter must have faced east, it may have lain in a rectangular enclosure at one of the eastern corners of the tower towards the nave, while the opposite corner would be a possible site for the altar of St Thomas, similarly enclosed. In the nineteenth century part of a wall painting of St Christopher was still extant on the inner south wall of the tower (Ashworth, 'St Mary Major', 24–8).

In 1402 and 1484 the church is mentioned as being used for meetings of the court of the archdeacon of Exeter (ECA, ED/M/568; BL, Add. Ch. 27631). Burials in the building included those of at least one rector and some important citizens and their wives of the parish (Lepine and Orme, *Death and Memory*, 85 (mentioning the font), 86, 89, 102, 111). Several obit masses or masses for one year were endowed, including those of Agnes de Woodleigh 1349 (ibid., 166), Andrew de Lappeflode 1373 (ECA, 51/1/2/7), Robert Taverner 1383 (D&C 23; ECA, 51/1/3/4–5), John Pytman 1411 (ECA, 51/1/2/10, 12), Richard Clerk 1474 (with a reference to the pulpit, ECA, 51/1/4/12), and Robert Russell 1488 (ECA, 51/1/5/4). In 1534 the Reformer Hugh Latimer used the pulpit to preach in favour of reform on the feast of the building's dedication, which by then was in June. The church was so crowded that the windows were broken to allow people outside to hear the sermon (ECA, Book 51 f. 342r–v). There were still three endowed obits in the church in 1548 (Orme, 'Dissolution of the Chantries', 107), and an inventory of ornaments and vestments survives from 1552. It mentions five bells, six rochets (simple vestments) 'for the children', and three other rochets, the latter being twice attributed to the (parish) clerk and once to 'clerks' (Cresswell, *Edwardian Inventories*, 50–8). The children may have been altar servers or members of a small choir, although one would expect more reference to adults if there was such a choir. A churchwardens' book survives, beginning in 1530, but apart from inventories of church goods, its annual accounts effectively start in 1580 (DHC, Exeter, St Mary Major, PW 1).

Other representations of the church include Robert Sherwood's map of the 1630s (Sherwood) and plans on the Chamber Maps of 1756×60 (ECA, Book 58/11, 13) and in Chanter, 'Custos and College', plate 17. Depictions of the exterior in the first half of the nineteenth century include those of Edward Ashworth (The Royal Albert Memorial Museum; illustration, p. 184) and George Townsend (*Sketches*, 2). The medieval church was wholly replaced in 1865–7 by one designed by Ashworth, but this church ceased to be used in 1970 and was then demolished. HER refs ECC11027, 11131. Location SX 9199 9225.

St Mary (3) Minor

First mentioned in 1194×1204 as a chapel (St Mary Minor) in the patronage of the cathedral (Barlow, *English Episcopal Acta XII*, 172–4) and included in Peter de Palerna's list *c*.1214, also as a chapel and called St Mary the Little (*Parve*) (D&C 2513). It was apparently made a parish church in 1222 (see below), and was still extant in *c*.1265 when it paid no dues to the cathedral, probably through poverty (D&C 3721). If the church had a parish beyond its own building, the parish must have been detached at some distance because this part of Exeter was crowded with other churches and parishes. The churches of St Mary Minor and St Mary Major (implying parish churches with parishes) were united by Bishop Quinil, probably on 5 September 1285; the year is mistakenly given as 1395 in the only known transcript of the document (Owen, *John Lydford's Book*, 105). St Mary Minor was demolished at some later date.

The church was very close to St Mary Major, and the names 'Major' and 'Minor' relate to the two churches. They are coupled together in the document of 1194×1294 and St Mary the Little follows St Mary the Great in Peter de Palerna's list (D&C 2513). In 1411 Robert Lingham, rector of St Mary Major, borrowed the charter of union from the cathedral exchequer as evidence in a legal dispute between himself and the vicars choral of Exeter, whose property adjoined St Mary Major on the south side (D&C 3550 f. 130v). The dispute was about a tenement of land 60 feet long by 12 feet wide, which both Lingham and the vicars claimed to possess (ECA, MCR 11 Hen IV m. 34). Judgment was subsequently given for Lingham (MCR 12 Hen IV mm. 35, 39). He evidently claimed the property as the site of the church of St Mary Minor, which suggests that it stood to the south or south-west of St Mary Major, bordering on the lands of the vicars choral. HER ref. 11039. Approximate location: as for St Mary Major.

St Mary (4) Steps

First mentioned as a church with this dedication in a deed of 1263×1267 (ECA, ED/M/109) and a will of 1269 (Lepine and Orme, *Death and Memory*, 145). However, Peter de Palerna's list of Exeter churches and chapels in *c*.1214, while not mentioning St Mary Steps, names the chapel of St Edward in the location where St Mary Steps should be: between the churches of St John Bow and St Edmund (D&C 2513). The best explanation is that the original dedication was something like Christ, Mary, Edward, and All Saints, and that Edward was superseded by Mary during the thirteenth century. Edward must have been Edward the Martyr (died 978), a saint popular in the eleventh century, suggesting that the church originated at that time. The cathedral owned relics of him by the later part of that century (Conner, *Anglo-Saxon Exeter*, 180–1), and there were other dedications to him in Devon at Egg Buckland, Holne, and Shaugh Prior (Orme, *English Church Dedications*, 237).

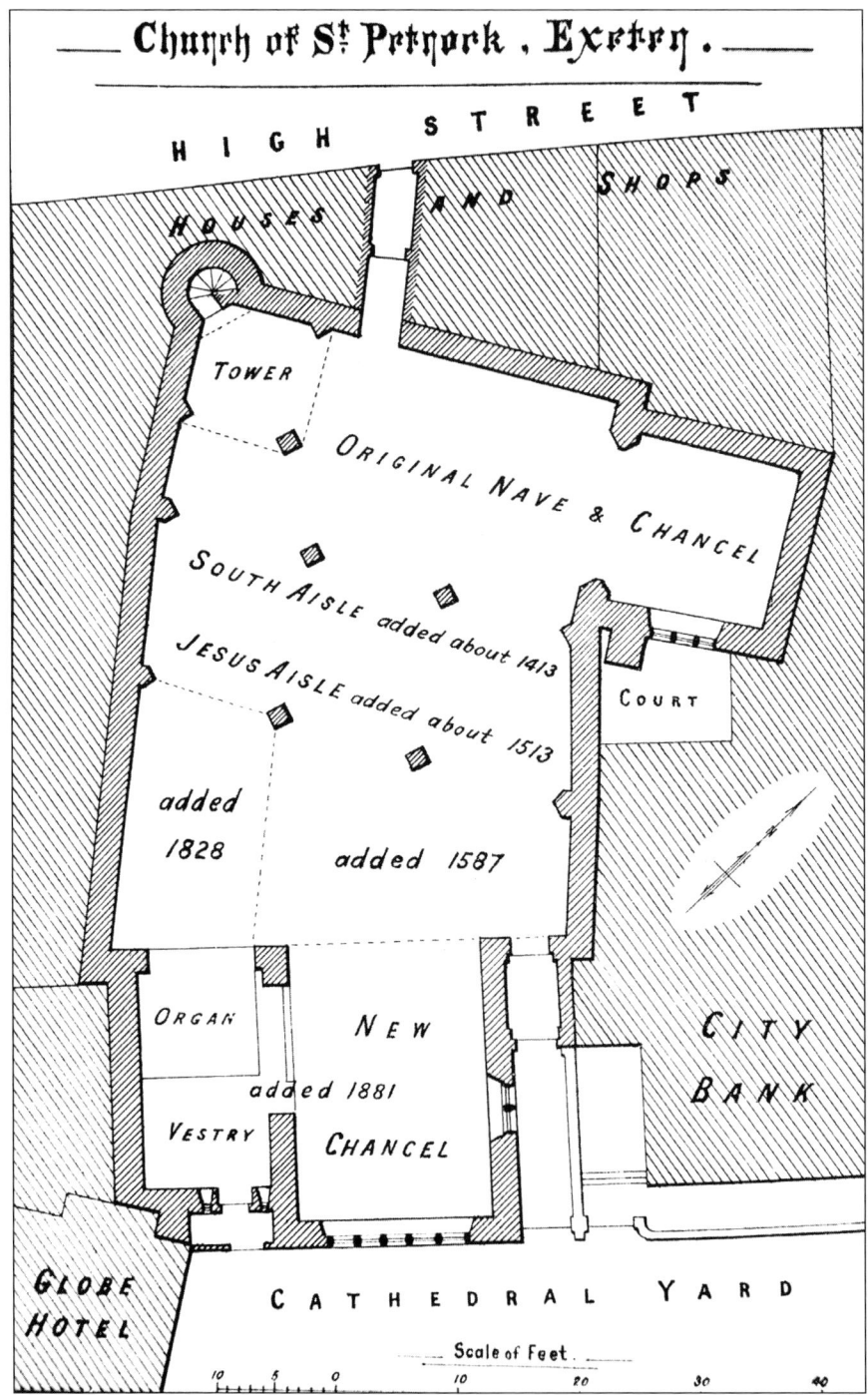

Plan of St Petroc church in 1882, showing the original nave and tower, the two aisles added before the Reformation, and the entrances from High Street and Cathedral Close.

The chapel occupied its present position at the west end of Stepcote Hill, a prominent place right opposite the West Gate, and was probably made a parish church in 1222. Its surname came either from the steps of which the adjoining street is composed or those up into the church itself, in Latin St Mary *de gradibus*, in French *de grysez* (TNA, C 1/11/20). In later centuries the parish lay mostly outside the city walls alongside the River Exe, including the islands of Millhay, Little Shilhay, and half of Shilhay. In 1291 the rector's annual income was rated at the locally high sum of £2 (*Reg. Bronescombe*, ed. Hingeston-Randolph, 451), but only at £8 6s. 8d. in 1535 (*Valor Ecclesiasticus*, ii, 317). The church was in lay patronage by 1273, the date of the first recorded institution of a rector (*Reg. Bronescombe*, ed. Hingeston-Randolph, 140); for much of the fourteenth and fifteenth centuries the patronage belonged to the local family of Shillingford. Bequests to the church and its clergy were made by members of the Collecote family in the late thirteenth century, with mentions of the church lights and a shop belonging to the church (Lepine and Orme, *Death and Memory*, 145, 147–8, 155–6). In 1349 William Mounteyn left money for a chaplain to celebrate mass in the church, probably for one year (ibid., 166–7).

Churchwardens' accounts survive from 1421 (DHC, DD 70884–9018 and Exeter, St Mary Steps, PW 1–6; those of 1553–8 are transcribed in Cresswell, 189–211). They refer to the roodloft, images of the Virgin Mary and St Katherine, and obits of Walter and Alice Dudbroke, John and Felicia Kyrton, and Thomas and Joan Trevylegh. An obit is also said to have been founded by Felicia Selman in 1462 (Cresswell, 121–2). The chantry survey of 1548 mentions endowments for two obit masses and a light before the picture of the Virgin Mary (Orme, 'Dissolution of the Chantries', 107). An inventory of the church's ornaments and vestments survives from 1552 when the church possessed two bells (Cresswell, *Edwardian Inventories*, 58–60), and after the Marian restoration of Catholicism in 1553 there were two altars in the church (Cresswell, 195). In 1865 the church acquired part of the roodscreen of St Mary Major when that church was demolished (Stabb, ii, plate 79).

St Mary Steps is depicted on Hooker's and Hogenberg's map of Exeter, 1587, with a tower topped by four pinnacles (Hooker, *Isca*), and on Robert Sherwood's map of the 1630s (Sherwood). The Chamber Maps of 1756×60 and other sources record it as having a nave, chancel, south aisle extending to the east end of the chancel, and south-west tower standing within the church (ECA, Book 58/9–10, 15; Jenkins, *History of Exeter*, 404–5; Hedgeland; Cresswell, 120–6). Photographs in Cresswell, 120, 123; Stabb, ii, plate 79. It remains in being, and is used for worship (first illustration, p. 185). HER refs ECC11029, 11154. Location SX 9176 9227.

St Mary (5) at St Mary Magdalene Hospital

In March 1220 Jordan Bestelabise granted rents in Exeter to the value of £2 11s. 10d. 'to God and St Mary in the chapel which is next the chapel of St Mary Magdalene of the house of lepers . . . to sustain the service of the Blessed Virgin Mary in the chapel for ever'. A sum of £2 was to be allocated to the chaplain there, 4s. to the clerk, and the rest to maintaining lights (ECA, ED/MAG/14). The grant has survived among the deeds of the hospital of St Mary Magdalene. The hospital's chapel, at least by the nineteenth century, consisted only of a chancel and nave (Devon and Exeter Institution, Diocesan Society Scrapbook, i, plate 19; Parker and Collings, 'St Catherine's Almshouses', 128–9). If the nave was originally occupied by the lepers, the chapel of St Mary may have been a closed aisle alongside their chapel where members of the public could worship with, but separately from, the lepers, and where perhaps service was done by the chaplain of the main chapel. No other reference to the chapel is known. HER ref. ECC11048. Approximate location SX 9249 9229.

St Mary (6) and St Francis

After the Franciscan friars moved from their original site in Frerenhay or Friernhay in Bartholomew Street soon after 1300 (p. 102), all or part of the church on the original site continued in use as a chapel. The chapel is described in 1421 as dedicated to St Francis and the Blessed Virgin Mary, but in 1434 to the same saints in the reverse order. The reference of 1421 is to damage caused to the chapel through the playing of games and vandalism, leading to the breaking of an image of the Virgin and the royal arms in the chapel windows (ECA, ED/M/685, printed by Oliver, *Monasticon*, 333–4). There is no reason to interpret this damage as indicative of Lollard anticlericalism, as suggested by Raymonde Foréville, 'Manifestations de lollardisme', 691–706. The document of 1434 is a grant by Bishop Lacy of an indulgence to those who visited the building for devotion or pilgrimage, or who contributed to its upkeep and repair (ECA, ED/SN/64; Little and Easterling, *Franciscans and Dominicans*, 59–60). The chapel was probably opened at times for the veneration of the images and access to the tombs therein, with regular or occasional masses celebrated by the friars. It may not have survived beyond the dissolution of the friary in 1538, and must have ceased to be used after 1548 or 1549. HER ref. 11074. Location SX 9164 9250.

St Mary (7) Mincinglake

The cathedral 'debt rolls' in the financial year ending at Michaelmas 1464 record offerings from 'the new chapel of Blessed Mary of Mincinglake [*Mynchinlake*]' (D&C 2753; 3754, i, sub 1468–9). The chapel was probably built in the previous twelve months, since it is not mentioned in the debt roll of the previous year. References to the chapel in the rolls indicate that the offerings centred on the feast of the Assumption of the Virgin Mary on 15 August, a dedication adopted shortly afterwards in 1471 by the guild of weavers and tuckers in Exeter (p. 176). The chapel was in Heavitree parish, hence the appropriation of its offerings by the cathedral as rector of the parish, and has been conjectured as lying near Polsloe Priory or even and quite improbably as having been an alternative name of the priory. Since late-medieval chapels were invariably sited beside roads to permit access and solicit donations from travellers, the likeliest locations are by one of the four roads that crossed the stream called Mincinglake, north or east of the city. Mincinglake Bridge near Stoke Hill on the old road from Exeter to Bradninch and Bristol is a particularly suitable candidate, since the chapel could have attracted travellers on that important route (Orme, 'Medieval Chapels of Heavitree', 126). During the 1460s and 1470s offerings in the chapel ranged from 1*s.* to 3*s.* 5*d.* annually, probably after deductions for expenses (D&C 3754). At Michaelmas 1480 the payment was standardised at 3*s.* 4*d.* until Michaelmas 1489, after which the chapel disappears from records (ibid.). HER ref. MDV55547. Location unknown.

St Mary (8) Bishop's Palace

In 1421 there is a reference to a chapel of St Mary within the bishop's palace in which the vicar-general of the diocese did legal business (*Reg. Lacy*, ed. Dunstan, i, 48). Ordinations were held in a chapel of the same name in 1509 and 1510, pointing to a chapel of significant size (DHC, Chanter XIII f. 101v). It is possible that this was a separate and more personal oratory of the bishop alongside his major chapel of St Faith (pp. 72–3); alternatively, it may have been another name for St Faith, perhaps because Mary shared the dedication and came to supersede Faith in common usage. No HER ref. Approximate location SX 9217 9252.

St Mary (9) Cathedral Cemetery

Ordinations of clergy in Exeter were usually held from 1510 to 1515 'in the chapel of Blessed Mary the Virgin within the cemetery of the cathedral church of Exeter' (DHC, Chanter XIII ff. 102v–22v). The only known chapel within the cemetery was the Charnel Chapel (p. 84), dedicated to St Edward. It may be that Mary was a co-patron of the chapel and came to replace Edward (compare St Mary Steps), or that the presence of an image of 'Mary of Pity', holding the dead body of Christ, outside the chapel led to its becoming associated with her. No HER ref. Location as for the Charnel Chapel.

St Mary (10) house of William Fawell

From 1539 to 1544 ordinations in Exeter were usually held in the chapel of the Blessed Virgin Mary in the house of Canon William Fawell, bishop of Hippo and suffragan bishop in Exeter diocese (DHC, Chanter XIV ordination lists). This was presumably the private chapel of his canon's house. No HER ref. Location unknown.

St Mary – see also Castle Chapel; Cathedral; Exe Bridge Chapel; St Katherine's Almshouse; Marsh, Priory of St Mary; St Roche; Tuckers Hall

St Mary Magdalene Hospital

First mentioned in 1177×1184 as a leper hospital, when Bishop Bartholomew made gifts to it and issued regulations for the thirteen leper brethren whom it was to accommodate (Barlow, *English Episcopal Acta XI*, 86–8). The fact that he confirmed it in possession of properties in and around the city that it had held for a long time suggests that it was founded in the first half or middle of the twelfth century. It was situated outside the South Gate of the city on the south side of Magdalen Street between that street and Fairpark Road, on the Fairpark Road side of the later Jewish cemetery. As the hospital had a dedication by 1184, it must also have had a chapel, and by 1220 this chapel was adjoined by one of St Mary (pp. 139–40).

From Bartholomew's time until 1244 the hospital was under the patronage of the bishop (or the cathedral in his absence), but in 1224 Bishop Brewer transferred his patronage to the mayor and citizens of Exeter in return for the patronage of the hospital of St John the Baptist. Subsequently the mayor and chamber appointed a lay warden to administer the hospital's affairs. A prior (perhaps elected by the inmates) was the authority on the site (ECA, ED/MAG/66), and by about 1220 there was a chaplain responsible for services in the chapel (ED/MAG/12, 14; Lepine and Orme, *Death and Memory*, 146). Fragments of a cartulary of the hospital's possessions survive along with three rolls of similar records (ECA, D/2, 20, 23; Davis, *Medieval Cartularies*, 45). There were still leper men and women in the hospital in 1391 when John Nymet made them a bequest (ECA, ED/M/527), and as late as 1458 Richard Orange, a former mayor of Exeter, was buried in the hospital chapel having retired to the premises after contracting leprosy. But by the early fifteenth century the inmates of the hospital were also described as 'infirm' (*decrepitorum*) which suggests that as the incidence or fear of leprosy declined, the hospital became more of an almshouse for the infirm of either sex. Brothers and sisters are again mentioned in the will of William Obley, 1505 (MCR 2–3 Hen VIII m. 26). The hospital was not dissolved at the Reformation and continued to exist until the early nineteenth century (Orme and Webster, *The English Hospital*, 226–31).

The earliest depictions of the hospital occur on Hooker's and Hogenberg's 1587 map of Exeter and Hooker's undated plan of St Sidwell's Fee outside the city. The former marks the site but represents it by a single small building (Hooker, *Isca*). The latter is more informative. It shows a courtyard having buildings on three and a half sides with a gatehouse fronting Magdalen Street, and a small chapel possessing a bell turret. A stream, the Shutbrook, runs a little way west of the property, and a garden is marked on the other side of the street (D&C 3530 ff. 37v–8r). The chapel appears on Robert Sherwood's map of the 1630s (Sherwood). The Chamber Maps of 1756×60 show the hospital as an enclosure with the gatehouse, three houses east of it along the street and by that time in lay occupancy, a wing pointing south at right angles to the gatehouse, the chapel in the middle of the enclosure, and a further building south of it. Much of the eastern and southern parts of the enclosure were covered with trees or bushes (ECA, Book 58/5). By the nineteenth century the chapel was an oblong building measuring about 61 by 18 feet (18.6 by 5.5 metres), with a three-light window at the east end and a two-light one at the west (illustration, p. 124). It had two entrances on the south side, and must once have functioned as a separate chancel and nave divided by a screen (Devon and Exeter Institution, Diocesan Society Scrapbook, i, plate 19; Harding, 'Account', 267; Parker and Collings, 'St Catherine's Almshouses', 128–9). If this arrangement went back to the era of the lepers, they would have occupied the nave while the public may have been allowed into a separate and possibly adjoining chapel (pp. 139–40). The main chapel was demolished in 1851. HER ref. ECC11048. Location SX 9249 9229.

St Michael (1) Cathedral Close

First mentioned in 1194×1204 as a chapel in the patronage of the cathedral (Barlow, *English Episcopal Acta XII*, 172–4). It was then listed between the chapels of St James and St Mary Major, and was therefore already on or near its later site off Palace Gate, a little way south of St Mary Major on part of what later became the location of the cathedral deanery. It is not included in Peter de Palerna's list of *c*.1214 (D&C 2513) and was apparently not made into a parish church in 1222. In *c*.1265 and 1408 it paid 4*d*. per annum to the cathedral (D&C 3721, 3642). Eventually it was absorbed within the deanery as the dean's private chapel; whether or not it was moved in this process is not known. The absorption may have happened by 1301 when an unspecified chapel is mentioned in the deanery (*Reg. Stapeldon*, 154; compare *Reg. Grandisson*, ii, 687), and had certainly taken place by 1408 when the chapel of St Michael is stated to have been 'within the house of the dean' (D&C 3642). It still existed in 1535 when the cathedral received 1*s*. 4*d*. per annum as a due from it (*Valor Ecclesiasticus*, ii, 294), but it probably ceased to function in 1548 or 1549 except as a place for private prayer. No medieval fabric appears to survive in the building that in later times was used as the chapel of the deanery. HER ref. ECC11038. Location SX 9202 9252.

St Michael (2) Cowick

First mentioned in 1278 (*Reg. Bronescombe*, ed. Robinson, ii, 116), but probably existing by 1261 when a reference is made to the 'chapels' belonging to Cowick Priory (*Reg. Bronescombe*, ed. Hingeston-Randolph, 127). It stood alongside or within the cemetery outside the priory gate in which the people of Cowick parish were buried, probably near Cowick Lane (Yeo, 'Where Was Cowick Priory?', 323–5; idem, *Monks of Cowick*, 11; illustration, p. 20). A field east of the priory was called Chapel Park in 1798 and 1838 (Allan et al., 'Site of Cowick Priory', 135–40; DHC, TA and TM St Thomas). The chapel was presumably used for funerals or masses for the dead in connection with the cemetery, the latter being said by Charles Worthy (*Suburbs of Exeter*, 155) to have stretched downwards from the chapel towards Exeter. When a new parish church of St Thomas was built in Cowick Street in 1412, this church was also provided with a cemetery but Bishop Stafford allowed the old one to remain in use if so desired (*Reg. Stafford*, 73). Bishop Oldham sanctioned the collection of alms for the chapel in 1507 (DHC, Chanter XIII f. 153v), and it is mentioned again in 1533–4 (DHC, W1258M/G4/53/1). In 1887 workmen found six graves on or near the site, two with stone coffins and a third containing a chalice, as well as tiles from a decorated pavement. Worthy (*Suburbs of Exeter*, 157–8) attributed them to the chapel, but he was not aware that the priory and its church were located close by, and the remains are more likely to have come from that church. Worship in the building probably ceased in 1548 or 1549, but the cemetery continued to be used until as late as 1729 (Yeo, 'Where Was Cowick Priory', 324; idem, *Monks of Cowick*, 11). HER ref. MDV17806. Location SX 9096 9115.

St Michael – see also Heavitree

More's and Fortescue's Almshouse

In 1477 the mayor and chamber of Exeter built two houses on the south side of Exe Bridge for two poor men who were directed to pray each day in the nearby Exe Bridge Chapel. The nomination of the men belonged to the mayor and chamber. In 1520 the houses were rebuilt and enlarged for three poor men by John More and Bartholomew Fortescue, who were allowed to nominate almsfolk during their lives, after which the nomination was to return to the mayor and chamber. There was no chapel other than usage of the Exe Bridge Chapel. The houses were demolished in about 1850 (Orme and Webster, *The English Hospital*, 246). HER ref. ECC11096. Location SX 9171 9219.

St Nicholas Priory

William the Conqueror visited Exeter in 1068 to establish his authority there, including the building of a castle. Later, at some point between 1070 and 1085, he granted the church of St Olave and its endowments at Sherford and Kenbury (Devon) to the monks of Battle Abbey, his new foundation in Sussex (*Regesta Regum Anglo-Normannorum: Acta of William I*, 132–4). He also gave them the church of Cullompton with lands there (ibid., 161–5) and probably the church of Pinhoe, all of which they held by 1086 (*Domesday Book*, ed. Thorn, 1/34, 1/52, 9/1–2). In due course Battle Abbey sent one of its monks named Cono to Devon to found a monastery, and he established the priory of St Nicholas as a daughter house in 1085–7, close to St Olave church and financed with the property that William had provided (Searle, *Chronicle of Battle*, 82–5).

The prior of St Nicholas was appointed by Battle and the priory paid the mother house an annual sum of money as a token of its dependency. For legal purposes the monks sometimes claimed that they were under the rule of the abbot of Battle, but for most of the time they had independent control of their own endowments, as Cowick Priory did under Bec. St Nicholas also resembled Cowick in being subject to the authority of the bishop of Exeter, who instituted the priors and occasionally intervened in their affairs, while the house also fell within the patronage of the crown as a royal foundation. At first, however, St Nicholas was regarded with hostility by the bishop of Exeter (Osbern) and the cathedral. They evidently feared the emergence of an independent foundation within the city walls and refused to allow it to have a burial ground or to ring its church bells. The monks appealed to the pope, probably through Battle Abbey, but two papal interventions were needed to settle the matter, the second of which was enforced by Anselm, the archbishop of Canterbury and himself a monk. He ordered the bishop and cathedral to give way on both issues and they did so in about 1100–2. Burials were allowed and ringing on all but three days of the year, and the monks undertook to join in the cathedral processions on Palm Sunday and Ascension Day (Barlow, *English Episcopal Acta XI*, 6–7).

The priory attracted the support of several Norman knights of Devon in the late eleventh and twelfth centuries, who no doubt saw it as a reassuringly familiar monastery with royal and Norman connections. One of them, Ruald, joined St Nicholas as a monk in later life and gave it his church of Poughill on the day that he did so in about 1100 (ibid., 5–6). The priory's endowments eventually included urban properties in Exeter given by various local people and known collectively as St Nicholas Fee, as well as half of the profits of the Lammas fair held in Southernhay on 1 August. Outside the city the priory owned land at Cullompton, Sherford, Bowley in Cadbury, and Bradham in Withycombe Raleigh, along with the

Polsloe Priory. Reconstruction by Stuart Blaylock of the west range of the cloister, the only remaining building of the priory.

Reconstruction of West Range c.1300
Axonometric Projection from N.W.

Reconstruction of West Range c.1300
Axonometric Projection from S.E.

Conqueror's churches of Cullompton, Pinhoe, and St Olave to which other benefactors added those of Affeton and Brampford Speke (with the chapel of Nether Exe), Butterleigh, and Cadbury, as well as Poughill. The priory had claims on five other churches – Clayhidon, Doddiscombsleigh, North Tawton, Rackenford, and South Tawton – but these were either lost or never secured. In 1291 the English lands were (under-)estimated to be worth £16 and the tithes and income of the English churches at about £20; the true total may have been twice as much (*Reg. Bronescombe*, ed. Hingeston-Randolph, 452–3, 455–6, 475). The history of the priory's English possessions may be studied in detail from the cartulary (the register of its charters) begun in the thirteenth century, which survives in the British Library (Cotton MS Vitellius D.ix; Davis, *Medieval Cartularies*, 45). Its contents were catalogued by Phillipps, 'List of Charters'.

The priory also established a foothold in Ireland. Two of the Anglo-Norman lords who conquered the island in the late twelfth century, Robert fitz Stephen and Miles de Cogan, granted property and churches near the south coast to St Nicholas between 1177 and 1182. The grants included an old monastic site at Begerin in Wexford harbour and the church of St Sepulchre (later St Nicholas) at Cork, after which a brother named Adam appears to have gone to organise the priory's affairs in these places. A daughter house may have been planned at one or the other and even initiated, but no permanent foundation was made. St Nicholas still owned some property in County Cork at the time of the Reformation, as well as four churches there and in County Kilkenny, but the value of the property seems to have been low and the priory may have been too weak to make much use of its church patronage (Brooks, 'Unpublished Charters', 313–66).

The priory staff consisted of a prior and five colleagues. Some of the early priors and monks were French like Cono and Ruald – it is usually hard to tell because only their forenames are recorded – but by the fourteenth century all of them were probably English. This reflected the fact that St Nicholas had an English mother house: a great advantage during the Hundred Years War when Cowick and St James encountered problems by being tied to monasteries in France. The priory buildings were dismantled or reshaped at the Reformation and much about them is unknown. The church faced east (in parallel with Fore Street) and included a choir, nave, and other areas (illustration, p. 131). There were chapels of Mary and of Thomas Becket (BL, Cotton MS Vitellius D.ix f. 115r–v), and altars of Martin and of Edward the Confessor (*Cal. Patent Rolls 1281–92*, 217), which are likely to be have been located in transepts, aisles, or in front of the stone screen that separated a monastic chancel from its nave. North of the church stood a cloister quadrangle with covered walks around it and a circular conduit house in the centre of the quadrangle for drawing water and washing. The water was conveyed at first from the cathedral and later from a well in Paul Street. The east range of the cloister included a chapter house and perhaps the monks' dormitory, and the north range the refectory. The buildings were of a high standard with much decorated stonework. Outside the cloister lay a hall for the feeding of servants, visitors, and the poor, accommodation for guests and servants, storage facilities, a garden, and a large orchard. Much rebuilding was done in about 1500 to improve the refectory, prior's chamber, guest hall, and guest rooms. The whole precinct of the priory was surrounded by walls with a gatehouse into Fore Street and possibly another into the lane called Friernhay (Allan, *St Nicholas Priory*, 4–12).

There was also a cemetery within the precinct. The cathedral's permission for this was given on condition that only monks were buried in it (D&C 2074), but approval was occasionally given for local gentry, citizens, or their wives to have graves there or in the church itself (Oliver, *Monasticon*, 126–7; Lepine and Orme, *Death and Memory*, 62, 75, 100, 107). Some wealthy people endowed religious services in the church. In the thirteenth century Robert Avenel of Broadclyst established a chantry for himself, and Robert fitz Robert of Cornwall an obit (or anniversary) mass for his benefit (Cotton MS Vitellius D.ix ff. 51v–2r, 54r–v). In 1464 Lady Maud Courtenay provided for an antiphon to be sung in honour of the Virgin Mary after compline (ECA, ED/M/838; Oliver, *Monasticon*, 124), and Stephen Ruygeway paid for a priest in 1496 to celebrate St Gregory's mass for one year and a standard mass for the year following (MCR 14–15 Hen VII m. 47d). Other obits were founded in the church by leading citizens (ECA, ED/SN/67, 72; Smith, *English Guilds*, 325–7).

An area around the priory formed a liberty which was not part of the city's parishes, and the church appears to have had a parochial role at least in terms of attracting visits from people of the neighbourhood who lived in other parishes. In the papal taxation of 1291 St Nicholas is listed both as a priory and as a parish church in the rural deanery of Exeter (*Reg. Bronescombe*, ed. Hingeston-Randolph, 452). Links with the community of the city included the wealthy laity who chose to be buried in the church, the Exeter guild of tailors which arranged to go there annually for the obit of its member John Hamelyn, formerly mayor, in 1482, and the guild of bakers which planned to hold its annual services in the church in the following year (Smith, *English Guilds*, 325–7, 335). That some local people worshipped in the church is attested by the hostility aroused when the priory was closed in 1536. An account of the charitable work of the monks written after the Reformation indicates that they gave bread, ale, and meat or fish to seven poor people every day, and the remains of the monastic dinner to other poor tenants or inhabitants of St Nicholas Fee (ECA, Chamber Act Book 4 f. 159v).

The income of the priory was reassessed by the crown in 1535, at which time its temporal lands were estimated to produce £103 2*s*. 8*d*. per annum, of which Sherford yielded £31 2*s*. 10*d*., Cullompton £27 1*s*. 7*d*., Bradham £9 5*s*. 5*d*., Bowley £7 18*s*. 0*d*., the city properties £6 2s. 1d., and other rents £21 12s. 9d. The income from the churches was £48 13s. 4d., of which Cullompton contributed £31, Pinhoe £10, Brampford Speke £3, Cadbury £2 13s. 4d., Nether Exe £2, and pensions from other churches £2 16s. 0d. The sum of £7 was still paid to Battle. This amounted to a net profit of £147 12s. 0d. (*Valor Ecclesiasticus*, ii, 313), and possibly a little more because the city revenues seem to have been undervalued (Oliver, *Monasticon*, 128). In June–July of the following year, however, Parliament enacted a statute dissolving monasteries worth less than £200 per annum, and royal commissioners came to close the priory soon afterwards, probably on 22 September (Smith, *Heads of Religious Houses III*, 109). The last prior, William Fawell alias Collumpton (who came from there and was also a suffragan bishop in the diocese), was granted a pension of £20 (*Letters and Papers, Henry VIII*, xiii part 1, p. 575), and the other monks were given the choice to move to a different monastery or become parish clergy.

According to John Hooker, the chronicler of Exeter who wrote half a century later, the closure provoked a riot. The commissioners went off to dinner, and a rumour spread that the images in the church were being removed. A group of local women, who were accustomed to worship there, heard the news and went angrily to the priory. They broke into the church and threw stones at a workman demolishing the images. Alderman John Blackaller arrived to pacify them, but Elizabeth Glandfield 'gave him a blow and sent him packing'. The women barricaded themselves in the building, and the mayor, embarrassed by the affront to the king's representatives, was obliged to come down with his officers. They forced open the church door, seized the offenders, and took them off to prison. Before the commissioners left, they asked the mayor to release the women, but the affair was still worrying the city authorities six months later (ECA, Book 51 f. 343r; *Letters and Papers, Henry VIII*, x, pp. 109–10).

Some of the buildings were pulled down very quickly, and the available stone was used to repair Exe Bridge in 1539. On 25 June 1540 the site of the monastery was granted to Sir Thomas Denys of Holcombe Burnell (*Letters and Papers, Henry VIII*, xv, 410). For the later history of the site, see Allan, *St Nicholas Priory*, 14–21, and for a more detailed history of the monastery, Orme, 'St Nicholas Priory'. The priors of St Nicholas are listed in Knowles et al., *Heads of Religious Houses I*, 89; Smith and London, *Heads of Religious Houses II*, 100–1; and Smith, *Heads of Religious Houses III*, 108–9. HER ref. ECC11054, 11170. Location SX 9177 9248.

Obley's Almshouse

In 1519 the cleric William Reygny, rector of Plymtree, bequeathed three sums of 13d. to the inmates of the almshouses of St Katherine and John Palmer and 'likewise they to have that dwelleth or should dwell within the almshouse founded by Oblegh by St Sidwell's church' (TNA, PROB 11/20/186). 'Oblegh' was either William Obley, mayor of Exeter in 1478 and 1494 who died in 1510, or a member of his family. No other reference to this almshouse has yet been found, and the phrase 'should dwell' makes it possible that a project to build one was envisaged but did not achieve completion. No HER ref. Location unknown.

St Olave

In existence by 1063, according to the texts of two Latin charters, allegedly made in that period and preserved in the fourteenth-century cartulary of St Nicholas Priory (BL, MS Cotton Vitellius D.ix ff. 39r–v, 167v; Sawyer, *Anglo-Saxon Charters*, nos 1037, 1236). The church of St Olave came into the ownership of the priory in 1087. One charter (Sawyer, no. 1236) represents Countess Gytha, widow of Godwin, earl of Wessex, and mother of the future King Harold II, granting land at Sherford (Devon) to 'the church of St Olave, king and martyr' at an undisclosed date which would have to fall between 1057 and 1065. The text explains that the land was part of her dower and that she gave it for her soul and that of Godwin. It is followed by a confirmation attributed to Bishop Leofric of Exeter and is witnessed by her sons Tostig and Gyrth together with Sa[e]win the priest. The other charter (Sawyer, no. 1037) claims that King Edward the Confessor gave two small pieces of land at Kenbury in Exminster parish (Devon) and *Lan* (an uncompleted word) to 'SS Mary, Thomas the Apostle, and Olave' in the year 1063, 'at the request of a certain priest by the name of Scepio'.

Both texts have been suspected of being later creations based on a list of charters or a prose account of the priory's lands and donors, but if they are not fully original, they do not appear to be wholly artificial productions either. If Gytha's charter was such a production, the maker might have put in Tostig and Gyrth as witnesses and Leofric as confirmator, but he would be unlikely to know or bother about Saewin. The Kenbury charter must have been derived from an earlier text containing Anglo-Saxon names that were difficult to read in later times, because it fails fully to reproduce the word *Lan* or the name of Saewin, the priest who also witnessed Gytha's grant, which the writer misread as Scepio through confusing the letter 'p' with the rune used for 'w'. The charter's mention of three patron saints of the church, including Mary, accords with the appearance of multiple saints in some church dedications elsewhere (p. 24), and an inventor would hardly have hit upon Thomas the Apostle because he occurs so rarely as a church saint. It is reasonable to conceive that Gytha's charter (or an earlier form of it) was executed at King Edward's court in 1063 and that Saewin was a priest in her retinue: a man of sufficient status to petition the king for the grant of Kenbury on the same occasion. He may be identical with Saewin the priest who held a small estate at Swimbridge (Devon) in 1086, which takes its name from him (*Domesday Book*, ed. Thorn, 13a/2).

The evidence of the charters seems acceptable too because it accords with what else is known about St Olave. The fabric of the church includes Saxon stonework that points to its existence in the eleventh century. The church site near the top of the north side of Fore Street was not far from an area behind the later priory of St Nicholas known by the twelfth century as *Irlesbery*, 'the earl's enclosure', indicating that it belonged to Godwin or Harold, earls of Wessex (ECA, ED/SN/5; Higham, *Anglo-Saxon Devon*, 187). The lands of the priory were known in later times as 'Harold's Fee' (Moore, *Shillingford Letters*, 10). Gytha was certainly the owner of Sherford, and both it and Kenbury were confiscated from her and her church by William the Conqueror, probably in 1068, and given by him to Battle Abbey, the mother house of St Nicholas Priory, between 1070 and 1085 (*Regesta Regum Anglo-Normannorum: Acta of William I*, 132–3; Searle, *Chronicle of Battle*, 80–3; *Domesday Book*, ed. Thorn, 1/4, /34). All this makes it likely that Gytha founded or endowed the church by 1063 to serve her family and its servants and tenants in Exeter.

St Olaf king of Norway (died 1030) was a recent saint widely venerated in Scandinavia, from which his fame had spread to England. Gytha came from a noble Danish family, and would have been well aware of his cult. Indeed Tostig, who was earl of Northumbria, occupied another Earlsburgh outside the walls of York which contained a church of St Olave founded by 1055 (*VCH Yorkshire: City of York*, 15, 347). It was customary to give relics to a new church, and Gytha's Scandinavian contacts would have enabled her to provide one relating to Olaf. The mention of Thomas the Apostle (placed before Olave because of his status as an apostle) suggests that she also acquired and gave the church a relic of him, and as he is an unusual saint in England this was perhaps one procured in Rome by her son Harold who may have gone there in 1056 or Tostig who certainly did so in 1061. The relics seem to have been highly regarded, because after the Norman Conquest it is said that they were taken on journeys, probably through Devon, during which sermons were preached and donations received (Searle, *Chronicle of Battle*, 82–3; compare Orme, 'Parish Processions', 73–82).

Gytha was the most exalted of the church founders of medieval Exeter, apart from the king at the minster and perhaps at St Stephen, and her church's endowments suggest that it was intended to possess both status and resources. All the churches in Exeter other than the cathedral were technically chapels (as they would come to be called in the twelfth century). They did not have parishes with secure incomes from tithes until 1222, and seem at first to have depended on voluntary donations. St Olave was favoured in this respect since the Sherford and Kenbury properties were valued at £3 2s. per annum in 1086 and supported at least one priest in 1066 (*Domesday Book*, ed. Thorn, 1/4, /34). This was not much less than the £3 15s. estimated as the total income of the four canons of the Castle Chapel in 1086 (p. 74). By 1535 the two properties were worth over £33 per annum, enough for three priests, suggesting that they were intended by Gytha to support either a very well-paid cleric (perhaps with a clerk or two) or a small body of clergy (*Valor Ecclesiasticus*, ii, 313). Sherford is in the South Hams, a good distance from Exeter, but Kenbury is only three and half miles away and looks like a glebe that was meant to supply the church's cleric or clergy with produce and fodder. One would expect a house for their accommodation as well, but if one was built it was lost as a result of subsequent events.

The Conqueror's grant of the church and its two estates to Battle Abbey was followed by the foundation of St Nicholas Priory as a daughter house of the abbey on the hill below St Olave in 1087. The priory thereafter held the patronage of the church, or rather chapel, and appropriated its estates, the clergyman presumably becoming reliant on a payment from the priory or on voluntary donations. William Bellus, 'chaplain of St Olave', occurs *c*.1200 (D&C 228) and Payne with a similar title *c*.1210–20 (BL, Cotton MS Vitellius D.ix ff. 70r, 77r, 77v–8r). St Olave is included in Peter de Palerna's list of chapels, *c*.1214 (D&C 2513), and was probably made a parish church in 1222. In 1291 it is recorded as paying a pension of 8*s*. to the priory although the rector's income in that year was described as 'scarcely sufficient to sustain a chaplain' (*Reg. Bronescombe*, ed. Hingeston-Randolph, 451–2). Despite this insufficiency, the priory continued to take the pension and in 1333 Bishop Grandisson allowed the rector to act as a chantry priest for a year to improve his income (*Reg. Grandisson*, ii, 555, 710). The rector had no house in 1408, and in that year the parishioners allowed him to build a room under the roof of the church where he might live and sleep; the room was still in being in 1539 (Oliver, 'Extracts', DD 23047–8; idem, *Ecclesiastical Antiquities*, i, 128). In 1476–7 he paid just over 10*s*. per annum to have meals with the monks of St Nicholas (Oliver, *Monasticon*, 125–6). By 1522 his income was estimated at £8 (Rowe, *Tudor Exeter*, 21) and in 1535 at £7 13*s*. 4*d*. (*Valor Ecclesiasticus*, ii, 316); the pension to the priory was still being paid in the latter year.

In 1310 Nicholas Page bequeathed property in Exeter to fund 'a chaplain celebrating divine service in perpetuity in the church of St Olave, taking five marks (£3 6*s*. 8*d*.) for his stipend', presumably as a chantry priest for Page's soul (MCR 4–5 Edw II m. 14). The subsequent history of the foundation is not known. Another local man, John Myrefyld, endowed a chaplain to celebrate for one year in 1478 (ECA, DD 22377). The church still contains the ledger-stone of Ricarda (died 1521), wife of Thomas Hoige or Hodge (Cresswell, 128–33). In 1536 the parishioners purchased a new pair of portative organs from Richard Chappinton of South Molton, 'organ builder', who undertook to maintain them and keep them in tune (Oliver, 'Extracts', DD 23048). These organs appear in the inventory of the church's ornaments and vestments made in 1552, along with three bells, a new font, and a new pulpit. The church was popularly known at this time as St 'Tooles' (Cresswell, *Edwardian*

Inventories, 61–6), a two-syllable word paralleled at churches with similar dedications in Britain.

The church is first depicted on Hooker's and Hogenberg's map of Exeter, 1587, with a tower surmounted by a low spire and four pinnacles (Hooker, *Isca*). Robert Sherwood's map of Exeter in the 1630s (Sherwood) and Hedgeland's model of Exeter, 1824, also feature a small spire. The building, the plan of which appears on the Chamber Maps of 1756×60 (ECA, Book 58/15), consists of a chancel, nave, inner north aisle, shorter outer north aisle, and tower at the south-east. Oliver mentions a former roodloft, but the religious cults in the medieval church are not recorded. The building remains in use for worship (illustration, p. 186). Photographs in Cresswell, 128, 130; Stabb, ii, plate 80. See also Parker, *Archaeological Recording at St Olave*. HER refs ECC11030, 11167. SX 9182 9246.

Palmer's Almshouse

This almshouse was founded by John Palmer, a property-owning citizen and baker of Exeter, at or shortly before his death in 1487. It lay on the north side of Magdalen Street between Wynard's Almshouse and the entrance to Southernhay, and consisted of a terrace of four small houses with a garden between them and the road (Chamber Maps, ECA, Book 58/5–6). Palmer issued a foundation deed in 1487, establishing a group of six feoffees to govern the almshouse and presumably to choose the almsfolk, the latter of whom was each to receive the modest sum of 6s. 8d. per annum. The deed and Palmer's will, in which he bequeathed each inmate a mattress, a pair of blankets, and a coverlet (DHC, Exeter, Holy Trinity/PFW 1–2), talk of the almsfolk merely as 'the poor', but by the late sixteenth century the foundation had come to cater for people of both genders. There is no mention of a chapel. The almshouse was demolished in about 1865 and rebuilt at a different site further east in Magdalen Road (Orme and Webster, *The English Hospital*, 246–7). HER ref. ECC11093. Location SX 9226 9231.

St Pancras

In existence by the 1160s when Gosfrid or Geoffrey, priest of St Pancras, witnessed grants to St Nicholas Priory (BL, Cotton MS Vit. D.ix ff. 31v, 33v), and recorded as a chapel in Peter de Palerna's grant of c.1214 (D&C 2513). It was not a cathedral possession in 1194×1204 (Barlow, *English Episcopal Acta XII*, 172–4) and was presumably already in the patronage of lay people, as it was from the time of the first recorded institution of a rector in 1324 (*Reg. Stapeldon*, 216). The chapel was probably made a parish church in 1222. Its ancient site was the same as the present one, and originally lay at the south-east corner of St Pancras Lane, leading off Paul

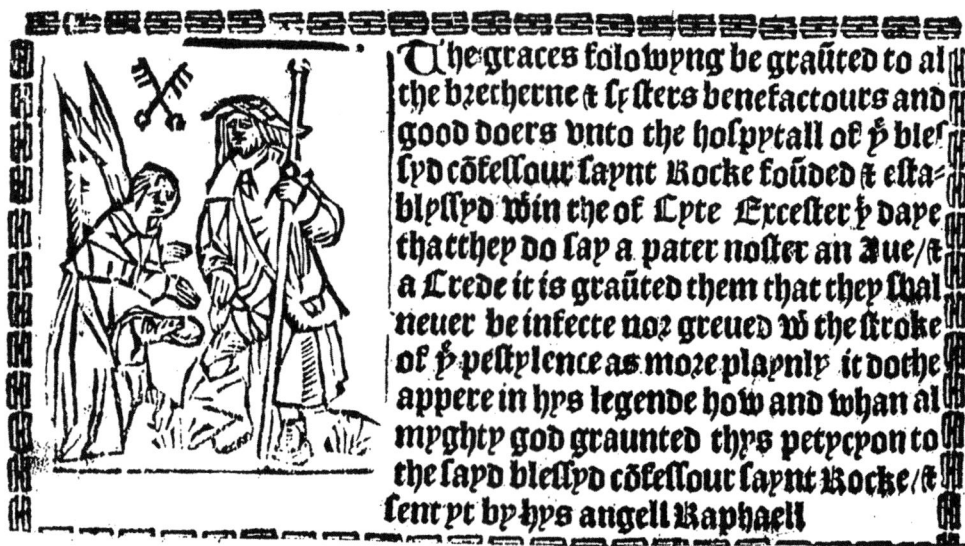

A printed letter of c.1510 offering benefits to supporters of the hospital of St Roche. The picture shows St Roche (right) and the angel and dog (carrying a loaf) who ministered to him during the plague.

Street, a little way behind the Guildhall. The ancient street pattern has been obliterated by the building of the Guildhall shopping centre. In 1291 the benefice was one of those described as 'scarcely sufficient to support a chaplain' (*Reg. Bronescombe*, ed. Hingeston-Randolph, 451). In 1522 the benefice income was valued at £5 6s. 8d. (Rowe, *Tudor Exeter*, 9) but in 1535 the rector was reckoned to be the poorest in the city with only £4 13s. 4d. (*Valor Ecclesiasticus*, ii, 316). In 1548 there were three endowed obit masses in the church (Orme, 'Dissolution of the Chantries', 107). An inventory of the church's ornaments and vestments survives from 1552, when the church possessed two bells (Cresswell, *Edwardian Inventories*, 66–9).

The church is depicted on Hooker's and Hogenberg's map of Exeter, 1587, with a small tower or bell turret (Hooker, *Isca*), on Robert Sherwood's map of the 1630s (Sherwood), and on the Chamber Maps of 1756×60 as a mere oblong (ECA, Book 58/12). Today it consists of a simple nave and narrower chancel with the bell turret at the west end and one bell (Cresswell, 134–7). The remains of a roodstair survive on the north side of the nave, indicating the usual roodscreen between chancel and nave. A glimpse of the interior in the early sixteenth century is provided by the will of John Chalmore in 1514, which provided for the donation of four tapers (large candles) to the church: to burn before the high altar, St Saviour (presumably Christ on the roodscreen), and the images of St Christopher and St Katherine (TNA, PROB 11/18/35). Photographs in Cresswell, 135–6; Stabb, ii, plate 81. The building remains in being and is occasionally used for worship (second illustration, p. 186). HER ref. ECC11031. Location SX 9192 9269.

St Paul

First mentioned *c.*1200 when the 'twenty brethren of the city of Exeter and the Kalendar brethren' transferred their rights in the chapels of St Paul and St Peter the Little to the cathedral chapter (D&C 2078). It stood in what was later called Paul Street on the east corner of the junction with Goldsmith Street. The church did not belong to the chapter in 1194×1204 (Barlow, *English Episcopal Acta XII*, 172–4), and may have been owned by the guild of Kalendars up to the time of transfer, after which it was in the patronage of the chapter. It is also mentioned as a chapel in Peter de Palerna's benefaction *c.*1214 (D&C 2513). In 1254 the guild of Kalendars owned a rent-charge on a piece of land near the church, which strengthens the case for St Paul's being its original place of meeting and perhaps for its ownership of the church (ECA, ED/M/80). Churches dedicated to Paul the Apostle on his own, as opposed to churches of Peter and Paul, are not common in medieval England, but they occur in other towns (Canterbury, Lincoln, Malmesbury, Norwich, and Stamford), and this was undoubtedly the case in Exeter. The theory that the church had a 'Celtic' origin and was dedicated to the Breton St Paul Aurelian, alias Paul de Léon, has no merit, since that saint was only venerated in England, if at all, at Paul in the far west of Cornwall (Orme, *Saints of Cornwall*, 212–13).

The chapel was probably made a parish church in 1222, and in 1285 its rector acquired the benefice and parish of St Cuthbert (p. 95). In 1291 it was one of the less poor city benefices, albeit rated at only 2*s.* (*Reg. Bronescombe*, ed. Hingeston-Randolph, 451), but after the Black Death there were difficulties in finding rectors and two were appointed *in commendam* on a provisional basis in 1349 and 1372 (*Reg. Grandisson*, iii, 1403; *Reg. Brantyngham*, i, 20). A sum of 12*d.* was bequeathed to support lights in the church in 1313 (ECA, MCR 6–7 Edw II, m. 26). In 1522 the rector's income was estimated at £10 (Rowe, *Tudor Exeter*, 14) and in 1535 at £8 2*s.* 6*d.* (*Valor Ecclesiasticus*, ii, 316). There was one endowed obit in 1548 (Orme, 'Dissolution of the Chantries', 107). An inventory of the church's ornaments and vestments survives from 1552, when the church possessed three bells, a little pair of organs, and an Easter sepulchre (Cresswell, *Edwardian Inventories*, 69–71).

The best depiction of the medieval church is on Hooker's and Hogenberg's Exeter map of 1587. This shows it as having a west tower incorporated into the nave of the church (as was usual in the city), the tower being topped by a low spire (Hooker, *Isca*). It is not clear if there were aisles. There is a less distinct image on Robert Sherwood's map of the 1630s (Sherwood). The church was rebuilt in the classical style in the late seventeenth century (Cresswell, 138–43) and its plan appears as a simple oblong on the Chamber Maps of 1756×60 (ECA, Book 58/12). It ceased to be used in 1934 and was demolished two years later. HER ref. ECC11053. Location SX 9192 9277.

St Paul – see also Cathedral

St Peter the Little

First mentioned *c.*1200 when the 'twenty brethren of the city of Exeter and the Kalendar brethren' transferred their rights in the chapels of St Paul and St Peter the Little to the cathedral chapter (D&C 2078). Since the guild of Kalendars seems to have been associated with St Paul, St Peter the Little may have been the venue of the 'twenty brethren', meaning a guild with twenty members. The chapel did not belong to the cathedral in 1194×1204 (Barlow, *English Episcopal Acta XII*, 172–4), but presumably did so after the transfer. 'Little' distinguished it from the cathedral, the great church of St Peter. It stood in the Cathedral Close near to and south-east of the chapel of SS Simon and Jude from which it was separated by a tenement, SS Simon and Jude itself lying a little south-east of Broadgate (Rose-Troup, *Lost Chapels*, 31–3, 51). The chapel appears in Peter de Palerna's list of *c.*1214 (D&C 2513) but it was apparently not made a parish church in 1222, and the loss of its guild link may have left it with little purpose. It still existed in 1281 but was transferred to lay ownership soon afterwards (Rose-Troup, *Lost Chapels*, 31–3), and had been turned into a dwelling house by 1308 (D&C 3712). A private chapel belonging to the house called 'The Eagle' stood on or near the site in the fifteenth century (p. 163). HER ref. ECC11046. Location SX 9199 9261.

St Peter – see also Cathedral

St Petroc (locally St Petrock)

First mentioned in 1194×1204 as a chapel in the patronage of the cathedral (Barlow, *English Episcopal Acta XII*, 172–4) and also as one in Peter de la Palerna's list *c.*1214 (D&C 2513). It has always occupied part of its present location in High Street. Peter, chaplain of St Petroc, occurs in 1228–9 (ECA, ED/M/38). The cult of Petroc was centred first at Padstow and later at Bodmin (Cornwall), and the saint became a popular choice as a patron saint in Devon from about the tenth century onwards. His presence in Exeter reflects that popularity and perhaps the fact that the bishops of Devon were also bishops of Cornwall and in control of Bodmin church from 1027 (Orme, *English Church Dedications*, 242). The chapel was probably made a parish church in 1222 but the rector's stipend was said, as usual in 1291, to be scarcely enough to sustain a chaplain (*Reg. Bronescombe*, ed. Hingeston-Randolph, 451). In 1366 the rector claimed that his annual income did not exceed £3 6s. 8d. (*Reg. Grandisson*, iii, 1253), but in 1426 it was valued at £5 6s. 8d. (*Reg. Lacy*, ed. Dunstan, i, 177). In 1522 it was estimated at an astonishing £26 (Rowe, *Tudor Exeter*, 18) and more realistically at £14 10s. 2d. in 1535, second only to St Mary Major within the city (*Valor Ecclesiasticus*, ii, 316). The church paid a pension of 4s. to the cathedral in c.1265 and 1408 (D&C 3721, 3642), and 16s. in 1535. In 1390 there was a proposal to unite the churches of St Mary Major, St Martin, and St Petroc but this came to nothing (D&C 3550 f. 61r–v/63r–v).

By the fifteenth century the church was one of the most flourishing within the city. It consisted of a chancel and nave to which a south nave aisle was added by 1413 when William Wilford bequeathed an annuity for the rector, priests, and other ministers to sing an antiphon before the image of the Virgin Mary in the aisle (*Reg. Stafford*, 401). Wilford's son Robert gave a pair of vestments, a missal, and a silver gilt chalice to the church in 1476 to be used in what he called 'the chapel of William Wilford' (MCR 17–18 Edw IV m. 7d), meaning this aisle, and John Kelly asked to be buried there in 1486 (MCR 3–4 Henry VII m. 10d). Wilford's reference to 'priests' beside the rector probably reflects the funding of temporary chantry chaplains to celebrate mass in the church for the souls of wealthy local people. In 1391 John Nymet left resources to maintain three such chaplains for three years, probably at least partly in St Petroc of which he was a parishioner (ECA, ED/M/527); in 1411 Simon Grendon left a bequest to every priest celebrating in the church (*Reg. Stafford*, 397); in 1420 John Talbot of Exeter instructed his wife to maintain one, probably for a limited period (ECA, Book 53A f. 84r); in 1495 William Nordon left money for a chaplain for one year (TNA, PROB 11/10/556); and Thomasia Davy did the same in 1517 (MCR 8–9 Hen VIII mm. 48–9). An outer south aisle was built in the early sixteenth century, known as the Jesus aisle, reflecting the presence of an altar of the Name of Jesus in the church at which a mass or antiphon of the Name is likely to have been celebrated like those at St George and St Mary Arches. On 22 July 1513 Bishop Oldham commissioned his suffragan bishop, Thomas Chard, to consecrate and bless the church, presumably following this enlargement (DHC, Chanter XIII f. 177v).

Churchwardens' accounts survive from 1428 (DHC, Exeter, St Petrock, PW 1–3; Dymond, 'Parish of St Petrock', 412–79). They mention, among other things, the high altar (of St Petroc) with a reredos, the rood and roodloft (with a seat thereon for the clerk who played the organs), the font and its cover, the chapel or aisle and altar of St Mary (the inner south aisle), an altar and a guild of Jesus (the outer south aisle), an image, altar, and guild of St Sythe, and images of St Anthony, St Christopher, St Dorothy, St Erasmus (patron of intestinal disorders), and St Jerome. George Oliver refers in addition to an altar of St Thomas (*Ecclesiastical Antiquities*, i, 79), possibly a shared altar because in 1483–4 there were only four altars in the church. In 1528–9 the feast-day of the dedication of the church building was changed, although the dates involved are not recorded. Meanwhile in 1505–6 liturgical material for the new feasts of the Visitation of the Virgin Mary and the

Transfiguration of Jesus was transcribed into a breviary given to the church. St Petroc, as noted above, had a small organ in its roodloft, and various people were paid to play it at major festivals such as Easter, including the rector, the parish clerk, one Saynthyll, and a certain Master John Germyn. In 1526–7 John Glasyer was employed to write masses, antiphons, the *Exultavit*, and sequences in five black books. The *Exultavit* was a polyphonic setting of the Magnificat, and the acquisition of five books suggests that the church held services with polyphonic music performed by several singers, at least on special occasions.

Altogether the church seems to have had an ambitious religious life by the end of the Middle Ages, no doubt because it was almost opposite the Guildhall in an area inhabited by some of the richer citizens. Even a chantry, rare in Exeter, was planned in the church by Thomas Elyott between 1485 and 1509, but the church's response to the Chantry Survey of 1546 claimed that it never became operative because the endowment was diverted to pay off a debt owed by Elyott to King Henry VII (Snell, *Chantry Certificates*, 10). The endowment, with an income of £4 3*s.* 6*d.*, reverted to the crown in 1548 along with that of Wilford's antiphon (Orme, 'Dissolution of the Chantries', 107). George Oliver provides a list of other obits and gifts to the church (*Ecclesiastical Antiquities*, i, 79–80). An inventory of the church's ornaments and vestments survives from 1552, when the church possessed four bells (Cresswell, *Edwardian Inventories*, 72–5). There were also internal burials of citizens, as there were in some other Exeter churches. Richard Vude asked to be buried before the image of the Virgin Mary in 1505 (TNA, PROB 11/15/487), and John Symon, mayor, beside his wife in 1524 (PROB 11/22/29). The church still contains the ledger stone of Thomas Hunt (died 1548), also mayor (Cresswell, 143–55).

The church originally consisted of a chancel and nave, to which a west tower was added above and at the north-west end of the nave (plan in Dymond, 'Parish of St Petrock', opposite 402; illustration, p. 138). As already noted a south aisle (Lady chapel, with altar of Mary) was appended by 1413, and an outer south aisle (Jesus aisle and altar) by 1513. The altar of St Sythe may have been sited within a screened area below the tower. She was a popular late-medieval Italian saint, patroness of servants, keys, and lost objects. One wonders if the guild in her name was created by or for the servants who would have abounded in the wealthy houses of the parish; if so, the ground floor of the tower would have been a suitably modest site for its altar. The church is depicted on Hooker's and Hogenberg's map of Exeter, 1587, with a battlemented tower (Hooker, *Isca*), and the tower also appears on Hooker's undated map of the Cathedral Close (D&C 3530 ff. 59–60). By the sixteenth century a row of houses had been built along High Street, against the north wall of the church, which was nevertheless still accessed from that street by a narrow entry between the houses as well as by an alley from the Cathedral Close (illustration, p. 138). An outline plan of the building, showing the two entrances, appears on the

Chamber Maps of 1756×60 (ECA, Book 58/11, 13). The church was enlarged in 1828, a new chancel added in 1881, and the adjoining houses removed in 1905. Photographs in Cresswell, 144; Stabb, ii, plate 83. The building survives but is partly used for secular purposes (first illustration, p. 187). See also Parker, *Archaeological Recording at St Petrock*. HER ref. ECC11032. Location SX 9194 9258.

Polsloe, Priory of St Katherine

Founded in or shortly after 1160 in view of the permission to have a cemetery granted in that year, discussed below, and also mentioned in 1161–2 (*Great Roll of the Pipe 8 Henry II*, 5). It was dedicated to St Katherine by 1201 (*Rotuli Chartarum*, 95). In the 1540s the foundation was attributed by the historian John Leland to William Brewer, bishop of Exeter, 1223–44 (Leland, *Collectanea*, i, 180), perhaps on the basis of a lost document involving the bishop and the priory, but not one of foundation which had happened long before the bishop's lifetime. Leland's attribution was repeated by monastic historians down to the year 1744, when John Tanner produced a revised edition of his brother Thomas's gazetteer of monasteries, *Notitia Monastica*, originally published in 1695 and now enlarged with the researches of both brothers. By this time they were aware that Polsloe had existed since at least 1200, ruling out Bishop Brewer as the founder, but being influenced by the tradition in favour of a William Brewer, they suggested rather cautiously that he was 'perhaps the nobleman' of that name who was the uncle of Bishop Brewer, a royal justice, and a wealthy land-owning magnate in Devon who founded the abbeys of Dunkeswell and Torre (Tanner, *Notitia*, 94). This new identification was repeated by subsequent monastic historians down to and including the Victorian historian of Devon, George Oliver (*Monasticon*, 162–30), who affirmed it decisively, and it has since become widely accepted although no evidence has been produced in support and the elder William Brewer, whose adult career stretched from 1179 to 1226, cannot have made a foundation in 1160.

In trying to identify the founder, it is important to note that Polsloe was the first house of nuns to be founded in the diocese of Exeter and remained the only one until shortly after 1200. It was founded near the episcopal city, albeit in a secluded place a mile away as was common when choosing a site for a nunnery, and it lay in the parish of Heavitree that belonged to the cathedral. These features point to a leading role by a bishop of Exeter who wished to provide a house in his diocese for women with religious vocations. The bishop must have been Robert II ('Robert of Chichester') who reigned from 1155 to 1160. Little is known about him, but it has been suggested that he 'gave Exeter a good shaking up; and suddenly the church appears livelier, less provincial, more cultured than before' (Barlow, *English Episcopal Acta XI*, p. xxxix). The priory's endowments came not from a single wealthy benefactor but a variety of people and consisted of fairly small properties scattered in south and east Devon. It looks as though Bishop Robert and his successor, Bartholomew, 1161–84, either initiated a project in which wealthy lay people joined, or added their support to a foundation by one or more moderately wealthy knights. The earliest records of the endowments point to the involvement of William de Tracy (probably the murderer of Thomas Becket, fl. 1155–74); Henry de Pomeroy (either Henry I, died c.1165, or his son Henry II, died 1207); Bishop Bartholomew himself; King Henry II, who granted an annuity in 1177–8; and King John while count of Mortain, 1189–99 (*Rotuli Chartarum*, 95; Barlow, *English Episcopal Acta XI*, 110; *Great Roll of the Pipe 24 Henry II*, 10).

The nuns of Polsloe followed the Rule of St Benedict. Their priory, as has been mentioned, lay in the cathedral's parish of Heavitree and was subject to the bishop and the cathedral, the bishop having the status of patron of the priory and the cathedral allowing it, by the grant of 1 March 1160, to have a cemetery for the sole use of its sisters and priests, in return for paying tithes to Heavitree church from its lands in the parish (D&C 1374). The priory's chief endowments consisted of land in Polsloe itself, Cokesputt in Payhembury, and Tudhays in Colyton, along with smaller properties in Withycombe Raleigh and the South Hams, together with the churches of Aylesbeare, East Budleigh, Holbeton, and (briefly) Upton Hellions (Devon), as well as Marston Magna (Somerset). In 1291 the lands and churches belonging to the priory were estimated to be worth about £40 per annum, and the true total may have been twice as much (*Reg. Bronescombe*, ed. Hingeston-Randolph, 456–7, 475). Seventeen nuns elected a prioress in 1347 (*Reg. Grandisson*, ii, 1016), but here as elsewhere numbers fell after the Black Death, and in 1438 there were only nine nuns at an election (*Reg. Lacy*, ed. Hingeston-Randolph, i, 241–3), although the complement increased a little by the time of the Reformation.

The priory was situated a little way north of the present Pinhoe Road and to the west of Mincinglake (meaning 'the nuns' stream'), near the present St Katherine's Road. Its church was apparently divided by a screen into a shorter nave and a longer chancel, without aisles. The nuns would have said the daily services in the chancel, but the celebration of mass at the high altar required a lay chaplain. One such man, Thomas Bannaster, asked to be buried in the chancel in 1534 (Oliver, *Monasticon*, 164). A chapel dedicated to St Thomas Becket adjoined the church by 1347 (*Reg. Grandisson*, ii, 1018), and in 1442 William Wynard of Exeter bequeathed the substantial sum of eighty marks (£53 6s. 8d.) to build a new bell-tower (TNA, PROB 11/1/181). South of the church stood a roofed four-sided cloister, with the chapter house and the domestic buildings of the nunnery on its east, south, and west sides. The west range of these buildings still survives, comprising a structure of three storeys. This range appears to have included a parlour and storage area on the ground floor, with the prioress's chamber and the hall for the use of servants and guests on the first floor

(Blaylock, *St Katherine's Priory*, 1–30; illustration, p. 146). Other discussions of the priory and its endowments may be found in Oliver, *Monasticon*, 162–9, and the works of Blaylock, Everett, Lega-Weekes, and Loe contained in the Bibliography.

In January 1320 Bishop Stapledon issued injunctions to the nuns which give a general sense of how they were expected to live (*Reg. Stapeldon*, 316–18). The convent day centred on the saying of the daily services in Latin but the women were not required to have a full understanding of the language. The bishop's injunctions were written in French, and he told the nuns that when they needed to ask one another for things in church, they should use simple Latin words such as *candela*, *liber*, and *vinum* without regard to grammatical rules. They were required to seclude themselves from outsiders as much as possible. No nun might leave the house except with the permission of its head, and only in the company of a colleague, chosen by the head of the house not the nun. If a nun gained leave of absence on another occasion, a different colleague should be assigned to go with her. Nevertheless, the nuns had a good deal of contact with the city of Exeter, and there are number of bequests to them in the wills of local clergy and men of the merchant class (*Reg. Stafford*, 382, 397, 399, 401, 411, 418, etc.).

The priory acquired a coat of arms of which three versions are known, including 'sable, a sword erect between two Katherine wheels argent' (Lega-Weekes, 'St. Katherine's Priory', 1937, 450–1). In 1535 its income was estimated at £164 8*s*. 11¼*d*. Its chief temporal possessions were then the manor of Polsloe producing £53 11*s*., Tudhays £12 14*s*. 8½*d*., and Cokesputt £8 15*s*. 11¼*d*., while the churches of Holbeton yielded £30 9*s*. 9*d*., East Budleigh £26 17*s*. 3*d*., Marston Magna £8, and Aylesbeare £6 13*s*. 4*d*. respectively (*Valor Ecclesiasticus*, ii, 315). In the following year religious houses with incomes of less than £200 were dissolved by act of Parliament, but Polsloe paid a large fine of £400 to escape (*Letters and Papers, Henry VIII*, xii (i), p. 144, 531; xiii (ii), p. 177). The fine had not been wholly paid when the priory was forced to surrender to the king on 19 February 1539 at the time that all the monasteries of Devon were closed. The act of surrender was signed by the prioress and thirteen nuns (ibid., xiv part 1, p. 124), who received pensions. On 1 February 1542 the site of the monastery and the manor of Polsloe were granted for life to Sir George Carew and his wife Mary at an annual rent of £29 3*s*. 1*d*. (Oliver, *Monasticon*, 168–9). On 19 July 1549 they were awarded, subject to the life interest of the Carews, to John Dudley, earl of Warwick (later duke of Northumberland), from whom they soon passed to other owners (*Cal. Patent Rolls 1549–51*, 2–4).

The earliest prioresses have not been recorded; those from 1216 are listed in Smith and London, *Heads of Religious Houses II*, 599–600, and Smith, *Heads of Religious Houses III*, 681–2. For more information on the priory, see Orme, 'Polsloe Priory'. HER ref. MDV15173. Location SX 9415 9383.

The medieval church of St Sidwell from the Chamber Maps of 1756×60, depicting the tower with a projecting staircase and the south aisle of the nave and chancel.

Private Chapels

As well as public chapels, there were private ones or oratories in the houses of the more important clergy and laity. The earliest recorded is the Castle Chapel, in being by 1086, although that was an unusually grand and perhaps semi-public institution. The Bishop's Chapel in his palace existed by 1142, and that of St Radegund in the house of the archdeacon of Cornwall did so by 1221; it is described in the next entry. Other cathedral clergy probably possessed chapels in their houses during the thirteenth century, and a survey of canons' houses in 1301 mentions five of them (*Reg. Stapeldon*, 153–4). Bishops of Exeter issued licences for several others in the houses of canons or other Exeter clergy during the fourteenth and fifteenth centuries (*Reg. Stapeldon*, 299; *Reg. Grandisson*, ii, 651, 687; *Reg. Brantyngham*, i, 231, 384; ii, 680; *Reg. Stafford*, 273, 275–6, 278–9, 282, 382, 384, 389; *Reg. Lacy*, ed. Dunstan, i, 101, 220; iii, 73). There was also a chapel at the house of the prebendary of Hayes in St Thomas (p. 78). After Bishop Lacy's time, licences are very rarely found: probably because they were not recorded rather than not granted. Remains of one chapel survive at No. 10 Cathedral Close, now the residence of the dean (Portman, *Exeter Houses*, 7, 9, 13, 69–70). It is not clear if all such chapels had dedications, the only ones recorded being St Radegund and that of St Mary in the house of William Fawell (p. 141).

Chapels in the houses of lay people in Exeter were less common, but acted as status symbols for people of wealth. Such chapels also needed to be licensed, and records of licences survive for Roger and Isabel atte Welle in Exeter in 1376 (*Reg. Brantyngham*, i, 366), Henry and Joan Tirelle at Wonford in 1387 (p. 127), Nicholas Bowedon at Larkbeare in St Leonard's parish in 1416 (*Reg. Stafford*, 272), Ricarda Grendon in St Petroc's parish in 1414 (ibid., 275), Isote, widow of Robert Wilford of the same parish in 1404 (ibid., 283), Richard Holand and his wife in Cowick Street (St Thomas) in 1429 and John Schaplegh in the same year (*Reg. Lacy*, ed. Dunstan, i, 220), and John Salter, saddler, in 1433 (ibid., i, 254). The Wilford chapel, also mentioned in 1437 and 1481, lay at the back of a major house in the High Street called 'The Eagle', and was originally built in about 1392 (Lega-Weekes, 'Hospitium de le Egle', 484; idem, *Topography of the Cathedral Close*, 15–16). Licences for lay people, like those for the clergy, cease to be recorded in the mid fifteenth century, so several others may have been issued to Exeter citizens between then and the Reformation.

St Radegund

In 1219–1221 there are mentions of a chapel of St Radegund (*Redegundis*), also referred to as an oratory, at the house of the archdeacon of Exeter (perhaps for a period that of the archdeacon of Cornwall) in Palace Gate (D&C 295; Lega-Weekes, *Topography of the Cathedral Close*, 112–14). Radegund, a Frankish queen of the sixth century, was popular among Normans, and religious houses dedicated to her were founded at Cambridge and Thelsford (Warws.) in the twelfth century. The chapel was presumably the private oratory of the archdeacon's house, but formal enough to have an altar and dedication. It should not be confused with the altar of SS Richard and Radegund in the cathedral, recorded in 1284, which seems to have prompted the dedication to Radegund of the chapel of Bishop Grandisson by the cathedral west door, although the linkage of Radegund with that chapel is only recorded in 1350 (Orme, *Exeter Cathedral*, 174–7). HER ref. ECC11126. Suggested location SX 9212 9238.

St Roche

A hospital of St Roche (pronounced in Exeter as 'Rock') is first mentioned in 1506, when the bishop of Exeter licensed the collection of alms for its support. In 1521 a similar licence refers to it as the hospital of Blessed Mary the Virgin, the Eleven Thousand Virgins, and St Roche, and mentions it as caring for poor infirm people. A printed letter of about 1510 survives which promised protection from the pestilence for all who became its brothers, sisters, or benefactors (Orme, 'A Letter of St Roche', 153–9; illustration, p. 154). St Roche was the patron saint of plague victims. The hospital was situated in Coombe Street, possibly towards the north-west end, the street being also known as St Rocke's Lane until the nineteenth century. It must have included a chapel in view of its dedication. The mention of 'brothers and sisters' points to the existence of a confraternity of supporters, perhaps even a guild. In view of the hospital's dependence on voluntary contributions, it does not appear to have had significant endowments, and seems to have been short-lived because there are no references to it before 1506 or after 1521 (Orme and Webster, *The English Hospital*, 247–8). HER ref. ECC11585. Suggested location SX 9200 9233.

St Sidwell

A religious building must have existed on this site by the eleventh century, when Sidwell (*Sativola* in Latin) is mentioned in two litanies and in a catalogue of relics belonging to the minster or cathedral of Exeter (Conner, *Anglo-Saxon Exeter*, 186–7), as well as in a national list of saints and their resting places. She was believed to have been a local virgin murdered by a mower or mowers, and was thought to be buried in the church (Orme, *Saints of Cornwall*, 234). There is no corroborative evidence with which to establish whether she existed and, if so, when, although a reference in the ninth-century Breton Life of St Paul de Léon to a virgin named Sitofolla living near the English Channel may indicate that her cult was in being by 900 (ibid.). It is unlikely that St Sidwell is the church mentioned in Domesday Book, 1086, as belonging to the bishop (p. 13), and the building is first formally recorded in 1153. It was then described as a church in the patronage of the cathedral (DHC, Chanter 1001; Oliver, *Lives of the Bishops*, 19), but a record of 1194×1204 calls it a chapel in the same patronage (Barlow, *English Episcopal Acta XII*, 172–4). The cathedral owned a large area of land around the church and outside the East Gate, known by the fourteenth century as 'St Sidwell's Fee'.

The church probably always occupied its later site beyond the gate and a little way off the north side of Sidwell Street. After the creation of parishes in 1222, it became a parochial chapel with a sub-parish within the parish of Heavitree, which also belonged to the cathedral (Orme, 'Medieval Chapels of Heavitree', 122; illustration, p. 15). It is called a chapel in Peter de Palerna's list *c*.1214 (D&C 2513) and John, 'chaplain of St Sidwell', occurs in a deed of the 1220s (ECA, ED/M/23). On the other hand a document of 1225 terms it a church whereas St David, with a similar status, was designated a chapel (Barlow, *English Episcopal Acta XII*, 224), and in the 'Taxation of Pope Nicholas IV', 1291, what appears to be the parish of Heavitree is described as 'St Sidwell' (*Reg. Bronescombe*, ed. Hingeston-Randolph, 465). This is also true in the *Valor Ecclesiasticus*, 1535 (ii, 293), possibly because St Sidwell's Fee was a prominent area within Heavitree parish. In 1401 St Sidwell was definitely described as a chapel dependent on Heavitree, whose vicar received all the offerings in return for bearing the burdens of the chapel, which presumably included the payment of its curate or parish chaplain (*Reg. Stafford*, 126). The chaplain and parish clerk are also mentioned in 1330 (Lepine and Orme, *Death and Memory*, 162).

The chapel contained the tomb of Sidwell, to which William Hodell gave a legacy to provide lights in 1400 (BL, Add. Ch. 27580) and Philip Courtour likewise in 1421 (ECA, ED/M/682). The saint was also associated with a well to the maintenance of which John de Doulys bequeathed an acre and a half of land in 1267 (Lepine and Orme, *Death and Memory*, 144; ECA, ED/MAG/47). On Hooker's late sixteenth-century map of St Sidwell's Fee, the well is shown as a small castellated structure in the middle of what is now Well Street, north of the chapel (D&C 3530 ff. 37–8). The chapel had its own cemetery by 1345 (ECA, MCR 18–19 Edw III m. 30), and seems to have prospered in the later Middle Ages, no doubt through the growth of the suburbs within its sub-parish. In 1299 Andrew Kilkenny, dean of the cathedral, gave a rent of 2*s*. to the 'vicar of St Sidwell' (presumably of Heavitree) to build an altar of St Andrew in the church of St Sidwell (D&C 394). Kilkenny was also responsible for the altar of St Andrew in the cathedral, but there is no subsequent reference to the altar in St Sidwell. An altar of St Mary is recorded in 1307 (MCR 34–35 Edw I m. 33), and the cross (i.e. the rood) together with the altars of St Mary and St Nicholas in 1314 (MCR 7–8 Edw II m. 27). Notes from a missal of the church copied into the cartulary of the hospital of St John mention lights before SS Sidwell and Mary, 'wardens' of St Mary (in charge of either a church store or a guild in her honour), and three endowed obits (ECA, Book 53A f. 36v). In 1395 William Rowe bequeathed money for several obits and for the lights of St Mary, St Michael, and St Katherine, as well as to the light of 'the old holy cross': perhaps a superseded but venerated crucifix from the roodscreen (ED/M/542). Hodell gave money to the fabric of the church in 1400 in return for an obit (BL, Add. Ch. 27580), and Courtour requested burial before the image of St Katherine and mentioned her 'store' of assets in 1421 (ED/M/682). In 1503 Robert Rawlens left money for a priest to sing mass for his soul for one year, probably in St Sidwell (TNA, PROB 11/13/487), and in 1548 there were twelve endowed obits in the church (Orme, 'Dissolution of the Chantries', 107). An inventory of the church's ornaments and vestments survives from 1552 when the church possessed four bells (Cresswell, *Edwardian Inventories*, 75–82).

Like most of the Exeter churches, St Sidwell was enlarged during the later Middle Ages, but the conjecture that it was 'wholly rebuilt and consecrated' by Bishop Lacy in 1437 (Cresswell, 156) is a mistake based on the consecration of Laneast church (Cornwall) which was also dedicated to Sidwell (*Reg. Lacy*, ed. Dunstan, ii, 44). The enlargement is more likely to have happened in stages. There must have been one or more aisles or chapels by the early fourteenth century to house the altars of Andrew, Mary, and Nicholas, and there was evidently one nave aisle by 1503 when Robert Rawlens bequeathed 'to the making of an aisle, 20*s*., with the condition that it be made according to the other' (PROB 11/13/487). This second nave aisle must have been built shortly afterwards since it is mentioned in later records. The fullest description of the medieval building occurs in a ground plan made by M. Nosworthy in 1793 with some elevations to show the proposed insertion of galleries. By this date the church consisted of a short chancel, a nave with north and south aisles, and a projecting west tower. Two arcades of five bays divided the aisles from the nave and the main entrance was on the south side towards the west with a smaller door, perhaps a priest's door, further east. The windows of the north aisle were in the Perpendicular style with three lights (DHC, Exeter, St Sidwell 34294–9/PW 9). There was a roodscreen between the chancel and nave, and early armorial bearings were glazed in the windows including the arms of Edward the Confessor (Polwhele, *History of Devonshire*, ii, 27; Jenkins, *History of Exeter*, 341–2; Cresswell, 155–63).

The church is depicted on Hooker's and Hogenberg's city map, 1587 (Hooker, *Isca*) and on Hooker's plan of St Sidwell's fee, in each case as a simple unit with a tower topped by four pinnacles (D&C 3530 ff. 37–8). On the Chamber Maps of 1756×60 the tower is depicted with a projecting south-east staircase (ECA, Book 58/7; illustration, p. 162). The medieval church was rebuilt in 1812 retaining the piers of the old arcade (Cresswell, 158), badly damaged by bombing in 1942, and built anew in 1957. HER ref. (church) ECC11033, 11198. Location SX 9245 9307. HER refs (well) ECC11020, 11560. Location SX 9255 9321.

SS Simon and Jude

First mentioned in 1194×1204 as a chapel in the patronage of the cathedral (Barlow, *English Episcopal Acta XII*, 172–4). However there is a suggestive reference to a local man named Simon of St Simon in 1159–60 (D&C 1374); perhaps he was the founder. The chapel stood in the Cathedral Close, a little way south-east of Broadgate, while on its other side a tenement separated it from the chapel of St Peter the Little (Rose-Troup, *Lost Chapels*, 40–1). It was not included in Peter de Palerna's list of chapels in *c.*1214 or apparently made into a parish church in 1222. However Geoffrey, 'chaplain of St Simon', is mentioned in *c.*1250 (D&C 178), and there are further allusions to the chapel in a deed of 1263 and a cathedral rental of 1265 (D&C 49, 3721). It may still have existed in 1275 when there is a reference to an entry to a cellar through its wall (D&C 3672, pp. 353–4), but it probably disappeared soon afterwards like its neighbours St Mary Minor and St Peter the Little. HER ref. ECC11040. Location SX 91979260.

St Stephen

The Exon text of Domesday Book in 1086 states that the bishop of Exeter owned one church 'in Exeter' (*Domesday Book: Additamenta*, ed. Ellis, p. 111 (f. 120v)), or 'in the city' according to the Exchequer text of the Book (*Domesday Book*, ed. Thorn, 2/1), and that the forty-seven houses and their inhabitants belonging to him there were linked with this church. The church has been conjectured as St Stephen, a possession of the bishop in later times and one that gave its name to St Stephen's Fee, the term for his properties in the city. Two charters attributed to Henry I (*c*.1107) and Stephen (1136) allege that William the Conqueror (died 1087) gave the church of St Stephen to Bishop William Warelwast (1107–37) while William was his chaplain (*Regesta Regum Anglo-Normannorum*, ii, 72; iii, 106–7). But Bishop William can hardly have been old enough for this post by 1087, and the charters appear to be fabrications produced on the bishop's behalf at a later date to justify and backdate his possession of the church so that St Stephen's Fee could be safely identified with the properties mentioned in Domesday Book. A more authentic charter of Henry I, dated 1123, confirmed a grant of the church of St Stephen (Exeter) to Bishop Warelwast which the king (i.e. Henry) had previously given him at some date from 1107 onwards (ibid., ii, 185). If Henry I gave (rather than restored or confirmed) it, the bishop would not have possessed it in 1086 and it cannot have been the church attributed to him, which was more probably the cathedral or rather that part of it represented by the church of St Mary Major (pp. 13–14). Instead St Stephen is likely to have been the unnamed church in Exeter that belonged in 1066 to King Edward the Confessor. From him it passed to William the Conqueror, who evidently gave it to his favoured half-brother Robert count of Mortain, the owner in 1086 (*Domesday Book*, ed. Thorn, 15/1). In 1106 Henry seized the property of Robert's son and heir William, and this would explain how the church came into his hands.

St Stephen is next mentioned by name as a chapel in 1177×1184 (Barlow, *English Episcopal Acta XI*, 87), and it appears again as a chapel in Peter de Palerna's list *c*.1214 (D&C 2513) in its present location on the south side of High Street. Oliver, 'chaplain of St Stephen', occurs in a deed of the 1220s (BL, Cotton MS Vitellius D.ix f. 104v). By the early thirteenth century the church was associated with St Stephen's Fee, the bishop's properties in the city (Curtis, *Disputes*, 14–15), and we have suggested that it took over this role from St Mary Major at some point during the twelfth century (p. 14). A manorial court, called the 'court of St Stephen' was held every three weeks by 1289 to administer the bishop's rights and properties (Hobbs, *Cartulary of Forde*, 107), and it is very likely that the court met in the church, which would explain the name of St Stephen's Fee. The name cannot have related to a parochial connection between the church and the bishop's properties after 1222, when the city was divided into parishes, because St Stephen was then given a parish limited to parts of High Street rather than one that embraced the scattered properties. The bishop continued to be the church's patron throughout the Middle Ages, but the benefice was not a wealthy one after 1222 since the rector's income was valued at only 2*s*. in 1291 (*Reg. Bronescombe*, ed. Hingeston-Randolph, 451) and was more truthfully only £7 16*s*. 11*d*. by 1535 (*Valor Ecclesiasticus*, ii, 316).

In 1320 John de Bovey granted a rent of 11s. in Exeter to the churchwardens of St Stephen. He was a chaplain who owned some property in Exeter (ECA, ED/M/163) and apparently functioned in the church by 1304 (MCR 32–33 Edw. I m. 3). Bovey instructed the wardens to pay a priest to celebrate mass every Saturday at the altar of St Gabriel in the church and to maintain lamps there and at the altar of St John the Baptist. An anniversary mass for the donor was also to be celebrated in the church. If any Saturday mass was not celebrated, 1d. was to be given to a poor person; the rest of the money was to be used for the benefit of the church (*Cal. Patent Rolls 1317–21*, 533). The altar of St Gabriel is likely to have been erected by Bishop Bronescombe (1258–80) who had a devotion to this saint and promoted his cult at the cathedral, at Bishop's Clyst east of Exeter, and at Stoke Gabriel. From the late fourteenth century the rectors of St Stephen were often also chaplains of the Bishop's Chapel in Exeter (p. 72). An inventory of the church's ornaments and vestments survives from 1552, when the church possessed three bells (Cresswell, *Edwardian Inventories*, 82–4).

The history of the church building has been reconstructed in detail by Stewart Brown, although it is likely that the chronology of its development is sometimes earlier than he suggests (Brown, *St Stephen's Church*, 17–24). He discerns the building as existing in the late Anglo-Saxon period when it probably comprised a chancel and a nave with the unusual feature of a crypt beneath the chancel, supporting the chancel floor on four columns and perhaps used for the display of relics. This mark of status would accord with a church belonging to the king in 1066. The crypt was reconstructed as a vaulted space in the twelfth century and may have had two staircases to reach it from the church above. Two Norman columns survive from the reconstruction, but the crypt is now sealed up and not visible. Later, perhaps in the late twelfth or thirteenth centuries, further changes were made, not necessarily all at the same time. The church was extended eastwards by building the 'bow' or archway across the adjoining street; this formed a chancel higher than the rest of the church and was reached by a flight of half a dozen steps. The nave was also extended laterally with the addition of arcades leading to narrow north and south aisles, and a new stair to the crypt was built on the north side of the church.

Brown suggests that the nave aisles date from the fifteenth century, but their narrow dimensions are more typical of the twelfth or thirteenth. Moreover one is likely to have been in place by 1280 in view of Bishop Bronescombe's probable foundation of the altar of St Gabriel by that date, and the other by 1320 when we hear of the altar of St John. Altars needed eastward-facing spaces, and the two could plausibly have stood at the east end of each aisle. George Oliver's conjecture that the altar of St John stood above the bow may be dismissed (*History of Exeter*, 157). During the fourteenth or fifteenth centuries a south chapel was built beyond the east end of the south aisle, with the likely purpose of providing a Lady chapel. Later still the south aisle was broadened for the whole of its length as far as the outer wall of this chapel, which was thereby incorporated in the larger aisle. This would still have left space for two altars at the east end of the aisle. A western tower was also built, extending west of the nave, but there was no evidence for further work on the crypt which may have become disused in the later Middle Ages. The ambitious scale of these enlargements suggests that the church had a higher than usual status among its sisters in the city. This no doubt reflected the fact that it belonged to the bishops, who had the resources to develop it, and its role in relation to St Stephen's Fee.

The church is first depicted on Hooker's and Hogenberg's map of Exeter, 1587, with a tower surmounted by a corner turret for access (Hooker, *Isca*). The tower also appears on Hooker's undated plan of the Cathedral Close (D&C 3530 ff. 59–60) and on Robert Sherwood's map of the 1630s (Sherwood). Much rebuilding took place in 1664–5, and the resulting ground plan of the church is shown on the Chamber Maps of 1756×60 (ECA, Book 58/13). Further alterations were made in the nineteenth and twentieth centuries. The building remains in being and in use (illustration, p. 187). See also Cresswell, 163–8 with photograph. HER refs ECC11034, 11194, 11397. Location SX 92119273.

Ten Cells – see Grendon's Almshouse

St Thomas

The foundation date of St Thomas may be narrowed down to the period between 1173 and 1190–1, since it was dedicated to Thomas Becket who was canonised in the former year and is first mentioned in the latter (DHC, W1258M/G6/46). Its original site was just beyond the west end of Exe Bridge, at the beginning of the east side of Alphington Street and almost opposite the opening of Cowick Street (ECA, ED/M/161; DHC, W1258M/G4/28). It was owned by the monks of Cowick Priory whose motive for building it may have been to serve the suburb centred on Cowick Street as well as to exploit the cult of a new and popular saint beside the recently rebuilt bridge at a focal point of roads where passers-by might pray and leave offerings. The cult of Thomas Becket aroused devotion in Devon soon after his death, an early supporter being Bishop Bartholomew (died 1184) (Orme, *Church in Devon*, 67–8). At first the building had only the status of a chapel, and it appears as such in Peter de Palerna's list *c.*1214 (D&C 2513) and in the reference that follows. Nothing is known about its structure or furnishings except for a record of 1259 concerning a piece of ground in the prebend of Hayes west of Exe Bridge which paid 3*d.* at Easter to the light of Blessed Mary in the chapel of St Thomas, indicating an image of the Virgin there (Oliver, 'Ancient Church', 157).

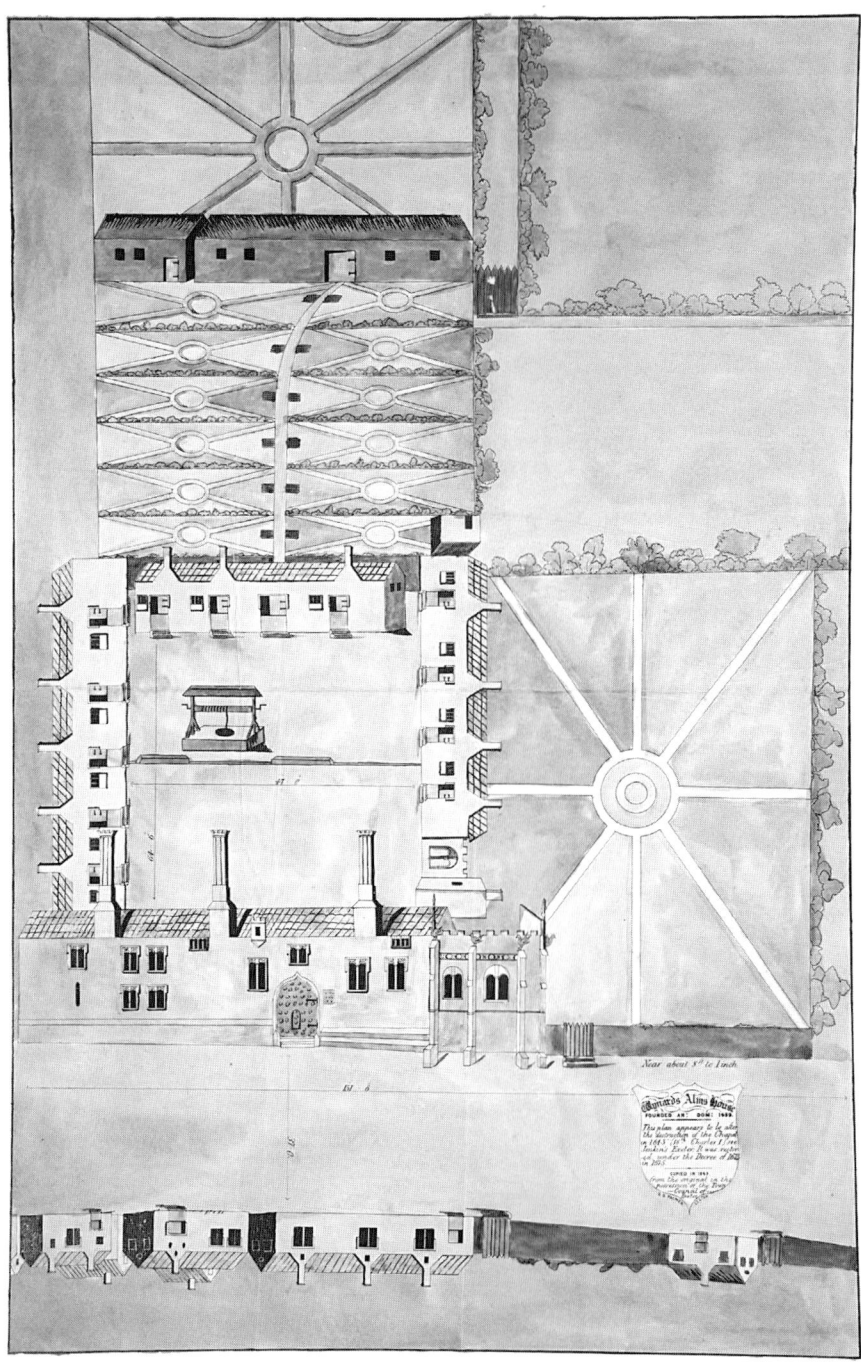

Wynard's Almshouse, from a seventeenth-century plan. The main frontage along Magdalen Street is shown towards the bottom, with the chapel to the right, a quadrangle of dwellings behind containing a well, and surrounding gardens.

The parish church of the area west of the bridge, i.e. Cowick, was the priory church of St Andrew (p. 90), which the parishioners shared with the monks and where they were buried in a churchyard outside the priory. In 1261 Bishop Bronescombe intervened to establish a vicar of the parish, observing that there had not previously been one; presumably the monks had paid a chaplain to do parish work. The bishop instituted a priest named Henry as vicar, but referred to his church as 'the church of St Andrew of Cowick', meaning the priory church and implying that Henry would chiefly officiate there, although he doubtless did so at St Thomas as well. The bishop ordered that the vicar and his successors should have a house and a stipend of £3 6s. 8d. (*Reg. Bronescombe*, ed. Hingeston-Randolph, 127); they were subsequently appointed by the monks of Cowick who held the advowson or patronage of the parish. At some point during the next eighty years, however, the vicar's activities moved to centre on St Thomas rather than St Andrew and the chapel came to be regarded unofficially as a parish church. This was the case by 1346 when the king claimed the right to appoint clergy to 'the vicarage of the church of St Thomas by Exeter' instead of the monks (who belonged to a French abbey) while the wars with France were in progress (*Cal. Patent Rolls 1345–8*, 108).

The chapel by Exe Bridge was damaged or destroyed by a flood in the first years of the fifteenth century, after which the monks of Cowick and the parishioners built the present church on a new site belonging to the priory in Cowick Street. Bishop Stafford dedicated and consecrated the building on 4 October 1412 and the high altar and cemetery on the following day. His record of the event supports the document of 1346 by stating that the vicar of Cowick had previously performed all parochial functions at the riverside chapel, except for burials which took place at the priory. He formally declared the new church to be the parish church of Cowick, and issued an indulgence of forty days' remission of penance to all who attended the church on 4 October, the feast-day of its dedication (*Reg. Stafford*, 73). The provision of a cemetery at the new church enabled parishioners to be buried there, but for a long time some people continued to be interred at the old burial ground by the priory (p. 144).

The late-medieval church seems to have come to consist of a chancel, a nave with north and south aisles (in order to accommodate the cults of SS Katherine, Mary, and Michael described below), and a west tower. In 1429 John Brygon of Cowick Street bequeathed money to the fraternity of the Virgin Mary in the church, implying a statue and probably an altar in her honour, and to the repair of the altar of St Katherine (TNA, PROB 11/3/342). In 1506 Roger Holand requested burial in the guild (i.e. aisle) of St Michael (PROB 11/15/2), and in 1521 Isabel Carew of the Cornish family of that name also asked for a grave in the church, giving money to the church store of St Thomas and the store of the Virgin Mary, and arranging for two friars to celebrate mass in the church for her soul on two days of the week for one year (Orme, *Cornish Wills*, 166). A third such request was that of John Rugge, the vicar in 1536, who wished to be buried in the chancel 'before the image of St Thomas', i.e. on the north side of the high altar (Cresswell, 'John Rugge', 166). In 1535 the vicar's stipend was estimated at £11 2s. 7½d. (*Valor Ecclesiasticus*, ii, 318). The vicar of the church in 1549, Robert Welch, was a leader of the 'Commotion' or 'Prayer-Book Rebellion' in Devon and was hanged from the church tower after its suppression (*Oxford Dictionary of National Biography*).

The monks of Cowick Priory were also patrons of the small nearby church of Oldridge. This was a separate parish in 1291 (*Reg. Bronescombe*, ed. Hingeston-Randolph, 455), but the income available to the clergyman was very small. The church probably ceased to have a resident rector after the Black Death of 1349 and is likely to have been served thereafter by a monk or chaplain from Cowick on an occasional basis. As a result the parish of Oldridge came to be regarded as an outlying part of St Thomas parish and its church as a subordinate chapel-of-ease. As for the church of St Thomas, it is first depicted on Hooker's and Hogenberg's map of Exeter, 1587, but only as a tower surmounted by four corner pinnacles (Hooker, *Isca*; illustration, p. 27). The church was burnt in the Civil War, rebuilt in 1646, and the north aisle extended in 1828 (Oliver, *Ecclesiastical Antiquities*, i, 52–9; Cresswell, 168–82). It remains in use as a parish church (illustration, p. 188). Photograph, Cresswell, 169. HER refs (old church by Exe Bridge) ECC11052. Location SX 9156 9209; (new church in Cowick Street) ECC11144, 11451. Location SX 9255 9320.

St Thomas – see also St Olave

Topsham, St Margaret

First mentioned in 1153 when it was described as a church dedicated to St Margaret and as the property of the cathedral (DHC, Chanter 1001; Oliver, *Lives of the Bishops*, 18–20). The building still possesses a Norman font, probably from the twelfth century, which is a sign of a parish church. In 1194×1204, however, the church was designated as a chapel in a list of the cathedral's possessions, showing that it was regarded as subject to the cathedral like the chapels within the city, having probably lain within the rural part of the large former parish of the Exeter minster and cathedral (Barlow, *English Episcopal Acta XII*, 172–4). Its location was doubtless always at its present site, and it is likely to have been formally made a parish church in 1222 along with the city churches. Three years later Bishop Brewer confirmed it as a possession of the cathedral (ibid., 224–5), and by 1295 it had its own cemetery (Lepine and Orme, *Death and Memory*, 148–9). The parish became a peculiar jurisdiction of the cathedral, in other words outside the normal administration of the diocese, and the cathedral appropriated all the tithes and revenues so that there was no vicar unlike Heavitree but merely a chaplain paid by the cathedral canon who 'farmed' or leased the parish revenues from the cathedral chapter. As a result no institutions of clergy are recorded in the bishops' registers of the Middle Ages. In 1295 Rosamund Kymming bequeathed small sums to the light of the church, the parish chaplain, and the parish clerk (ibid.).

A visitation of the church was made by two canons of the cathedral in 1281. It listed the books, ornaments, and vestments, stated that the glebe included thirty-two acres with a house and curtilage, and that two houses had been given to support the light in the church. The church's revenues were valued at £12 (D&C 3672A), which, of course, went to the cathedral not the chaplain. This estimate was more accurate than that of the 'Taxation of Pope Nicholas', 1291, which rated the church's income at only £5 (*Reg. Bronescombe*, ed. Hingeston-Randolph, 465). Records of a further visitation survive from 1330 and also list the contents of the church (*Reg. Grandisson*, i, 576). In 1436 Bishop Lacy allowed the dedication feast of the church (the anniversary of the building's dedication) to be changed from the Friday after Easter to 3 July, and granted an indulgence of forty days to those who attended the feast (*Reg. Lacy*, ed. Dunstan, ii, 3). In 1535 the tithes of grain and the glebe were said to be worth £12 per annum and the 'altarage' or other tithes and offerings a further £5 (*Valor Ecclesiasticus*, ii, 294).

Nothing remains of the medieval church except for the font and the tower (illustration, p. 189). The latter was built or rebuilt in the fifteenth or early sixteenth century of red sandstone without buttresses and containing a stair turret. A plan of the church in 1844 shows that it consisted of a nave, a north aisle with an arcade of five bays, and a south aisle which enfolded the tower and therefore consisted of two parts, east and west of the tower (DHC, Topsham 1417A add. 2/PW5). This church was replaced in 1874–6, except for the tower. HER ref. MDV9950. Location SX 9654 8803.

Trinity, Holy

First mentioned in 1194×1204 as a chapel in the patronage of the cathedral (Barlow, *English Episcopal Acta XII*, 172–4) and as a chapel in Peter de Palerna's list, c.1214 (D&C 2513). The building stood inside and close to the South Gate (see below) on the north-east side of South Street. It was probably made a parish church in 1222, and in later centuries the parish included a small area within the city walls (to which the parish of St James was added in the mid fourteenth century) and a larger one outside, stretching to the River Exe on the west and the Shitbrook or Shutbrook on the south, as far as St Mary Magdalene hospital. The rector's income was rated as poor in 1291 (*Reg. Bronescombe*, ed. Hingeston-Randolph, 451), but suburban development probably helped to raise his stipend to £11 16s. 4d. in 1535 (*Valor Ecclesiasticus*, ii, 317). The church paid a pension of 5*s.* to the cathedral in *c.*1265, 6*d.* in 1408 (D&C 3721, 3642), and 3*s.* 8*d.* in 1535. In 1302 Emma Wadekyng bequeathed £2 13*s.* 4*d.* to endow a chantry for one year in the church for her soul and those of her family (ECA, MCR 29–30 Edw I m. 43), and in 1334 a rent of 12*d.* was granted by a private householder in return for permission to build a house wall on the south wall of the church. The money was to provide a candle burning before the image of the Trinity (ECA, ED/M/317).

The church was partly rebuilt in 1404; during the rebuilding the rector and parishioners worshipped in the hall of Sir William Bonville's house in the parish (*Reg. Stafford*, 271). The church, 'newly erected and constructed', was relicensed for worship on 27 September 1404 (ibid., 100). Light is shed on the church before its rebuilding by an enquiry of 1442 which came about because the church's consecration and dedication with its right to keep a dedication festival were being called in question; it is not clear why. Nine lay jurors testified that the church was believed to have been consecrated and dedicated from time immemorial and that the dedication festival had been observed on 30 September; there was written evidence of this in the calendar of an old breviary in the church. Previous to the rebuilding, the church had an upper floor or solar where the parishioners heard mass at a stone altar, and a lower floor containing three altars, one of the Virgin Mary and one of St Loye whose statue stood in a niche beside it. There was also a stone font and the grave of John Susseter, formerly rector. While John Govys was rector (i.e. in 1404), the roof and the upper floor were demolished because of age, and the south and west walls were taken down and rebuilt so as to enlarge the church; the north wall remained as it was, but was raised a little to carry the roof. A new chancel was built, the old font was kept, and the mensa of the old high altar was reused in the new one. The church had always possessed a processional way (*Reg. Lacy*, ed. Dunstan, ii, 259–63).

Churchwardens' accounts of Trinity church survive from about 1428 (DHC, Exeter, Holy Trinity, PW 1–3). They reveal the existence of a substantial fraternity of St George in the church by 1478, which had its own wardens, raised money, procured an indulgence from the bishop in 1483 to assist in this respect, and paid for the saying of a weekly mass for the souls of its brothers and sisters. By 1519 there was a group of maidens who raised money called 'the maidens' silver' at Whitsuntide. An altar and image of St George stood in the church; by 1534 these were in an 'ambulatory', meaning a nave aisle which is mentioned in other sources. Reference is made to two altars outside the choir, to an image of St Katherine, and to an organ-player who functioned on the church's principal feasts: Christmas, Candlemas, Easter, Ascension Day, Whitsunday, Trinity Sunday, Corpus Christi, and the feast of the dedication of the church building. In 1487 John Palmer, the benefactor of the almshouse that bears his name, requested burial in the church before the high cross and founded an obit in his memory (DHC, Exeter, Holy Trinity, PFW 1–2). John Govys had already established an obit in 1416 (*Reg. Stafford*, 415) and Robert Were endowed another in 1465 (Holy Trinity, PFW 11). At the dissolution of the chantries in 1548 there were four such commemorations in the church (some of which are mentioned in the churchwardens' accounts) as well as an endowment for two candles to burn before the high cross (Orme, 'Dissolution of the Chantries', 107). An inventory of the church's ornaments and vestments survives from 1552 when the church possessed three or four bells and a little pair of organs (Cresswell, *Edwardian Inventories*, 85–7).

The nave aisle was an addition of the early sixteenth century. In 1516 the city chamber agreed that the wardens and parishioners might rent an area measuring 24 by 12 feet (7.3 by 3.6 metres) 'for the building of an ambulatory' (ECA, Chamber Act Book I f. 59v; II f. 22v). In 1529 the chamber made a grant of a slightly larger area 34½ feet long and 13¾ feet wide (10.5 by 4.1 metres) on the south side of the church, on which the 'new ambulatory' was now built (ECA, ED/M/1013). The earliest picture of the church is on Hooker's and Hogenberg's map of Exeter, 1587, where it is shown simply as a tower topped by four pinnacles next to the South Gate (Hooker, *Isca*). It appears in similar form on Hooker's undated map of the Cathedral Close (D&C 3530 ff. 59–60) and on Robert Sherwood's map of the 1630s (Sherwood). The Chamber Maps of 1756×60 depict the plan as a chancel, nave, and south aisle extending the whole length of the church. The tower was at the north-west corner of the nave, and the entrance was through the north side of the tower (ECA, Book 58/11, 14). Jenkins (*History of Exeter,* 376) describes the south aisle as separated from the nave by an arcade of six piers, and the tower as projecting into the street. An engraving of the church was published in 1831–2 (Sprake, *Gates*; compare illustration, p. 190). Meanwhile the late-medieval building was demolished in 1819 and rebuilt further north in the following year. The new church was closed in 1968 and transferred to secular use. HER ref. ECC11047. Location SX 9211 9231.

Trinity – see also Castle Chapel; Christchurch; Wynard's Almshouse

Tuckers Hall

The fraternity or guild of the Assumption of the Blessed Virgin Mary is first mentioned in 1471, when its wardens acquired a piece of land in the parish of St John Bow, probably where the modern Tuckers Hall stands on the north side of the lower part of Fore Street (ECA, 58/7/2/3/1). The fact that the wardens included two weavers, a fuller, and a shearman shows that this was a guild of these workers in the cloth industry. A later note in the city records states that a chapel was built between 13 May 1471 and 21 December 1472 (ECA, Chamber Act Book III, p. 2).

The chapel was definitely in existence by 1479 (ECA, MCR 19–20 Edw IV mm. 3–4), and was also dedicated to the Assumption of the Virgin (compare St Mary Mincinglake, p. 141). In 1494–5 the guild appears to have hired a priest to serve in the chapel on an occasional basis (ECA, 58/7/2/3/2), but in 1523 it received permission from Bishop Veysey and Plympton Priory (patron of St John Bow, the parish in which the chapel lay) to maintain a priest in the chapel and to receive all the profits. The priest was forbidden to minister the sacraments in the parish or to celebrate mass until the gospel and offering were over at the high mass at St John Bow, and the guild promised to pay 3s. 4d. per annum to the parish church (ECA, ED/M/1004).

When the first chantry survey was made in 1546, the guild was still employing a priest, oddly described as functioning in the church of St Mary Arches (perhaps a mistake for the chapel of St Mary), with an income of £6 0s. 6d. gross, £5 5s. 0d. net (Orme, 'Dissolution of the Chantries', 107). In 1547, however, the guild, foreseeing the dissolution of chantries, converted the chapel into its guildhall (the wagon roof of the chapel still survives above the hall) and did not report the endowment at the chantry survey of 1548. As a result, much later on, the chapel was granted by the crown to Anthony Kynwelmersh in 1574, probably having been seized as a piece of concealed chantry property, but it was eventually returned to the guild (for secular use and no doubt at a price) in 1578 (ECA, Misc. Roll 22 m. 38). The document of return contains another odd feature in referring to the chapel's cemetery, which it ought not to have had because of the monopoly of burials by the cathedral. See also Youings, *Tuckers Hall*, 9–20. HER ref. ECC11163. Location SX 9173 9235.

Vicars Choral, College

Planned in 1382 and built by 1387 as dwellings for the twenty vicars choral of the cathedral, largely on the initiative of Bishop Brantingham. The site in Kalendarhay had an unspecified connection with the guild of Kalendars, probably as their private graveyard, possibly as the site of a guildhall; the Kalendars apparently transferred their property to the vicars choral during the fourteenth century (p. 120). The buildings consisted of a gatehouse towards the cathedral, leading to a lane fringed by a double row of houses for the vicars. At the end of the lane stood a common hall, backing on to South Street but without entry to it. In 1401 the vicars were legally incorporated as a college, and the buildings subsequently came to be known as 'the college' as well. The site never had its own place of worship. Between 1547 and the 1560s the number of vicars was reduced to four priests and eight laymen, and the resident community gradually declined until by the mid nineteenth century only one house was occupied by a vicar and the rest by lay tenants. The houses, which by this time were regarded as unsatisfactory, were demolished between 1850 and 1893; the college was abolished as a legal entity in 1933; and the hall was damaged by bombing in 1942 and never rebuilt. Its ruins are the only visible remnant of the community. Further information will be found in Chanter, 'Custos and College', 1–52; Orme, 'The Medieval Clergy of Exeter Cathedral: I, The Vicars and Annuellars', 79–91; idem, 'The Kalendar Brethren', 158–9; John Allan, 'The College of the Vicars Choral', 29–43; and Orme, *Exeter Cathedral*, 32, the latter two works with a reconstruction of the buildings. HER ref. ECC11121. Location SX 9199 9252.

Wells, Holy

The history of holy wells is difficult to reconstruct, because most of the information about them comes from the nineteenth and twentieth centuries (Brown, 'Holy and Notable Wells', passim) when folklore and romance often attributed sanctity to wells without ancient historical evidence (Orme, 'Medieval Holy Wells', 130). At least two wells in Exeter were regarded as holy before the Reformation. St Sidwell's Well in Well Street (p. 165) probably dated back to late Anglo-Saxon times. Its water was used for general purposes, but seems to have had a reputation for sanctity and the well eventually acquired a substantial well-house to protect it. Parker's Well in Matford Lane, as we have seen, was linked with the chapel of St Clair by the fifteenth century (p. 88). A third well, at the junction of Paris Street and Heavitree Road, is described as that of St Catherine in 1806 and has a separate entry (p. 83). It was said to have once had an adjoining chapel, but the existence of the chapel and the antiquity of the well have yet to be established.

Wynard's Almshouse

Founded in the 1430s by William Wynard, a lawyer who was recorder of Exeter from 1418 to 1442. Its site was that of its surviving buildings: at the north-east end of Magdalen Street, outside and beyond the South Gate. In 1436 Wynard issued an ordinance prescribing how the almshouse was to operate, followed by a deed or charter in 1439 which specified its endowments and provided for Wynard and his heirs to act as patrons of the foundation with power to appoint the inmates (Oliver, *Monasticon*, 404–7). The patronage passed to the Stonor family of Oxfordshire and later to the Spekes of Somerset. The statutes laid down that the almshouse should be known as 'God's House' and should provide lodgings for twelve poor and sick people in separate houses; these were built round a quadrangle. Each inmate, most of whom were men, received an allowance of 8*d*. a week. The buildings included a chapel dedicated to the Holy Trinity and staffed by a chaplain nominated by the patron. Wynard's ordinance required the inmates to attend one mass daily in the chapel and another daily in the nearby Franciscan Friary, at which the literate almsfolk were to say a seventh part of the psalter while the illiterate repeated the Paternoster (Lord's Prayer) and Ave Maria.

The chapel consisted of a nave with two small windows leading (probably through a screen) to a chancel containing five large windows (Parker and Collings, 'St Catherine's Almshouses', 129). There was still a chaplain in 1548 with a stipend of £5 6s. 8d., but the dissolution of the chantries in that year led to the confiscation of the chaplain's share of the endowment by the crown (Orme and Webster, *The English Hospital*, 242–4). The almshouse and chapel were damaged during the Civil War, rebuilt thereafter, and again rebuilt in medieval style in the nineteenth century. The layout of the buildings, however, is largely the original one. A seventeenth-century plan shows the buildings arranged in a quadrangle with the chapel at the south-west corner. A well stood in the quadrangle, and there were gardens on the south and east sides (Devon and Exeter Institution, D17; illustration, p. 170). The Chamber Maps of 1756×60 depict the almshouse as a similar quadrangle with gardens only to the east (ECA, Book 58/5). The almshouse community continued in being until the second half of the twentieth century, but the buildings are now a centre for community projects. The chapel survives. HER ref. ECC11092. Location SX 9235 9231.

John Hooker's map of St Sidwell's Fee, late sixteenth century. The left-hand fold includes (left) St Mary Magdalene hospital and above it Wynard's Almshouse. The right-hand fold shows (top) the Castle Chapel and (centre left) St Sidwell with its well tower nearby.

St Anne's chapel, from the west end of the building.

St David. The medieval church as it was in 1756×60, with tower, nave, chancel, and a north aisle that may have included an eastern Lady chapel.

Dominican Friary. Head of an effigy of a knight, one of several of the aristocracy formerly buried in the church.

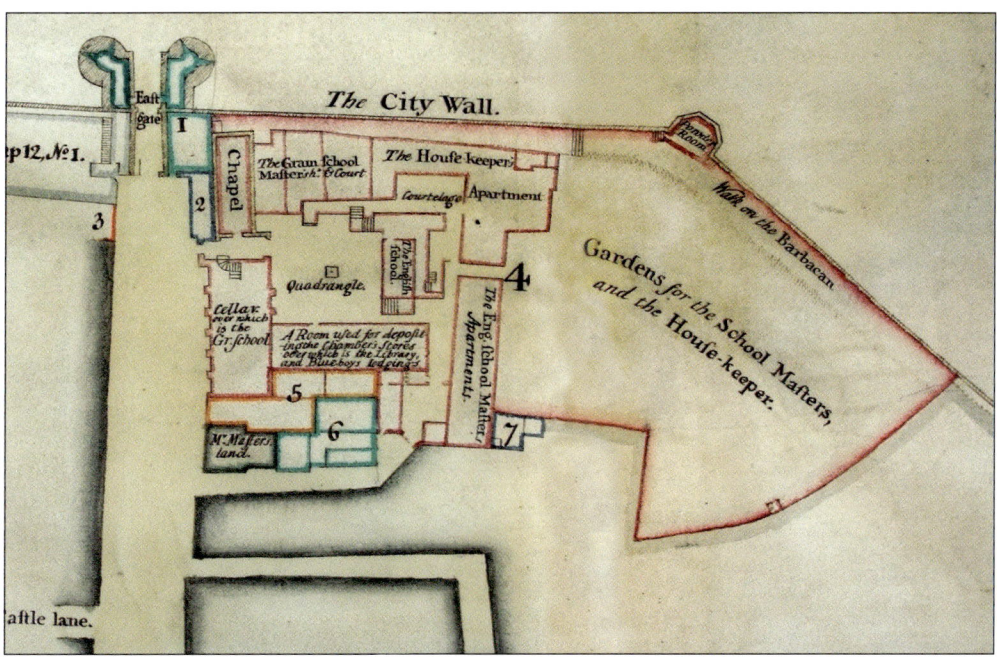

The hospital of St John from the Chamber Maps of 1756×60. By this time the chancel was a chapel and the nave a grammar school, while vestiges of the cloister remain to their right.

The frontage of St Katherine's Almshouse, Catherine Street. Behind it lay a kitchen, rooms along alleys for almsfolk, and a chapel.

A rare image of St Kerrian church from the Chamber Maps of 1756×60, showing the west end of the church in North Street with a small bell turret above the west window.

St Martin's church, consecrated in 1065 and substantially rebuilt in the fifteenth century when the tower was added.

St Mary Major before its replacement in 1865. The original tower was much higher and carried an impressive steeple.

St Mary Steps, sited opposite what was once the West Gate of the city and the approach to Exe Bridge.

St Olave church, Fore Street, founded in about the early 1060s but much enlarged in later times.

St Pancras, one of Exeter's smallest churches, with the nave left, the chancel right, and a small bell turret.

The original nave and tower of St Petroc church from the north. The high windows reflect the former presence of houses against the church wall.

St Stephen, originally a smaller church of nave and chancel, later enlarged with a chancel across the 'bow' or arch, aisles, and a tower.

The second church of St Thomas, built in 1412 in Cowick Street. The exterior is largely work of the seventeenth and nineteenth centuries.

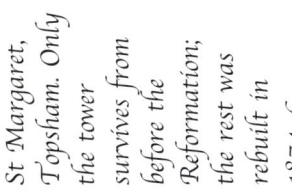

St Margaret, Topsham. Only the tower survives from before the Reformation; the rest was rebuilt in 1874–6.

The medieval church of Holy Trinity by the South Gate, c.1820. The church was entered under the tower, and its nave, chancel, and aisle lay left of the tower.

Bibliography

UNPUBLISHED SOURCES

Cambridge, King's College
    KCAR/3/3/1/1/1, Ledger Book 1
    SJP, St James Priory documents
Exeter, Cathedral Archives
    D&C 23, Deed
    D&C 49, Deed
    D&C 178, Deed
    D&C 228, Deed
    D&C 287, Deed
    D&C 295, Deed
    D&C 394, Deed
    D&C 1374, Grant of cemetery to Polsloe Priory
    D&C 2074, Agreement regarding St James Priory
    D&C 2078, Grant to guild of Kalendars
    D&C 2099, Deed
    D&C 2111, Union of churches of St Cuthbert and St Paul
    D&C 2513, Peter de Palerna bequest
    D&C 2538/2, Will of John Bradeworth
    D&C 2737, 2753, Debt rolls
    D&C 3518, Martyrology and list of obituaries
    D&C 3530, John Hooker's maps of Exeter
    D&C 3550, Chapter act book 1383–1434
    D&C 3642, Reference by Frances Rose-Troup to an unlocated financial record
    D&C 3672, General cartulary
    D&C 3675, Obit book of the vicars choral
    D&C 3712, Accounts of stewards of the exchequer
    D&C 3721–2, Rental of cathedral property
    D&C 3750/1–4, Excrescence books
    D&C 3773, Ordinary and extraordinary expenses and exchequer views
    MS 3515, Missal
    VC/3074, Deed
    VC/3219, Deed

Exeter, Devon and Exeter Institution
　　Diocesan Architectural and Archaeological Society Scrapbooks
Exeter, Devon Heritage Centre (formerly Devon Record Office)
　　Chanter XIII, The register of Hugh Oldham
　　Chanter XIV, The register of John Veysey, part i
　　Chanter XV, The register of John Veysey, part ii
　　Chanter 1001, Papal bull of 1153
　　DD 3204, Deed
　　DD 22377, Will of John Myrefyld
　　DD 36765–9, St John Bow, Churchwardens' accounts
　　DD 38034, Lease
　　DD 67952, Deed
　　DD 70884–9018, St Mary Steps, Churchwardens' accounts
　　ECA, 48/series, Deeds
　　ECA, 51/series, St Mary Major deeds
　　ECA, 58/series, Deeds
　　ECA, Book 51, Hooker's Annals of Exeter
　　ECA, Book 53A, Cartulary of St John's Hospital
　　ECA, Book 58, Chamber maps of 1756×60
　　ECA, Chamber act books
　　ECA, D/2, 20, 23, St Mary Magdalene records
　　ECA, Drawer 2, Hooker's map of St Sidwell, late sixteenth century
　　ECA, Mayor's court rolls
　　ECA, ED/AWL series, Awliscombe deeds
　　ECA, ED/BC series
　　ECA, ED/M series, Exeter deeds
　　ECA, ED/MAG series, St Mary Magdalene deeds
　　ECA, ED/SN series, St Nicholas Priory deeds
　　ECA, L618, Robert Sherwood's map of Exeter, 1630s
　　ECA, L619, John Hooker's manuscript map of Exeter, 1590s
　　ECA, Miscellaneous Rolls
　　Exeter, Holy Trinity, PW 1–3, Churchwardens' accounts
　　Exeter, Holy Trinity, PFW 1–11, Parish documents
　　Exeter, St Leonard, 1862A/PW 113
　　Exeter, St Mary Arches, deeds
　　Exeter, St Mary Major, PW 1–5, Churchwardens' accounts
　　Exeter, St Petrock, PW 3, Churchwardens' accounts
　　Exeter, St Sidwell, PW 9, Churchwardens' records
　　TA and TM, Tithe apportionments and maps, listed under parishes
　　Topsham, 1417A add. 2/PW 5
　　W1258M Bedford deeds
Exeter, Royal Albert Memorial Museum
　　Caleb Hedgeland's model of Exeter, 1824
Exeter University Library
　　M. P. D. Collison, 'The Courtenay Cartulary', MA Thesis 1972 COL 1–2

London, British Library
    Additional Charters 13913, 27580, 27631, 32988–9
    Additional MS 6027, Plans of John Norden
    Additional MS 49359, Courtenay Register
    Cotton MS Cleopatra C.vii, Cartulary of Merton Priory
    Cotton MS Vitellius D.ix, Cartulary of St Nicholas Priory
London, Lambeth Palace Library
    The Register of William Courtenay
    MS 721, Taxation list *c*.1490
London, The National Archives
    C 1, Chancery, Early chancery proceedings
    C 143, Chancery, Inquisitions ad quod damnum
    E 36, Exchequer, TR, Books
    E 40, Exchequer, TR, Ancient deeds
    E 199, Sheriffs' accounts
    E 315, Exchequer, Augmentations, Miscellaneous books
    PROB 11, Probate Court of Canterbury, Registered copy wills
    SC 6, Special collections
Oxford, Bodleian Library
    MS Digby 81
Powderham Castle
    Courtenay Cartulary, Q4/282, used in the transcript by M. P. D. Collison, above

PUBLISHED SOURCES

Allan, John P. *Medieval and Post-Medieval Finds from Exeter, 1971–1980*, Exeter Archaeological Reports, 3 (Exeter, 1984).

Allan, John P. *St Nicholas Priory*, Exeter (Exeter, 1999).

Allan, John P. 'The College of the Vicars Choral of Exeter', in *Vicars Choral at English Cathedrals*, ed. Richard Hall and David Stocker (Oxford, 2005), 29–43.

Allan, John P. *An Archaeological Survey of the South Wall of St Stephen's Church, Exeter* (Exeter, Exeter Archaeological Report, 5097, 2005), summarised in *Post-Medieval Archaeology*, 39 (2005), 345, 348.

Allan, John P., Austin, Jeremy, and Collings, Anthony S. 'Observations on the Site of Cowick Priory, Exeter', *Devon Archaeological Society Transactions*, 66 (2006), 135–40.

Allan, John P., Henderson, C. G., and Higham, R. A. 'Saxon Exeter', in *Anglo-Saxon Towns in Southern England*, ed. J. Haslam (Chichester, 1984), 385–414.

Archaeological Assessment and Field Evaluation of the Princesshay Redevelopment Scheme, Exeter (Exeter, Exeter Archaeology Report, 02.15, 2002).

Ashworth, Edward. 'Account of the Church of S. Mary Major, Exeter', *Exeter Diocesan Architectural Society*, 2nd series 2 (1867–71), 24–8.

Barlow, Frank. (ed.) *English Episcopal Acta*, vol. XI: *Exeter 1046–1184* (London and Oxford, 1996).

Barlow, Frank. (ed.) *English Episcopal Acta*, vol. XII: *Exeter 1186–1257* (London and Oxford, 1996).

Barlow, Frank, and others. *Leofric of Exeter* (Exeter, 1972).

Bearman, Robert. (ed.) *Charters of the Redvers Family and the Earldom of Devon*, Devon and Cornwall Record Society, new series 37 (1994).
Biddle, Martin. (ed.) *Winchester in the Early Middle Ages*, Winchester Studies 1 (Oxford, 1976).
Bidwell, P. T. *The Legionary Bath-House and Basilica and Forum at Exeter* (Exeter, 1979).
Blair, John. *The Church in Anglo-Saxon Society* (Oxford, 2005).
Blair, John, and Orme, Nicholas. 'The Anglo-Saxon Minster and Cathedral at Exeter: Twin Churches?', *Friends of Exeter Cathedral 65th Annual Report* (1995), 24–6.
Blaylock, Stuart R. 'Exeter Guildhall', *Devon Archaeological Society Proceedings*, 48 (1990), 123–78.
Blaylock, Stuart R. *St Katherine's Priory, Polsloe: fabric survey of the west range 1979–80*, Exeter Museums Archaeological Field Unit, Report 91.57 (Exeter, 1991).
Blaylock, Stuart R., Higham, Robert A., and Passmore, Andrew. *Excavations and Building Recording at Exeter Castle, 1984–2009* (Exeter Archaeology Reports, forthcoming).
Blaylock, Stuart R., and Westcott, K. A. 'Late Saxon Fabric in St Martin's Church, Exeter', *Devon Archaeological Society Proceedings*, 47 (1989), 119–22.
Bowers, Roger. 'Liturgy and Music in the Role of the Chantry Priest', *Journal of the British Archaeological Association*, 164 (2011), 130–56.
Brooks, E. St J. 'Unpublished Charters Relating to Ireland, 1177–82, from the Archives of the City of Exeter', *Proceedings of the Royal Irish Academy*, 43 (1935–7), 313–66.
Brown, Stewart. *St Stephen's Church, Exeter: archaeological fabric recording and excavation during reordering works 2011–12* (Stuart Brown Associates, March 2012).
Brown, Stewart. *Excavations on the Medieval Exe Bridge, St Edmund's Church and Frog Street Tenements* (Exeter, Exeter Museums Archaeological Field Unit Report 91.52, 1991); to be republished as *The Medieval Exe Bridge, St Edmund's Church, and Excavation of Waterfront Houses* (Exeter, 2014).
Brown, Theo. 'Holy and Notable Wells of Devon', *Devonshire Association Transactions*, 89 (1957), 205–15; 90 (1958), 60–1; 91 (1959), 36–7; 92 (1960), 101–3; 95 (1963), 131–4; 98 (1966), 154–6; 107 (1975), 43–5.
Buck, Samuel and Nathaniel. *The South West Prospect of the City of Exeter* (London, 1736).
C., E. I. 'Church of St. Edmund on the Bridge, Exeter', *The Gentleman's Magazine* (February, 1835), 148–50.
Calendar of Close Rolls, 1272–1509, 47 vols (London, Public Record Office, 1892–1963).
Calendar of Inquisitions Post Mortem (London, Public Record Office, 1904–, in progress).
Calendar of Patent Rolls (London, Public Record Office, 1891–, in progress).
Chanter, J. F. *The Bishop's Palace Exeter and Its Story* (London, 1932).
Chanter, J. F. 'The Custos and College of the Vicars Choral of the Choir of the Cathedral Church of St. Peter, Exeter', *Exeter Diocesan Architectural and Archaeological Society*, 3rd series, 5 part 1 (1933), 1–52.
Cheney, Mary, et al. (ed) *English Episcopal Acta*, vol. XXXIII: *Worcester: 1062–1118 5* (London and Oxford, 2007).
Cherry, Bridget, and Pevsner, Nikolaus. *Devon*, The Buildings of England, 2nd edn (London, 1989).
Cherry, John. 'The Silver Seal of Thomas Dene, Prior of St James in Exeter', *Devon Archaeological Society Proceedings*, 41 (1983), 138–9.
Clarke, Kate M. 'Records of St. Nicholas Priory, Exeter', *Devonshire Association Transactions*, 44 (1912), 192–205.

Conner, Patrick W. *Anglo-Saxon Exeter: a tenth-century cultural history* (Woodbridge, 1993).
Cramp, Rosemary. *Corpus of Anglo-Saxon Stone Sculpture, VII: South West England* (London, 2006).
Cresswell, Beatrix F. *Exeter Churches* (Exeter, 1908).
Cresswell, Beatrix F. (ed.) *The Edwardian Inventories for the City and County of Exeter*, Alcuin Club, 20 (1916).
Cresswell, Beatrix F. 'John Rugge, Vicar of St Thomas by Exeter', *Devon and Cornwall Notes and Queries*, 17 (1932–3), 166–7.
Crocker, James. *Sketches of Old Exeter* (London, 1886).
Curtis, Muriel E. *Some Disputes between the City and the Cathedral Authorities of Exeter* (Manchester, 1932).
Davis, G. R. C. *Medieval Cartularies of Great Britain: a short catalogue* (London, 1958).
Dickinson, F. H. (ed.) *Missale ad Usum Insignis et Praeclarae Ecclesiae Sarum* (Burntisland, 1861–83).
Dictionary of Medieval Latin from British Sources, ed. D. R. Howlett and others (London, 1975–2013).
Documents Preserved in France, Illustrative of the History of Great Britain and Ireland, 918–1206, ed. J. H. Round (London, 1899).
Domesday Book, IX: Devon, 2 vols, ed. C. and F. Thorn (Chichester, 1985). Original text and translation of the Exchequer Domesday.
Domesday Book: Additamenta, ed. H. Ellis (London, Record Commission, 1816). Original text of the Exon Domesday.
Duckett, G. F. *Visitations of English Cluniac Foundations* (London, 1890).
Dymond, Robert. *History of the Suburban Parish of St Leonard, Exeter* (Exeter, 1873).
Dymond, Robert. 'The History of the Parish of St. Petrock, Exeter, as shown by its churchwardens' accounts and other records', *Devonshire Association Transactions*, 14 (1882), 402–92.
Edwards, Kathleen. *The English Secular Cathedrals in the Middle Ages*, 2nd ed. (Manchester, 1967).
Emden, A. B. *A Biographical Register of the University of Oxford A.D. 1501–1540* (Oxford, 1974).
English Episcopal Acta, vol. XXXIII: *Worcester: 1062–1185*, ed. Mary Cheney et al. (London and Oxford, 2007).
Everett, A. W. 'St Katherine's Priory, Exeter', *Proceedings of the Devon Archaeological Exploration Society*, 2 (1934), 110–19.
Everett, A. W. 'Polsloe Priory: a remarkable architectural feature', *Devon and Cornwall Notes and Queries*, 18 (1934–5), 170–1.
Everett, A. W. 'Ancient Tiles at St. Katherine's Priory, Polsloe', *Devon and Cornwall Notes and Queries*, 18 (1934–5), 212–13.
Everett, A. W. 'Polsloe Priory', *Devon and Cornwall Notes and Queries*, 20 (1938–9), 42–3.
Everett, A. W. 'St John's Church, Exeter', *Devon and Cornwall Notes and Queries*, 20 (1938–9), 176–7.
Everett, A. W. 'St Loye's Chapel, Wonford', *Devon and Cornwall Notes and Queries*, 21 (1940–1), 62–5, 131.
Everett, A. W. 'St. Lawrence Church, Exeter', *Devon and Cornwall Notes and Queries*, 22 (1942–6), 314–16.

Falla, Trevor. *Heavitree* (Exeter, 1983).
Fiennes, Celia. *The Journeys of Celia Fiennes*, ed. Christopher Morris (London, 1947).
Fizzard, Allison D. *Plympton Priory. A House of Augustinian Canons in South-Western England in the Later Middle Ages* (Leiden and Boston, 2008).
Foréville, Raymonde. 'Manifestations de lollardisme à Exeter en 1421', *Le Moyen Age*, 69 (1963), 691–706.
Fox, Aileen. *Roman Exeter* (Manchester, 1952).
Francis, David. *Lost Churches* (Exeter, 1995).
Gover, J. E. B., Mawer, A., and Stenton, F. M. *The Place-Names of Devon*, 2 vols, English Place-Name Society, 8–9 (1931).
Graham, Rose. 'The Cluniac Monastery of St Martin des Champs, Paris, and its Dependent Priories in England and Wales', *Journal of the British Archaeological Association*, 3rd series, 11 (1948), 35–59.
The Great Roll of the Pipe for the Eighth Year of the Reign of King Henry the Second, A.D. 1161–2, Pipe Roll Society, 5 (1885).
The Great Roll of the Pipe for the Twenty-Fourth Year of the Reign of King Henry the Second, A.D. 1177–1178, Pipe Roll Society, 27 (1906).
Hale, W. H., and Ellacombe, H. T. (ed.) *Account of the Executors of Richard Bishop of London 1303, and of the Executors of Thomas Bishop of Exeter 1310*, Camden Society, new series 10 (1874).
Harding, William. 'An Account of some of the Ancient Ecclesiastical Edifices of Exeter', *Transactions of the Exeter Diocesan Architectural Society*, 4 (1835), 266–88.
Heales, Alfred. *The Records of Merton Priory in the County of Surrey* (London, 1898).
Henderson, C. 'The City of Exeter from A.D. 50 to the Early Nineteenth Century', in *Historical Atlas of South-West England*, ed. R. J. P. Kain and W. L. D. Ravenhill (Exeter, 1999), 482–98.
Henderson, C., and Bidwell, P. T. 'The Saxon Minster at Exeter', in *The Early Church in Western Britain and Ireland*, ed. Susan M. Pearce (Oxford, 1982), 145–76.
Higham, Robert A. *Making Anglo-Saxon Devon* (Exeter, 2008).
Higham, Robert A. 'William the Conqueror's Siege of Exeter in 1068', *Devonshire Association Transactions*, 145 (2013), 67–106.
Higham, Robert A. 'The Origins and Context of Exeter Castle', in *Exeter Castle: history, fabric analysis and excavation*, ed. S. R. Blaylock (forthcoming).
Hill, Francis. *Medieval Lincoln* (Cambridge, 1948, repr. Stamford, 1990).
Hobbs, Steven. (ed.) *The Cartulary of Forde Abbey*, Somerset Record Society, 85 (1998).
Hooker, John. *Isca Damnoniorum* ([London?], 1587): a map, *Short Title Catalogue* 24886.3.
Hooker, John. *The Description of the Citie of Excester*, ed. W. J. Harte and others, 3 parts, Devon and Cornwall Record Society (1919–47).
Hope, V., Lloyd, J., and Erskine, Audrey M. *Exeter Cathedral: a short history and description*, 2nd ed. (Exeter, 1988).
Hoskins, W. G. (ed.) *Exeter in the Seventeenth Century: tax and rate assessments 1602–1699*, Devon and Cornwall Record Society, new series 2 (1957).
Hoskins, W. G. 'Early Churches in Exeter', *Friends of Exeter Cathedral 29th Annual Report* (1959), 20–5.
Hoskins, W. G. *Two Thousand Years in Exeter* (Exeter, 1960).
Jenkins, Alexander. *The History and Description of the City of Exeter and its Environs, Ancient and Modern, Civil and Ecclesiastical* (Exeter, 1806).

Juddery, J. Z. *Exebridge Wardens' Accounts, 1450–1556: financial summaries and property rentals* (Exeter Museums Archaeological Field Unit, Report No. 90.30, December 1990).

Kain, R. J. P., and Ravenhill, W. L. D. (ed.) *Historical Atlas of South-West England* (Exeter, 1999).

Keene, Derek. *Survey of Medieval Winchester*, part 1, Winchester Studies, 2 (Oxford, 1985).

Ker, N. R. *Medieval Manuscripts in British Libraries*, 5 vols (Oxford, 1969–2002).

Kerslake, T. 'The Celt and the Teuton in Exeter', *Archaeological Journal*, 30 (1873), 211–25, reprinted in *Saint Richard the King of Englishmen and his Territory A.D. 700–720* (Clevedon, 1890), 75–96.

Knowles, David, Brooke, C. N. L., and London, Vera C. M. (ed.) *The Heads of Religious Houses: England and Wales, I. 940–1216*, 2nd ed. (Cambridge, 2001).

Lapidge, Michael. (ed.) *Anglo-Saxon Litanies of the Saints*, Henry Bradshaw Society, 106 (1991).

Lega-Weekes, Ethel. 'An Account of the Hospitium de le Egle, some Ancient Chapels in the Close, and some Persons Connected therewith', *Devonshire Association Transactions*, 44 (1912), 480–511.

Lega-Weekes, Ethel. *Some Studies in the Topography of the Cathedral Close* (Exeter, 1915).

Lega-Weekes, Ethel. 'Saint Loye's, East Wonford, Devon', *Devonshire Association Transactions*, 52 (1920), 360–6.

Lega-Weekes, Ethel. 'The Pre-Reformation History of St. Katherine's Priory, Polsloe', *Devonshire Association Transactions*, 66 (1934), 181–99; 67 (1935), 349–59; 69 (1937), 447–70; 70 (1938), 423–32.

Leland, John. *The Itinerary of John Leland*, ed. L. Toulmin Smith, 5 vols (London, 1907–10).

Leland, John. *De Rebus Britannicis Collectanea*, ed. T. Hearne, 2nd ed., 6 vols (London, 1774; repr. Farnborough, 1970).

Lepine, David. *A Brotherhood of Canons Serving God: English secular cathedrals in the later middle ages* (Woodbridge, 1995).

Lepine, David, and Orme, Nicholas. *Death and Memory in Medieval Exeter*, DCRS, new series, 46 (2003).

Letters and Papers, Foreign and Domestic, Henry VIII, ed. S. J. Brewer, J. Gairdner, and R. H. Brodie, 21 vols in 33 parts (London, 1864–1932).

Liebermann, F. (ed.) *Ungedruckte Anglo-Normannische Geschichtsquellen* (Strasbourg, 1879).

List of Inquisitions Ad Quod Damnum Preserved in the Public Record Office, 2 vols, Public Record Office, Lists and Indexes, 17, 22 (London, 1904–6).

Little, A. G., and Easterling, R. C. *The Franciscans and Dominicans of Exeter* (Exeter, 1927).

Lobel, Mary D. *Historic Towns* (also *Atlas of Historic Towns*), 3 vols (London and Oxford, 1969–89).

Loe, Louise. *Human Remains from St Katherine's Priory, Polsloe, Exeter, 1976–8*, Exeter Archaeology Report No. 98.69, 1998, revised 1999 (Exeter, 1999).

M., R. B. 'Hayes Prebend', *Devon and Cornwall Notes and Queries*, 12 (1922–3), 46.

MacCaffrey, Wallace T. *Exeter, 1540–1640: the growth of the English country town* (Cambridge, Mass., 1958).

Moore, Stuart A. (ed.) *Letters and Papers of John Shillingford, Mayor of Exeter 1447–50*, Camden Society, new series 2 (1871).

Morgan (later Chibnall), Marjorie M. *The English Lands of the Abbey of Bec* (London, 1946).

Oliver, George. *Ecclesiastical Antiquities in Devon: being observations on several churches in Devonshire, with some memoranda on the history of Cornwall*, 3 vols (Exeter, 1839–42).

Oliver, George. *Monasticon Dioecesis Exoniensis*, with supplement (Exeter and London, 1846).
Oliver, George. *Additional Supplement to the Monasticon Dioecesis Exoniensis* (Exeter, 1854).
Oliver, George. 'Ancient Church within the Castle of Exeter', *Archaeological Journal*, 11 (1854), 157–64.
Oliver, George. *Lives of the Bishops of Exeter and a History of the Cathedral* (Exeter, 1861).
Oliver, George. *The History of the City of Exeter*, 2nd ed. (Exeter, 1861).
Oliver, George. 'Extracts from Devon and Cornwall Deeds made by George Oliver in 1825 from a Manuscript in Powderham Castle', Devon Heritage Centre, unpublished volume.
Ordinale Exon, ed. J. N. Dalton and G. H. Doble, 4 vols, Henry Bradshaw Society, 37–8, 63, 79 (1909–40).
Orme, Nicholas. *Education in the West of England, 1066–1548* (Exeter, 1976); 'Education in the West of England: Additions', *Devon and Cornwall Notes and Queries*, 34 (1978), 22–5.
Orme, Nicholas. 'The Kalendar Brethren of the City of Exeter', *Devonshire Association Transactions*, 109 (1977), 153–69.
Orme, Nicholas. 'The Guild of Kalendars, Bristol', *Bristol and Gloucestershire Archaeological Society Transactions*, 96 (1978), 33–52.
Orme, Nicholas. 'The Dissolution of the Chantries in Devon, 1546–8', *Devonshire Association Transactions*, 111 (1979), 75–123.
Orme, Nicholas. *The Minor Clergy of Exeter Cathedral, 1300–1548* (Exeter, 1979).
Orme, Nicholas. 'The Medieval Clergy of Exeter Cathedral: I, the Vicars Choral and Annuellars', *Devonshire Association Transactions*, 113 (1981), 79–102.
Orme, Nicholas. 'The Medieval Clergy of Exeter Cathedral: II, the Secondaries and Choristers', *Devonshire Association Transactions*, 115 (1983), 79–100.
Orme, Nicholas. 'A Letter of St Roche', *Devon and Cornwall Notes and Queries*, 36 (1989), 153–9.
Orme, Nicholas. 'Saint Walter of Cowick', *Analecta Bollandiana*, 108 (1990), 1–7.
Orme, Nicholas. 'The Charnel Chapel of Exeter Cathedral', in *Medieval Art and Architecture at Exeter Cathedral*, ed. F. Kelly, The British Archaeological Association, Conference Transactions, 11 (1991), 162–71.
Orme, Nicholas. 'The Medieval Chapels of Heavitree Parish', *Devon Archaeological Society Transactions*, 49 (1991, publ. 1993), 121–9.
Orme, Nicholas. *English Church Dedications* (Exeter, 1996); 'English Church Dedications: Supplement No. 1', *Devon and Cornwall Notes and Queries*, 38/10 (Autumn, 2001), 305–7; 'English Church Dedications: Supplement No. 2', ibid., 40 part 2 (Autumn 2007), 40.
Orme, Nicholas. 'Church and Chapel in Medieval England', *Transactions of the Royal Historical Society*, 6th series, 6 (1996), 75–102.
Orme, Nicholas. *The Saints of Cornwall* (Oxford, 2000).
Orme, Nicholas. *Medieval Children* (New Haven and London, 2001).
Orme, Nicholas. *Medieval Schools* (New Haven and London, 2006).
Orme, Nicholas. (ed.) *Cornish Wills 1342–1540*, Devon and Cornwall Record Society, new series 50 (2007).
Orme, Nicholas. *A History of the County of Cornwall:* vol. ii: *Religious History, 500–1560* (Victoria County History, Woodbridge and London, 2010).
Orme, Nicholas. 'Parish Processions in Medieval and Tudor Cornwall', *Journal of the Royal Institution of Cornwall* (2011), 73–82.

Orme, Nicholas. *The Minor Clergy of Exeter Cathedral: Biographies, 1250–1548*, Devon and Cornwall Record Society, new series 54 (2013).
Orme, Nicholas. *English School Exercises 1420–1530* (Toronto, 2013)
Orme, Nicholas. *The Church in Devon, 400 to 1560* (Exeter, 2013).
Orme, Nicholas. 'Medieval Holy Wells in Devon', *Devonshire Association Transactions*, 145 (2013), 129–54.
Orme, Nicholas. 'The Early History of Tiverton Church', *Devonshire Association Transactions*, 146 (2014).
Orme, Nicholas. 'The Dominican Friars of Exeter' (Exeter Archaeology Reports, forthcoming).
Orme, Nicholas. 'The Franciscan Friars of Exeter' (Exeter Archaeology Reports, forthcoming).
Orme, Nicholas. 'St James Priory' (Exeter Archaeology Reports, forthcoming).
Orme, Nicholas. 'Polsloe Priory' (Exeter Archaeology Reports, forthcoming).
Orme, Nicholas. 'St Nicholas Priory' (Exeter Archaeology Reports, forthcoming).
Orme, Nicholas, and Webster, Margaret. *The English Hospital, 1070–1570* (New Haven and London, 1995).
Owen, Dorothy (ed.) *John Lydford's Book: the fourteenth-century formulary of the archdeacon of Totnes*, Devon and Cornwall Record Society, new series 20 (1975).
The Oxford Dictionary of National Biography, ed. C. Matthew and B. Harrison, 60 vols (Oxford, 2004); updated electronic edition (including further biographies): http://www.oxforddnb.com
Parker, R. W. *Archaeo-Historical Assessment of 5 The Close, Exeter* (Exeter, Exeter Archaeology, Report No. 97.30, 1997).
Parker, R. W. *Archaeological Recording at St Olave's Church, Exeter* (Exeter, Exeter Archaeology Report No. 99.67, 1999).
Parker, R. W. *Archaeological Recording at St Petrock's Church, Exeter* (Exeter, Exeter Archaeology Report No. 00.90, 2000).
Parker, R. W., and Collings, A. G. 'St Catherine's Almshouses and the Medieval Canonry in Catherine Street, Exeter', *Devon Archaeological Society Proceedings*, 60 (2002), 75–205.
The Parliament Rolls of Medieval England 1275–1504, ed. C. Given-Wilson and others, 16 vols (Woodbridge and London, 2005).
Parry, H. Lloyd. *The History of the Exeter Guildhall and the Life Within* (Exeter, 1936).
Peskett, Hugh. *Guide to the Parish and Non-Parochial Registers of Devon and Cornwall 1538–1837*, Devon and Cornwall Record Society, extra series 2 (1979).
Phillipps, Sir Thomas. 'List of Charters in the Cartulary of St. Nicholas Priory at Exeter', *Collectanea Topographica et Genealogica*, 1 (1834), 60–5, 184–9, 250–4, 374–88.
Phillips, E. Masson. 'The Ancient Stone Crosses of Devon: Part II', *Devonshire Association Transactions*, 70 (1935), 299–340.
Polwhele, Richard. *The History of Devonshire*, 3 vols (Exeter and London, 1793–1806; repr. Dorking, 1977).
Ponsford, Michael. 'Post-Medieval Britain and Ireland in 1991', *Post-Medieval Archaeology*, 26 (1992), 95–156.
Portman, D. *Exeter Houses 1400–1700* (Exeter, 1966).
Powicke, F. M., and Cheney, C. R. (ed.) *Councils & Synods A.D. 1205–1313*, 2 vols (Oxford, 1964).
Ravenhill, Mary R., and Rowe, Margery M. (ed.) *Early Devon Maps* (Exeter, 2000).
Ravenhill, Mary R., and Rowe, Margery M. (ed.) *Devon Maps and Map-makers: manuscript maps before 1840*, 2 vols, Devon and Cornwall Record Society, 45–6 (2000–2).

Reed, Harbottle. 'Allhallows Church, Goldsmith Street, Exeter', *Devonshire Association Transactions*, 35 (1903), 581–616.
Regesta Regum Anglo-Normannorum, ed. H. W. C. Davis et al., 4 vols (Oxford, 1913–59).
Regesta Regum Anglo-Normannorum: The Acta of William I (1066–1087), ed. David Bates (Oxford, 1998).
The Register of Thomas de Brantyngham, Bishop of Exeter, ed. F. C. Hingeston-Randolph, 2 vols (London and Exeter, 1901–6).
The Registers of Walter Bronescombe and Peter Quivil, Bishops of Exeter, ed. F. C. Hingeston-Randolph (London and Exeter, 1889).
The Register of Walter Bronescombe Bishop of Exeter 1258–1280, ed. O. F. Robinson, 3 vols, Canterbury & York Society, 82, 87, 94 (1995–2003).
The Register of John de Grandisson, Bishop of Exeter, ed. F. C. Hingeston-Randolph, 3 vols (London and Exeter, 1894–9).
The Register of Edmund Lacy, Bishop of Exeter, ed. F. C. Hingeston-Randolph, 2 vols (London and Exeter, 1901–15). Vol. ii is now superseded by the edition of G. R. Dunstan, next following.
The Register of Edmund Lacy, Bishop of Exeter: Registrum Commune, ed. G. R. Dunstan, 5 vols, Devon and Cornwall Record Society, new series 7, 10, 13, 16, 18 (1963–72).
The Register of Edmund Stafford, ed. F. C. Hingeston-Randolph (London and Exeter, 1886).
The Register of Walter de Stapeldon, Bishop of Exeter, ed. F. C. Hingeston-Randolph (London and Exeter, 1892).
Reichel, O. J., and others. (ed.) *Devon Feet of Fines*, 2 vols, Devon and Cornwall Record Society (1912–39).
Rose-Troup, Frances. *Lost Chapels of Exeter* (Exeter, 1923).
Rose-Troup, Frances. 'Lists Relating to Persons Ejected from Religious Houses', *Devon and Cornwall Notes and Queries*, 17 (1932–3), 81–96, 143–4, 191–2, 238–40, 285–8.
Rose-Troup, Frances. *Exeter Vignettes* (Exeter, 1942).
Rotuli Chartarum in Turri Londinensi Asservati, ed. T. D. Hardy, vol. i, part i (London, Record Commission, 1837).
Rotuli Hundredorum temp. Hen. III et Edw. I, 2 vols (London, Record Commission, 1812–18).
Rowe, Joseph Hambley. (ed.) *Cornwall Feet of Fines*, 2 vols, Devon and Cornwall Record Society (1914–50).
Rowe, Margery M. (ed.) *Tudor Exeter. Tax assessments 1489–1595 including the military survey 1522*, Devon and Cornwall Record Society, new series 32 (1977).
Rowe, Margery M., and Cochlin, J. J. 'Evidence of the Existence of St John's Hospital, Exeter, in the Late Twelfth Century', *Devon and Cornwall Notes and Queries*, 29 (1962–4), 211–13.
Salisbury Cathedral: Perspectives on the Architectural History, Royal Commission on Historical Monuments of England (London, 1993).
Salter, H. E. *Medieval Oxford*, Oxford Historical Society, 100 (1936), 113–31.
Sanders, I. J. *English Baronies: a study of their origin and descent 1086–1327* (Oxford, 1960).
Sawyer, P. H. *Anglo-Saxon Charters: an annotated list and bibliography* (London, Royal Historical Society, 1968); online updated version http://www.trin.cam.ac.uk/sdk13/chartwww/charthome.html
Searle, Eleanor. (ed.) *The Chronicle of Battle Abbey* (Oxford, 1980).
Smith, David M. (ed.) *The Heads of Religious Houses: England and Wales, III. 1377–1540* (Cambridge, 2008).

Smith, David M., and London, Vera C. M. (ed.) *The Heads of Religious Houses: England and Wales, II. 1216–1377* (Cambridge, 2001).
Smith, Toulmin. *English Gilds*, Early English Text Society, original series, 40 (1870).
Snell, Lawrence S. (ed.) *The Chantry Certificates for Devon and the City of Exeter* (Exeter, [1960]).
Somers Cocks, J. V. *Devon Topographical Prints 1660–1870: a catalogue and guide* (Exeter, 1977).
Somerset Medieval Wills (1383–1500), ed. F. W. Weaver, Somerset Record Society, 16 (1901).
Sprake, C. J. G. *Gates and Other Antiquities of the City of Exeter* (Exeter, 1831–2).
Stabb, John. *Some Old Devon Churches*, 3 vols (London, 1908–16).
Staniforth, P. R., and Juddery, J. Z. *Exeter Property Deeds 1150–1450*, 4 vols (Exeter Museums Archaeological Field Unit, Report Nos. 91.45–8, October 1991).
The Statutes of the Realm, from Magna Carta to the end of the Reign of Queen Anne, 11 vols (London, Record Commission, 1810–28).
Tanner, Norman P. *The Church in Late Medieval Norwich 1370–1532* (Toronto, 1984).
Tanner, Thomas. *Notitia Monastica*, ed. John Tanner (London, 1744).
Tatton-Brown, T., and Crook, J. *Salisbury Cathedral: the making of a medieval masterpiece* (London, 2009).
Townsend, George. *Sketches of Bygone Exeter* (Exeter, 1908).
Urry, William. *Canterbury under the Angevin Kings* (London, 1967).
Valor Ecclesiasticus tempore Henrici VIII auctoritate regia institutus, ed. J. Caley, 6 vols (London, Record Commission, 1810–24).
Victoria County History: A History of the County of Cornwall – see above, Orme, Nicholas.
Victoria County History: A History of the County of Devon, vol i, ed. William Page (London, 1906).
Victoria County History: A History of the County of York: The City of York, ed. P. M. Tillott (London, 1961).
Weaver, F. W. (ed.) *Somerset Medieval Wills 1383–1500*, Somerset Record Society, 16 (1901).
Whitelock, Dorothy. (ed.) *English Historical Documents c.500–1042*, 2nd ed. (London and New York, 1979).
Whitley, H. Michell. 'An Inventory of the Goods of St Kieran's Church, Exeter, A.D. 1417', *Devonshire Association Transactions*, 43 (1911), 309–18.
William of Malmesbury, *Gesta Regum Anglorum*, ed. R. A. B. Mynors, R. M. Thomson, and M. Winterbottom, 2 vols (Oxford, 1998–9).
Worthy, Charles. *The History of the Suburbs of Exeter* (Exeter, 1892).
Yeo, Geoffrey. 'Where was Cowick Priory?', *Devon and Cornwall Notes and Queries*, 35 part 10 (1986), 321–6.
Yeo, Geoffrey. *The Monks of Cowick* (Exeter, 1987).
Youings, Joyce. *Devon Monastic Lands: calendar of particulars for grants, 1536–1558*, Devon and Cornwall Record Society, new series 1 (1955).
Youings, Joyce. *Tuckers Hall Exeter: the history of a provincial city company through five centuries* (Exeter, 1968).

Index

The word St is ignored in the indexing of churches and chapels. References to illustrations are in bold type.

Acclom, Thomas, cleric 49
Adeliz, daughter of Richard fitz Baldwin 35, 75, 118, 128
advowsons – *see* churches, parish: patronage
Æthelstan, king 7, 11, 81
Alexius, saint 67
St Alexius, hospital **32**, 67; mentioned 16, 18, 23, 26, 35–6, 101, 114
Alfred, king 81
Algar, chapel founder 22, 86–7
All Hallows (Goldsmith Street), church **37**, 68; mentioned 16–17, 23, 26, 50, 56–7
All Hallows-on-the-Wall, church 68–9; mentioned 16–17, 23
almshouses 42, 70 – *and see* named foundations
Alphington, Devon 3, 128–9
anchoresses 59, 115, 126–7
Andrew, saint 90, 165
Andrew, Thomas, mayor 132–3
Anne, saint 69, 122
St Anne, chapel 69–70, **180**; mentioned 44, 65, 108
annuellars – *see* chantry priests
Annuellars' House 70–1
Anselm, archbishop 16, 145
Anthony of Egypt, saint 157
antiphons, votive 53, 148, 157–8
Apollonia, saint 135
archdeacons 17, 34, 45, 47, 136

Arundell, Lady Katherine 103
Ashclyst, Devon, prebend 74–6, 79
Asser, bishop 81
Attehole (Hole), Nicholas 68
Avenel family 75, 118, 148
Ayssh, William, cleric 107

Baker family 71–2, 117
Baker's Almshouse 71–2; mentioned 42
bakers' guild 44, 148
Baldwin fitz Gilbert, magnate 14–15, 22, 74, 89, 118
Banyster (Bannaster), Thomas, cleric or clerics 49, 160
Bartholomew, saint 72
St Bartholomew, chapel 72; mentioned 17, 23, 29, 125
Bartholomew, bishop of Exeter 142, 160, 169
Battle, Sussex, abbey 16, 35–6, 145, 151–2
Bec-Hellouin, France, abbey 16, 35–6, 89–91
bede-rolls 60
Bedford – *see* Russell
bells, church 48
Bellus, William, cleric 152
Benbow, Thomas, cleric 50
Bernard, Alice, anchoress 59, 126
Bernard, Roger, cleric 51–2
Bestelabise, Jordan 139
Billeford, William 70

bishops of Exeter 1, 12–14, 22, 25, 28, 30, 34, 36, 39, 50, 57, 63, 132, 166–7 – *and see* individual names
Bishop's Chapel 72–3; mentioned 16, 23, 25, 45, 162
Bitton, Thomas, bishop 114
Blackaller family 133, 149
Black Death 33, 61
Bole, John le 130
Boniface, saint 7, 81
Bonville, Sir William 73, 174
Bonville's Almshouse 73; mentioned 42
books 18, 28, 38, 52–3, 60, 70, 107, 115, 120, 130, 165, 173 – *and see* cartularies
Bovey, John de, cleric 168
Bowedon, Nicholas 45, 163
Boyecote, William de 126
Bradeworth, John 131
Brantingham, Thomas, bishop 82–3, 120, 127
Braylegh, Richard, cleric 87, 109
Brewer, William, bishop 95–6, 107, 114, 132, 142, 159, 172
Brewer, William, magnate 159
Bridgwater, Somt. 38
Bristol, Gloucs. 23, 30, 41, 120
Broadclyst, Devon 15, 75
Bronescombe, Walter, bishop 30, 72, 98, 168, 171
Brown, Stuart 168
Browne, Robert 85
Brygon, John 171
Budwyke, Philip 99
burials – *see* funerals
Buttes, Alice, anchoress 59, 115
Bysshop, John, cleric 50

Calwoodleigh family 99, 107
Cambridge, Cambs. 30
  King's College 112
Canterbury, Kent 24–5, 30–1
Caperoun, Henry, cleric 87
cappers' or haberdashers' guild 44
Carew families 115, 161, 171
Carswill, Devon, prebend 75–7, 80
cartularies 38, 115, 142, 147, 150
Castle, Exeter 1, 10
Castle Chapel **41**, 73–80; mentioned 10–12, 14–15, 19, 21–3, 25–6, 30–1, 34, 45, 55, 65, 162

Cathedral, Exeter 81–3; mentioned 7–9, 13–14, 17, 19–21, 33, 44–5, 49, 53, 60, 64, 70, 87, 107, 110, 126, 133–4, 145, 172–3 – *and see* Charnel Chapel
  vicars choral of 176–7; mentioned 33, 42, 120, 137
St Catherine's Well 83–4; mentioned 46
'Celtic' saints 10–11, 25, 122, 155–6, 164
Chalmore, John 86, 96, 154
chantries and chantry priests 50, 61–2, 64, 70–1, 100, 131–2, 148, 152, 158
chapels 5–6, 21–8, 40–5, 64–5
  private 162–3; mentioned 45, 65
chaplains – *see* clergy, parish
Chapman, Christine 100
Chappinton, Richard 152
Chard, Thomas, bishop 157
charity and poor relief 39, 56, 148 – *and see* almshouses
Charnel Chapel 84–6; mentioned 18, 41–3, 55, 65, 83, 131
children and adolescents 53, 58, 136 – *and see* parish clerks
Christ and Holy Trinity, cults of 18, 86–7, 115, 122, 127, 132–3, 173, 177
Christchurch, chapel 86–8; mentioned 17–19, 22–3, 26, 43, 49, 64, 109
Christopher, saint 122, 136, 154, 157
churches, parish
  buildings 25–6, 47–8, 57
  calendar of observances 56–7
  chronology of 19–20
  clergy – *see* clergy, parish
  dedications 11, 24–5, 54–5
  guilds in – *see* guilds
  legal status 34
  locations 23–4
  parishes of 19–21, 28–34
  patronage of 21–2, 26
  Reformation and 64–5
  stores and companies in 57–8
  worship in 52–7, 57–63, 64–5
churchwardens' accounts 118, 136, 139, 157, 174
Ciarán of Saighir, saint 122
Clair, saint 88
St Clair, chapel 88; mentioned 44, 108
Clement, saint 44, 89
St Clement, chapel 89; mentioned 17–18, 24, 29, 108

clergy, parish 18, 28, 31–3, 48–57, 61–2
    chapels in houses of 162
    housing 49, 78, 123, 152
    stipends and wages 31, 49–50
Clerk, Richard 136
Cobethorne, John, cleric 113
Coffin, James 130
Cogan, Miles de 147
Collecote family 139
Collecote, Nicholas, cleric 52
Colles, Humphrey 104
Collumpton, William, cleric – see Fawell
Colshill family 99
Corpus Christi, cult of 43, 86, 131
Courtenay family 26, 38, 69, 75–80, 90,
    92–3, 99, 104, 126, 128, 132, 148
Courtenay, William, archbishop 113
Courtour, Philip 165
Cowick (nowadays St Thomas) 3, 20, 29, 45,
    47, 74, 94 – and see Hayes
  priory and original parish church (St
    Andrew) **20**, 48, 89–93; mentioned 3,
    16, 21, 24, 26, 30, 34–40, 49, 64, 90,
    169–71
  later parish church (St Thomas) – see
    St Thomas
Crediton, bishops of 7, 81
Cremell, William 122
Cresswell, Beatrix, historian 3, 132
crosses, standing 46–7, 93–4; mentioned 10
Crugge, Anna, vowess 59
Crugge, William, mayor 60
Cuthbert, saint 25, 94–5
St Cuthbert, church 94–5; mentioned 17, 23,
    33, 155
Cutton, Devon, prebend 75–7, 80

David, saint 25, 95–6
St David, chapel 95–6, **180**; mentioned
    17–18, 21, 24, 29, 34, 48, 55–7, 107–8
Davy, Thomasia 157
dedications – see church dedications; saint
    cults
Delabere, John 112
Dene, Thomas, prior 111–12
Denys, Sir Thomas 149
Devon, earls of – see Courtenay, Redvers
Dinham family 98–9
Dobell, Laurence, cleric 50
Domesday Book 12–14

Dominic, saint 98
Dominican Friary **51**, 96–9, **181**; mentioned
    35–6, 38–9, 55, 64
Dorothy, saint 157
Doulys, John de 95, 122
Doun, William 105
Dudbroke family 139
Dudley, John, earl of Warwick 161
Duke, William 131
Dunstan, saint 68
Dynyngton, John, abbot 91

Edgar, king 7, 81
Edmund, saint 84, 99
St Edmund, church **62**, 99–100; mentioned
    17, 19–20, 22–4, 26, 29, 30, 41, 48, 62,
    101
St Edward, church 12, 17–19 – and see St
    Mary Steps
Edward the Confessor, king and saint 7, 12,
    21, 42, 82, 84, 123, 147, 150, 167
Edward the Elder, king 81
Edward the Martyr, king and saint 12, 25,
    137
Edward I, king 41–2, 84
Edward IV, king 91
Elyott, Thomas 158
Erasmus, saint 122, 157
Esterpeny, William, prior 91
Eton (Bucks.), college 91
Everett, A. W., historian 125
Exe Bridge 59, 99, 144
    chapel on 101; mentioned 40–1, 49, 62, 64
    – and see St Edmund
Exeter, city of 1–3, **4**, **8**, **27**
    city government (mayor and chamber) 2,
      22, 72, 99, 101, 105–7, 119, 175
    other topics – see individual names
Exeter, John of, alias Picot, cleric 41, 84,
    86

Faith, saint 72
Fawell alias Collumpton, William, bishop
    45, 141–2, 149, 162
Fayreman, Robert, cleric 50
Fenton, Thomas, cleric 50
Ford, John 108
Foréville, Raymonde, historian 140
Fortescue, Sir John 104
Francis, saint 102, 140

Francis, David 3
Franciscan Friary **32**, 101–4, 140; mentioned 35–6, 38, 47, 64, 67, 93, 177
friaries 34–6, 38–9, 52, 58–60, 63–4, 171
funerals and burials
    castle 9–10, 21, 73–4, 80
    cathedral 10, 21, 24, 34, 39, 59–60, 84–6
    parish churches 10, 17, 21, 24, 40, 59–60, 90–1, 125, 133, 136, 144, 152, 157, 165, 171–2, 174
    religious houses 16, 21, 34, 39–40, 59–60, 90, 92, 98–9, 102–3, 110–11, 114, 116, 129, 145, 148, 159–60

Gabriel, saint 168
Gamonte, John, cleric 50
Gascoigne, John 70
Geffrey, Richard 105
Geoffrey of Coutances, bishop 22
George, saint 98, 104, 106, 174
St George, church **71**, 104–5; mentioned 11, 17, 19, 23–6, 31, 47–8, 57
Germyn, John, organist 53, 158
Gervas, Walter 40, 101, 113
Glandfield, Elizabeth 149
Glasyer, John, scribe 53
God's House – *see* Wynard's Almshouse
Godwyn, Thomas 79, 130
Govys, John, cleric 52, 174–5
Grandisson, John, bishop 109, 114–15, 135, 152
graves – *see* funerals and burials
Grendon, Ricarda 45, 163
Grendon, Simon, mayor 106, 157
Grendon's Almshouse **78**, 106; mentioned 42
Grey family, marquesses of Dorset 73
Guildhall Chapel 106–7; mentioned 43, 49, 64, 101
guilds 10, 22–3, 42–4, 58–9, 86–8, 106, 119–20, 148, 155, 174
Gytha, countess 14, 21, 150–1

Hamelyn, John, mayor 148
Hamond, John 122
Harold II, king 21, 150
Harvey, Anthony 79
Hayes, Cowick, prebend and manor 45, 74–80, 169
Hayes Barton 78, 162

Heavitree, church and parish **15**, **85**, 107–8; mentioned 3, 6, 15, 17–18, 21, 24, 29–30, 34, 44–5, 48, 95, 128, 160, 164
Hendeman, Thomas, cleric 76
Henderson, C. G. 18
Henry I, king 12, 167
Henry II, king 160
Henry III, king 96
Henry VI, king 91
Henry VII, king 96
Hewet, Richard 125
Heynes, Simon, cleric 135
Higham, Dr R. A. 74
High School 108–9; mentioned 40
Hille, Sir John, justice 116
Hodell, William 117, 165
Hoige (Hodge) family 152
Holand family 45, 163, 171
Holby, Christine, anchoress 126
Hooker, John, historian 149
Hoskins, W. G. 13, 134
hospitals 16, 18, 22, 29, 35–6, 42 – *and see* individual foundations
Huddesfeld, Lady Katherine 102–3
Hull, Henry 105
Hull, John 104
Hunt, Thomas, mayor 60, 158

images, religious 53–6
indulgences 57; mentioned 64, 69, 92–3, 100, 105, 126, 130, 132, 140, 171, 173–4
Innocent III, pope 21
Ireland 147
Irlesbery, district 21, 35–6, 151

James the Great, saint 109, 113, 118
St James (South Street), parish church 113; mentioned 17, 23, 33, 48, 173
St James (Topsham Road), priory and chapel **32**, 48, 109–112; mentioned 5, 12, 16, 19, 24, 34–8, 45, 63
Jerome, saint 157
Jesus, images and cults of the Name of 92, 105, 133, 157
John the Baptist, saint 98, 106, 114, 118, 122, 168
John the Evangelist, saint 118
St John, hospital **32**, 114–17, **181**; mentioned 16, 18, 23–4, 29, 33, 35–6, 38, 40, 43, 52, 58–60, 63–4, 68, 77, 109, 125

St John Bow, church **92**, 117–19; mentioned 5, 16–17, 22–3, 26, 44, 47–8, 51, 57, 63, 105, 129, 175–6
John, king 160
Jude the Apostle, saint 166

Kalendars, guild of 119–20; mentioned 22–3, 28, 42, 60, 86, 155–6, 176
Katherine, saint 83, 116, 118, 121, 139, 154, 159, 165, 171
St Katherine's Almshouse 121, **182**; mentioned 42, 65
Katherine of Aragon, queen 135
Keilway, Robert, royal servant 79
Kelly, John, mayor 60, 107, 157
Kenbury, Devon, 145, 150–2
Kerrian, saint 122
St Kerrian, church 121–3, **182**; mentioned 16–17, 23, 31, 48–50, 56–7, 59
Kerslake, Thomas, historian 11
Kerswell – *see* Carswill
Kilkenny, Andrew, cleric 165
Kynwelmersh, Anthony 176
Kyrton family 139

Lacy, Edmund, bishop 69, 96, 105, 126, 132, 140, 165, 173
Lappeflode, Andrew de, cleric 136
Larkbeare, Exeter 45, 104, 163
Latimer, Hugh, reformer 85, 136
Laurence, saint 97
St Laurence, church **97**, 123–5; mentioned 12, 16–17, 23, 26, 33, 40, 48, 52–3, 72, 87, 114
Lechlade, Walter de, cleric 41
Legh family 108
Leland, John, antiquary 65, 86, 159
Leofric, bishop 82, 150
Leonard, saint 103
St Leonard, church **103**, 126–7; mentioned 6, 16–17, 21, 24, 26, 29, 31, 34, 48, 59
lepers 142
Lercedekne family 116
Lincoln, Lincs. 24, 30
Lingham, Robert, cleric 52, 137
Livery Dole, chapel and almshouse 127; mentioned 45, 65
London 30, 41, 48
 St Paul's Cathedral 65, 86
Long, Gilbert and John 114

Loye, saint 127, 174
St Loye, chapel **110**, 127–8; mentioned 44–5, 47, 108
St Lucy's Lane, Exeter 128
Luysshant, Gervase 132

Mainwaring, George and Oliver 70
Malmysbury, Robert de 113
Margaret, saint 172
Marsh (Barton), St Mary, priory 128–30; mentioned 5, 16, 34–6, 38, 64, 75, 118
Marshal, Henry, bishop 17
Martin, saint 105, 130, 147
St Martin, church 130–2, **183**; mentioned 11, 17, 19, 23–5, 31, 33, 43, 48–9, 57, 62
 missal of 18, 130
St Martin-des-Champs, France, abbey 16, 36, 110–11
Martyn, Sir William and Eleanor 98
martyrologies 22, 60, 121
Mary, saint 53–6 and passim
St Mary Arches, church **117**, 132–3; mentioned 13, 17, 22, 25, 48, 51, 57, 62–3, 176
St Mary, at St Mary Magdalene hospital, chapel 139–40
St Mary, Bishop's Palace, chapel 141; mentioned 73
St Mary, cathedral cemetery, chapel 141
St Mary, house of William Fawell, chapel 141–2
St Mary Major, church 133–6, **184**; mentioned 9, 14, 17, 19, 23, 25, 28–30, 33, 47–50, 52–3, 56–7, 73, 81, 83, 106, 137
St Mary Mincinglake, chapel 140–1; mentioned 44–5, 55, 63, 108
St Mary Minor, church 137; mentioned 17, 23, 33, 134
St Mary Steps (St Edward), church 137–9, **185**; mentioned 12, 19, 23, 26, 29–31, 48, 135
St Mary and St Francis, chapel 140
Mary Magdalene, saint 142
St Mary Magdalene, hospital **32**, **124**, 142–3; mentioned 16–17, 21, 24, 35–6, 38, 63, 114, 139–40
Ste-Marie-du-Val, France, abbey 26, 123–5
Marys, William, cleric 50
Maynard, John 132

Merton, Surrey, priory 26, 123–5
Michael, saint 107, 116, 118, 143–4, 165, 171–2
St Michael (Cathedral Close), chapel 143; mentioned 17–18, 23, 29, 65
St Michael (Cowick), chapel 144; mentioned 24, 40, 90
Mincinglake – *see* St Mary Mincinglake
minsters 7–9
monasteries 7–9, 15–16, 19, 21, 24, 34–40, 63–4 – *and see* individual houses
   dissolution of 63–4
   pastoral roles of 38–40
   wealth of 36–7
More's and Fortescue's Almshouse 144; mentioned 42
Mortain, counts of
   John – *see* John, king
   Robert 12, 22, 123, 167
   William 12, 167
Mounteyn, William 139
music, church 53, 136
Myrefyld, John 152

Nicholas, saint 145
St Nicholas, priory **32**, **131**, 145–9; mentioned 16, 19, 24, 26, 34–40, 44, 49, 60, 64, 151–2
   St Nicholas Fee 145
Nordon, William 71, 85, 157
Norwich, Norf. 24–5, 30–1, 48
Nosworthy, M., architect 166
nuns 159–61
Nymet, John 142, 157

obits (obit masses) 60–1; mentioned 18–19, 56, 96, 100, 116–17, 119–20, 122, 125, 131, 133, 136, 139, 148, 154–5, 165, 175
Obley, William, mayor 105, 116–17, 133, 142, 149–50
Obley's Almshouse 149–50; mentioned 42
Okehampton, Devon 77
Olaf, saint 150
St Olave, church 150–3, **186**; mentioned 11–12, 14, 16–17, 19, 21, 23–6, 30, 48–9, 53, 57, 62, 145
Oldham, Hugh, bishop 86, 144, 157
Oldridge, Devon 172
Oliver, George, historian 84, 88, 108, 111, 127, 133, 135, 153, 157–9, 168

Orange, Richard, mayor 142
oratories – *see* chapels, private
organs, church 53, 125, 152, 157–8, 174
Osbern, bishop 16, 72, 145
Oxford, Oxon. 24, 30

Page, Nicholas 152
Palerna, Peter de 17–18
Palmer, John, citizen 153, 174–5
Palmer's Almshouse 153; mentioned 42
Pancras, saint 153
St Pancras, church 153–4, **186**; mentioned 16–17, 23, 25–6, 30, 49–50, 57
parish churches – *see* churches, parish
parish clerks 50–1
parishes, creation of 28–9
Parker, Thomas 102
Parker's Well, Exeter 46
Paul the Apostle, saint 156
Paul Aurelian (Paul de Léon), saint 10, 25, 155, 164
St Paul, church 156; mentioned 17, 23, 25–6, 28, 30–1, 33, 48, 50–1, 53, 57, 95, 120
Peter the Apostle, saint 81, 156
Peter Martyr, saint 98
St Peter the Little, chapel 156; mentioned 17, 23, 25–6, 29, 120
Petroc, saint 156
St Petroc, church **138**, 156–9, **187**; mentioned 17, 23, 30, 33, 48–9, 53, 56–8, 60, 63, 89
Picot, John – *see* Exeter, John of
Piran, saint 122
Plymouth, Devon 52
Plympton, Devon, priory 16, 22, 26, 35–6, 47, 63, 75, 118–19, 128–30, 176
Pollard, Sir Richard 130
Polsloe Priory **146**, 159–61; mentioned 16, 34–40, 58, 64
Pomeroy family 12, 22, 123, 160
poor relief – *see* almshouses; charity
population of Exeter 2
Poughill, Corn. 25
preaching 39, 42, 85
Preston Street, Exeter 28, 49
processions, religious 56–7
Pytman, John 136

Quinil, Peter, bishop 33, 57, 114, 137

Radegund, saint 163
St Radegund, chapel 163; mentioned 45,162
Radway, Henry 105
Ralegh family 98, 116
Rawlens, Robert 71, 165
Redvers, Baldwin de, earl of Devon 35, 109–10
Redvers, Richard de, earl of Devon 111
Redway, William, cleric 50
Reformation, the 63–5, 149
Reichel, O. J., historian 123
Reygny, William, cleric 115, 121
Richard fitz Walter 111
Rivers, Sir Richard 104
Robert of Chichester, bishop 35, 159–60
Robert fitz Robert of Cornwall 148
Robert fitz Stephen 147
Robin Hood plays 58
Roche, saint 163
St Roche, hospital **154**, 163–4; mentioned 24, 42, 58, 63
Rose-Troup, Frances, historian 3, 18
Rouen, Robert de, prior 91
Rowe, William 165
Rugge, John, cleric 172
rural deanery of Exeter 34, 107, 126
Russell family, later earls of Bedford 64, 92–3, 99
Russell, Robert 136
Ruygeway, Stephen 148
Ryse, John, cleric 71

Saewin the priest 150
saint cults 52–7, 64–5, 85 – *and see* individual names
Salter, John 45, 163
Saynthill, organist 158
Schaplegh, John 163
seals **32**, 76, 112
Seler, Richard, mayor 99
Sherford, Devon 14, 145, 150–2
Shillingford family 139
shoemakers' guild 43, 62, 64, 87–8
Sideman, abbot 81
Sidwell, saint 10–11, 164
St Sidwell, church **162**, 164–6; mentioned 10–11, 13, 17, 19, 21, 24, 29, 34, 48, 63, 107–8
    well of 46
St Sidwell's Fee 164, **179**

Simon the Apostle, saint 166
Simon de Apulia, bishop 28
SS Simon and Jude, chapel 166; mentioned 17–20, 23, 29
St Simon, Simon of 166
skinners' guild 43, 86, 131
Spec, Walter le 135
Speke family 116
Stafford, Edmund, bishop 83, 126, 130, 144, 171
Stapledon, Walter, bishop 79, 86, 109, 114, 161
Stephen, saint 166
St Stephen, church 166–9, **187**; mentioned 5, 11–12, 14, 16–17, 19, 21–3, 25, 31, 47–8, 57, 63, 72, 121, 134
St Stephen's Fee 14, 47, 134, 167
Stephen, king 167
Stevens, John, cleric 42, 121
Stevyns, John, cleric 79
Susseter, John, cleric 174
Symon, John, mayor 60, 158
Sythe, saint 157–8

tailors' guild 43–4, 148
Talbot, John, mayor 116, 157
Tanner, John and Thomas, historians 159
Taverner, Robert 136
Tavistock, Devon, abbey 34, 36, 91, 93
Taxation of Pope Nicholas (1291) 30–1
Taylour, John, merchant 103
Thomas the Apostle, saint 150–1
Thomas Becket, saint 116, 135, 147, 157, 160, 169
St Thomas, churches of, Cowick 169–72, **188**; mentioned 17, 19–20, 24, 39–40, 48, 58, 90–1
St Thomas, suburb – *see* Cowick
Tirell, Henry and Joan 44, 127, 163
Topsham, Devon 1
    church 172–3, **189**; mentioned 3, 6, 17–18, 21, 24, 29, 34, 48–9
Torre, Devon, abbey 75–6
Torre, William, cleric 49
Tracy, William de 160
Tregethew, John, cleric 50
Tregonwell, Robert 86
Trevylegh family 139
Trinity, the Holy – *see* Christ and Holy Trinity

Trinity, Holy, church 173–5, **190**; mentioned 17, 23, 25, 29, 33, 47–50, 52–3, 56, 58, 63, 113
Tuckers Hall – *see* weavers' and tuckers' guild
Turner, Richard 107

Uphome family 108
Ursula and the 11,000 Virgins, saints 163

Vener, John 108
Veysey, John, bishop 95, 176
vowesses 59
Vude, Richard 158

Wadekyng, Emma 174
Wadham, Nicholas 79–80
Walter of Cowick, popular saint 92
Walter of Douai, magnate 22
Walter son of Wulward 109–10
Warelwast, Robert, bishop 128
Warelwast, William, bishop 12, 72, 82, 167
weavers' and tuckers' guild 175–6; mentioned 43, 55, 57, 62, 141
Welch, Robert, cleric 172
Welle, Roger and Isabel atte 45, 163
wells, holy 45–6, 177; mentioned 44, 88, 165
Were, Robert 175

West Clyst, Devon 74
Weston, Nicholas, cleric 86
Wilford family 45, 107, 157, 163
William I, king 1, 10, 19, 35, 74, 145, 151–2, 167
William II, Rufus, king 19
William fitz Baldwin, magnate 35, 89
William fitz Ralph, alias Prodom 67
William of Malmesbury 11
wills 51–2, 59
Winchester, Hants. 21, 23–6, 29–31, 48, 120
Winkleigh, Devon 52
Wolsey, Thomas, cardinal 57
women 39, 58–60, 70, 149, 164–5, 174 – *and see* anchoresses, nuns, vowesses
Wonford, Devon 44, 127
Woodleigh, Agnes de 136
Worcester, Worcs. 9, 21
Worthy, Charles, historian 144
Wygwar, John, priest 44, 69–70
Wynard, William, lawyer 42, 102–3, 160, 177
Wynard's Almshouse **170**, 177–8; mentioned 42, 49, 62, 64–5

Yeo, John 68
York, Yorks. 24, 29–31, 41, 48
Yott (Hyott), John, cleric 70